In this excellent book, Dr Sean McGever of
which has as yet eluded it: a deeply theolog
the theologies of conversion with which Joh.
founders of the evangelical movement in the English speaking world) operated
in relation to other central doctrinal loci, this work is deeply historical, carefully
systematic, and a bold and much needed contribution to contemporary theology
and evangelicalism.

—**Tom Greggs**,
The Marischal Chair of Divinity,
University of Aberdeen

I am happy to recommend Sean McGever's *Born Again*, which gives readers a precise
and illuminating assessment of what the all-important doctrine of "conversion"
actually meant to the founders of the Anglo-American evangelical movement.

—**Thomas S. Kidd**,
Vardaman Distinguished Professor of History,
Baylor University

McGever argues convincingly that Wesley and Whitefield shared a theology of
conversion that is best understood as an inaugurated teleology—with the emphasis more on the telos of salvation than on its initial roots. This nuanced study is
highly recommended.

—**Randy L. Maddox**,
William Kellon Quick Professor of Wesleyan and Methodist Studies,
Duke Divinity School

McGever introduces us to two giants of early Evangelical theology and practice,
focusing on the former to illumine the latter. I know of no other volume that
unpacks this kind of theological focus in thinkers as fundamental as Wesley and
Whitefield. Read this to understand the theological underpinnings driving much
of early Evangelicalism, and read it to attend to the call to consider conversion
theologically today.

—**Kyle Strobel**,
Associate Professor of Spiritual Theology,
Talbot School of Theology, Biola University

We are in great debt to Sean McGever for his careful reading and wonderfully anno-
tated study of John Wesley and George Whitefield. This significant work illuminates
the dynamic and maturing nature of their respective theologies of conversion,
reflecting their many points of similarity as well as some unique distinctives. Most
revealing is how their balanced understanding of this topic challenges contemporary evangelicals in their major neglect of sanctification. I highly recommend it!

—**Tom Schwanda**,
Associate Professor Emeritus of Christian Formation and Ministry,
Wheaton College

Evangelical religion is still shaped by a view of conversion that reached its classic form in the eighteenth century. McGever's patient analysis of the two leading preachers of conversion, Wesley and Whitefield, is especially helpful at showing the broad common ground they shared regarding what conversion is for, and how it is fulfilled. In doing so, it also clarifies their points of disagreement, especially regarding how conversion begins.

—**Fred Sanders**,
Professor of Theology,
Torrey Honors Institute, Biola University

BORN AGAIN

The Evangelical Theology of Conversion
in John Wesley and George Whitefield

BORN AGAIN

*The Evangelical Theology of Conversion
in John Wesley and George Whitefield*

SEAN MCGEVER

STUDIES IN HISTORICAL AND SYSTEMATIC THEOLOGY

LEXHAM PRESS

Born Again: The Evangelical Theology of Conversion in John Wesley and George Whitefield
Studies in Historical and Systematic Theology

Copyright 2020 Sean McGever

Lexham Press, 1313 Commercial St., Bellingham, WA 98225
LexhamPress.com

Print ISBN 9781683593300
Digital ISBN 9781683593317
Library of Congress Control Number 2019950873

Lexham Editorial: Todd Hains, Tom Parr, Danielle Thevenaz, Abigail Stocker
Cover Design: Bryan Hintz
Typesetting: Danielle Thevenaz

CONTENTS

ACKNOWLEDGMENTS

—

I undertook this project to dive further into the depths of the gospel, which God used to change my life profoundly. When I first heard the gospel as a teenager, I knew nothing of Wesley and Whitefield—and I did not need to. I am glad to have now met them. I realize now that I was impacted as a teenager in a way that was shaped through their legacy and understanding of evangelical conversion.

I am indebted to my PhD supervisor, Professor Tom Greggs. Tom's guidance, consistency, encouragement, and correction provided me exactly what I needed in each step of my journey—both academically and in a spirit of friendship. I am grateful to the divinity faculty of King's College at the University of Aberdeen for their support, especially Professor Phil Ziegler and Professor Paul Nimmo. The continuing support from my friends at the University of Saint Andrews—Dr. Eric Stoddart, Dr. Andrew Torrance, and Dr. Andrew Marin—has been invaluable.

I would not have been able to undertake this task without the full support of my supervisors (and friends) from Young Life—in particular, Marty Caldwell, Larry Anderson, John Irwin, Rick Wilson, Chris Eaton, Jorge Lujan, Matt Hock, Chris McGuire, Ken Knipp, Pam Moore, Newt Crenshaw, as well as the Paradise Valley Young Life committee. The College of Theology at Grand Canyon University, including Dean Dr. Jason Hiles and Associate Dean Anna Faith Smith, have supported me thoroughly. I am grateful to Dr. Joel Houston, Dr. Ian Maddock, and Professor Randy Maddox for their expertise in all things Wesley and Whitefield and encouragement in many stages of my research, as well as the staff at the archives at the British Library and the Dr. Williams Evangelical Library in London. Todd Hains and Jesse Myers at Lexham Press have been fantastic to work with in bringing this project to print. You believed in me, and we had a lot of laughs together along the way—perhaps gifs will be printable one day and genuine maple syrup will be readily accessible in all of the lower states.

I received unending support from my mother, Carol, and my father and mother-in-law, John and Connie. My children, Caleb, Lilly, and Molly, have enjoyed the ups (fun travel) and downs (dad reading yet another book) for their entire lives; you are the best. Most of all, I am thankful to my wife, Erin. Her commitment to this project outweighs mine and has far fewer people recognizing her contribution (which is the way she prefers). Only I know the depth of her investment. Thank you, Erin.

1
—

INTRODUCTION

This book examines John Wesley and George Whitefield's theologies of conversion.[1] It synthesizes their operant theologies of conversion to produce an espoused theology of conversion for each figure. This allows me to state and analyze what has not previously been articulated systematically and directly—their conversion *theologies*. Their theologies of conversion often set the table for contemporary evangelical discussions of conversion because Wesley and Whitefield were foundational for the evangelical revival of the eighteenth century and evangelical theology more broadly. Despite the centrality of Wesley and Whitefield for evangelicalism and of conversion as a foundational topic for evangelicalism, there is currently no sustained work articulating and comparing their *theologies* of conversion.

To address this gap, this study articulates what John Wesley and George Whitefield understood as the meaning of conversion, of instantaneous conversion, and of ongoing conversion. Wesley and Whitefield were not systematic theologians. Thus, I address the way conversion operates as a theological category in their works to uncover their underlying theological understanding of conversion. But to understand conversion as a theological category in Wesley and Whitefield demands attention be given to related theological themes such as baptism, regeneration, justification, sanctification, and salvation. Therefore, this study deals directly with the specific, direct discussions of instantaneous and ongoing conversion, as well as those attendant themes in Wesley and Whitefield's theologies. Furthermore, it does not merely deal directly with the articulated theological statements about conversion which Wesley and Whitefield offered

---

1. In this study, John Wesley will also be referred to as "Wesley." To avoid confusion with John Wesley's brother Charles Wesley, all references to Charles Wesley will state explicitly "Charles Wesley."

but also with the way in which conversion functions as an operant trope within their theologies.

Wesley and Whitefield's overarching theologies of conversion are best understood in terms of inaugurated teleology with an emphasis on the *telos* of salvation rather than the *arché* of salvation. Nine synoptic espoused statements can be made from the operant theologies of conversion of John Wesley and George Whitefield.[2]

1. Conversion is initiated and sustained by the grace of God.

2. Conversion is the experiential correlate to salvation.

3. Conversion is a turning *from* self and *to* Christ.

4. Conversion is foreshadowed by a deep sense of sinfulness.

5. Conversion arrives by faith in an instant.

6. Conversion is instantaneous but is not always recognizable on behalf of the convert.

7. Conversion is marked by ongoing good works.

8. Baptism marks one's entrance to the church but is not chronologically tied to conversion.

9. Assurance of salvation is available but not required for a genuine convert.[3]

These nine statements clarify what is meant by inaugurated teleology. While these nine statements reveal overlap regarding conversion between Wesley and Whitefield, there are also critical areas of divergence between them: election, predestination, irresistible grace, imputation, perseverance, and Christian perfection.

---

2. These statements are not articulated directly by Wesley and Whitefield but derive from analysis of the way in which conversion operates theologically within their corpora.

3. The final two statements can be considered attendant to the preceding statements since the final two attend more narrowly to topics which are subservient theologically but are necessary to discuss.

1. MOTIVATION

This study is not just an exercise in excavating an antiquarian theological topic. I want to provide tools for ongoing constructive systematic theology among evangelicals through the analysis of two figures who spurred the evangelical movement that currently counts about half a billion people.[4]

Part of the motivation of this study, therefore, is to provide clarity for the understanding of early evangelical theology as a stepping-stone toward a reappraisal of evangelical conversion theology. David Bebbington provided what has become the standard morphology of early evangelicalism, commonly called the "Bebbington Quadrilateral," consisting of four areas: biblicism, activism, crucicentrism, and conversionism.[5] Despite the broad acceptance of the Bebbington Quadrilateral, little attention has been devoted to the topic of conversionism theologically; instead, sustained

---

4. For recent estimates of the size of evangelicalism see the research published by the Pew Research Center. Pew Research Center, "The Size and Distribution of the World's Christian Population (2010)," accessed February 20, 2017, www.pewforum.org/2011/12/19/global-christianity-exec/.

5. David W. Bebbington, *Evangelicalism in Modern Britain: A History from the 1730s to the 1980s* (London: Routledge, 2004), 2–19. The Bebbington Quadrilateral's definition of evangelicalism, while firmly established, has been subject to recent debate. Recent interest in the definition of what it means to be an "evangelical" has further prompted examination. I see these conversations orbiting around four topics. First, the origins of evangelicalism have been reassessed. For example, a collection of seventeen essays assessed the emergence of evangelicalism in light of Bebbington's work; see Michael A. G. Haykin and Kenneth J. Stewart, eds., *The Emergence of Evangelicalism: Exploring Historical Continuities* (Nottingham: Apollos, 2008). Second, questions have been raised regarding the continuity of evangelicalism from its origins until now. For example, Kidd insists that the Holy Spirit should be a fifth aspect of Bebbington's definition. Dochuk agrees with Kidd and adds fellowship and eschatology. Bebbington responded to these additions, and others, and concludes that: "All of them prevailed at a particular time, but not throughout the course of evangelical history." He concluded: "There is no persuasive call to add to their number and certainly no reason to drop any of them." See Thomas S. Kidd, "The Bebbington Quadrilateral and the Work of the Holy Spirit," *Fides et Historia* 47, no. 1 (Winter 2015): 54–57; Darren Dochuk, "Revisiting Bebbington's Classic Rendering of Modern Evangelicalism at Points of New Departure," *Fides et Historia* 47, no. 1 (Winter 2015): 63–72; David W. Bebbington, "The Evangelical Quadrilateral: A Response," *Fides et Historia* 47, no. 1 (Winter 2015): 93, 96. Third, the quadrilateral has been challenged in light of modern political questions related to American politics and evangelicals following Donald Trump's election. This issue has received sustained attention for the last several years in the Evangelical Studies Unit of the American Academy of Religion, with no apparent consensus or conclusion. Fourth, there is a need for theological analysis that prioritizes theological articulation over historical locatedness. This is not to mute the essential voice of historicity but to focus more on the theological work of the theologian over the historical work of the historian as a matter of emphasis (and not exclusion). This book is concerned with the first and fourth issues in the Bebbingtonian arena: the theological articulation of conversion in early evangelicalism.

studies on conversion have focused on psychological, sociological, and historical perspectives.[6] The historical theology offered herein is offered in the hope of renewed reflection and response to the issues raised by evangelical theologians on the topic of conversion.

2. APPROACH

This study synchronically identifies motifs that bring together the assumptions about the theology of conversion with which Wesley and Whitefield work. Within these synchronic motifs, the arcs of historical development of the ideas are explicated. Thus, this study balances the twin aspects of historical theology: synchronically, it espouses the operant themes in Wesley and Whitefield's theologies of conversion in a way that has not yet been done; diachronically, it attends to the historical context of Wesley and Whitefield and the literary form of their writings as they develop.

A precipitous balance between biographic and primary source details is needed because the abundant literature and vast time frame of Wesley and Whitefield's entire careers have been considered in order to provide a robust analysis of the conversion theologies of Wesley[7]

---

6.   A 1992 collection of essays on conversion considers four areas: conversion in comparative religions, theological perspectives on conversion, conversion in the social/behavioral sciences, and conversion in culture and church. The section on theological perspectives has four essays which cover biblical theology and conversion, the Catholic view of conversion, the mainline Protestant understanding of conversion, and the evangelical Protestant understanding of conversion. The chapter on evangelical Protestant conversion covers seven pages and contains no footnotes; it leaves much to be desired. See H. Newton Malony and Samuel Southard, eds., *Handbook of Religious Conversion* (Birmingham, AL: Religious Education Press, 1992); see a similar approach in Walter E. Conn, ed., *Conversion: Perspectives on Personal and Social Transformation* (New York: Alba House, 1978).

7.   The current critical edition of Wesley is the Bicentennial Edition of the Works of John Wesley, including twenty volumes in print of a planned thirty-five volume collection. John Wesley, *Sermons*, ed. Albert C. Outler, The Bicentennial Edition of the Works of John Wesley, vols. 1–4 (Nashville: Abingdon Press, 1984); John Wesley, *A Collection of Hymns for the Use of the People Called Methodists*, ed. Franz Hildenbrandt and Oliver A. Beckerlegge, The Bicentennial Edition of the Works of John Wesley, vol. 7 (Nashville: Abingdon Press, 1983); John Wesley, *The Methodist Societies: History, Nature, and Design*, ed. Rupert E. Davies, The Bicentennial Edition of the Works of John Wesley, vol. 9 (Nashville: Abingdon Press, 1989); John Wesley, *The Methodist Societies: The Minutes of Conference*, ed. Henry D. Rack, The Bicentennial Edition of the Works of John Wesley, vol. 10 (Nashville: Abingdon Press, 2011); John Wesley, *The Appeals to Men of Reason and Religion and Certain Related Open Letters*, ed. Gerald Cragg, The Bicentennial Edition of the Works of John Wesley, vol. 11 (Nashville: Abingdon Press, 1989); John Wesley, *Doctrinal and Controversial Treatises I*, ed. Randy L. Maddox, The Bicentennial Edition of the Works of John Wesley, vol. 12 (Nashville: Abingdon Press, 2012); John Wesley, *Doctrinal and Controversial Treatises II*, ed. Paul Wesley Chilcote and Kenneth J. Collins, The Bicentennial

and Whitefield.[8] Engagement with these primary sources is a significant task.

The study has attempted to consider the entire careers of Whitefield and Wesley, who lived to be 55 and 87 years old respectively, and the diachronic discussion within the synchronic motifs seeks to speak to and address the historical complexities involved in this theological task.

As an exercise in historical theology, this study seeks to offer an account of the theologies of conversion in Wesley and Whitefield in a manner which is thoroughly historical, and attentive to the contexts (ecclesial and otherwise) in which they lived and wrote, and to the operative conditions in which their theologies were expressed.[9] However, the account offered is

---

Edition of the Works of John Wesley, vol. 13 (Nashville: Abingdon Press, 2013); John Wesley, *Journals and Diaries*, ed. W. Reginald Ward and Richard P. Heitzenrater, The Bicentennial Edition of the Works of John Wesley, vols. 18-24 (Nashville: Abingdon Press, 1988); John Wesley, *Letters*, ed. Frank Baker and Ted A. Campbell, The Bicentennial Edition of the Works of John Wesley, vols. 25-27 (Nashville: Abingdon Press, 1980). In situations where the bicentennial texts have yet to be published, reliance on other sources has been utilized. Specific, non-bicentennial sources include the following: John Wesley, *A Plain Account of Christian Perfection*, ed. Randy L. Maddox and Paul Wesley Chilcote (Kansas City, MO: Beacon Hill Press, 2015); John Wesley, *Explanatory Notes upon the Old Testament* (Salem, OH: Schmul Publishers, 1975); John Wesley, *Explanatory Notes Upon the New Testament* (New York: J. Soule and T. Mason, 1818); John Wesley, *The Complete English Dictionary Explaining Most of Those Hard Words, Which Are Found in the Best English Writers* (London: W. Strahan, 1753); John Wesley, *The Letters of John Wesley*, ed. John Telford (London: The Epworth Press, 1931); John Wesley, *The Works of John Wesley*, ed. Thomas Jackson, 3rd ed., 14 vols. (London: Methodist Reading Room, 1872); John Wesley, ed., *Thoughts Upon Infant-Baptism (Extracted from a Late Writer)* (Bristol: Felix Farley, 1751). The letters written to Wesley are being added to the following website: wesley-works. org/john-wesleys-in-correspondence. Sources consulted for the study include the digital collections at Southern Methodist University, the Wesley Center Online hosted by Northwest Nazarene University, as well as documents made available via emails with Professor Randy Maddox at Duke Divinity School. Where sources are not in the public domain, unpublished letters and diaries of Whitefield have been located and transcribed on-site at the British Library and the Dr. Williams Evangelical Library in London.

8. The broadest recent collection of Whitefield's works is found in John Gillies's 1771 seven-volume collection of journals, letters, and sermons. Gillies's work is incomplete; it does not include fifty-four additional sermons identified for this study. In addition, many letters have been identified since 1771 which are not included by Gillies but have been included in this exposition. This study has also attended to another layer of complexity in relation to the sources, seeking to address at relevant points the fact that it is known that Whitefield went back and edited his early sermons and journals to add nuance to overtly Calvinistic points and to make other key linguistic adjustments. For the sake of this study, original documents were compared to those published by Gillies. George Whitefield, *The Works of the Reverend George Whitefield*, ed. John Gillies, 6 vols. (London: Printed for Edward and Charles Dilly, 1771).

9. For the social and historical context of Wesley and Whitefield, see W. Reginald Ward, *Early Evangelicalism: A Global Intellectual History, 1670-1789* (Cambridge: Cambridge University Press, 2006); Thomas S. Kidd, *The Great Awakening* (New Haven, CT: Yale University Press,

also thoroughly theological in that it seeks, in relation to a theology of conversion, to espouse what is operant for Wesley and Whitefield in a clear and systematic way.

To do this I have drawn upon the morphology of the four voices of theology as presented by Deborah Bhatti et al.[10] This morphology recognizes and categorizes theological communication as a product of its origin and form. Bhatti et al. outline the four voices as: normative theology, that is, the theology dictated by Scripture, creeds, and liturgies; formal theology, that is, the theology constructed by a theologian; espoused theology, that is, the theology embedded in a group's statement of its beliefs; and operant theology, that is, the theology embedded in the actual practices of a group.[11]

The primary *materials* of the study are the operant theologies of conversion of Wesley and Whitefield.[12] Exegeting and analyzing this operant

---

2007); David Ceri Jones, Eryn Mant White, and Boyd Stanley Schlenther, *The Elect Methodists: Calvinistic Methodism in England and Wales, 1735-1811* (Cardiff: University of Wales Press, 2012); David Ceri Jones, *The Fire Divine: An Introduction to the Evangelical Revival* (Nottingham: InterVarsity Press, 2015); D. Bruce Hindmarsh, *The Spirit of Early Evangelicalism: True Religion in a Modern World* (Oxford: Oxford University Press, 2018); Mark A. Noll, *The Rise of Evangelicalism: The Age of Edwards, Whitefield, and the Wesleys* (Downers Grove, IL: InterVarsity Press, 2003); Hughes Oliphant Old, *The Reading and Preaching of the Scriptures in the Worship of the Christian Church: Moderatism, Pietism, and Awakening*, vol. 5, 7 vols. (Grand Rapids: Eerdmans, 2004); Mark Chapman, *Anglican Theology* (London: T&T Clark, 2012); Haykin and Stewart, *The Emergence of Evangelicalism: Exploring Historical Continuities*; David W. Bebbington, "Evangelicalism in Modern Britain and America: A Comparison," in *Amazing Grace: Evangelicalism in Australia, Britain, Canada, and the United States*, ed. Mark A. Noll and George A. Rawlyk (Grand Rapids: Baker, 1993); Bebbington, *Evangelicalism in Modern Britain*.

10. Deborah Bhatti et al., *Talking about God in Practice: Theological Action Research and Practical Theology* (London: Hymns Ancient and Modern, 2010).

11. Normative theology is found in the Scripture, creeds, and liturgies to which an individual or group adhere. Formal theology is the product of a theologian, for example Calvin's *Institutes*. Espoused theology is what many Presbyterian churches do when they ascribe to the Westminster Confession of Faith. Operant theology is, as Ward argues, "often slightly hidden from view, or taken as 'just the thing that we do.' " It is often only revealed when the everyday teaching and practices are examined to reveal their theological nature. Pete Ward, "Seeing and Believing," in *The End of Theology: Shaping Theology for the Sake of Mission*, ed. Jason S. Sexton and Paul Weston (Minneapolis: Fortress Press, 2016), 162; see also Bhatti et al., *Talking about God in Practice*, 54; Michael Armstrong, "Ordinary Theologians as Signal Processors of the Spirit," in *Exploring Ordinary Theology: Everyday Christian Believing and the Church*, ed. Leslie J. Francis and Jeff Astley (London: Routledge, 2016), chap. 7; Jeff Astley, *Ordinary Theology: Looking, Listening, and Learning in Theology* (London: Ashgate, 2002).

12. Wesley and Whitefield did not compile complete systematic theological texts, but this should not demote them to secondary status as theologians. To do so would be to apply a largely anachronistic and biased rubric upon them. Maddox argues: "The early church influence may also account for the fact that Anglican theologians of the seventeenth and eighteenth centuries focused more on clarifying issues of theological method than on constructing 'systems' of

material is this study's primary task. It allows us to state what Wesley and Whitefield did not state explicitly about their theologies of conversion. The methodology of this study speaks through two of the four voices because Wesley and Whitefield left largely operant material on conversion and this study produces a work of espoused theology.

While this study aims to capture the theology of conversion of early evangelicalism by attending to Wesley and Whitefield, the limited scope of this study does not allow for the inclusion of other prominent voices of early evangelicalism. Early evangelicalism originated nearly simultaneously in Massachusetts with Jonathan Edwards (1734–1735), in Wales with Howell Harris and Daniel Rowland (1735), in England with George Whitefield (1735–1737) and John Wesley (1738), and in Scotland at Cambuslang (1742).[13] Other individuals figured prominently in early evangelicalism, foremost among them being Charles Wesley.

John Wesley and George Whitefield have been isolated in this study on early evangelical conversion theology for two reasons. The first reason John Wesley and George Whitefield are being examined is due to their commonalities. Both Wesley and Whitefield were Church of England ministers, born in England, educated at Oxford, and committed to the basic premises of Methodism. These men, additionally, left a similar trail of documents in the same era, including a prolific abundance of published sermons, tracts, journals, and diaries. Further, both men had expansive public ministries in which they traveled extensively. The commonalities of these men provide a robust shared baseline upon which their theologies

---

theology (the contemporaneous preoccupation of Continental theology). Indeed, they actively distrusted systems. As such, the fact that Wesley never constructed a 'system' would not have implied to them that he was not a serious theologian. By their standards, a serious theologian would strive to clarify the sources of theology and the methods for utilizing and weighting these sources. Judged accordingly, Wesley was not only conversant with the issues involved, he made an important contribution concerning the role of experience in formulating and testing theological assertions." Randy L. Maddox, "John Wesley—Practical Theologian?," *Wesleyan Theological Journal* 23 (1988): 130. See also Randy L. Maddox, *Responsible Grace: John Wesley's Practical Theology* (Nashville: Kingswood Books, 1994); Randy L. Maddox, "The Recovery of Theology as a Practical Discipline: A Contemporary Agenda," *Theological Studies* 51 (1990): 650–72; Randy L. Maddox, "An Untapped Inheritance: American Methodism and Wesley's Practical Theology," in *Doctrines and Disciplines: Methodist Theology and Practice*, ed. Dennis Campbell (Nashville: Abingdon Press, 1999), 19–52, 292–309. Whitefield largely mirrors Wesley's theological approach, so it is fair to classify Whitefield as a practical theologian. See Stuart C. Henry, *George Whitefield: Wayfaring Witness* (New York: Abingdon Press, 1957), 96.

13. Bebbington, "Evangelicalism in Modern Britain and America: A Comparison," 186.

can be examined with precision due to their abundant overlap in life context, terminology, and personal interaction. The second reason these men
are being examined is due to their well-known points of departure, namely,
Wesley's Arminianism and the mature Whitefield's Calvinism. Both men
remained committed to the Church of England while providing two different trajectories that pushed past the edges of the established norms of their
church. For Wesley, this movement became Methodism. For Whitefield,
this movement became Calvinistic Methodism early in his ministry, but
also a general ecumenism in his warm embrace of any church that would
embrace his teaching of the new birth.

Charles Wesley's theology of conversion could be examined, but, while
differences exist, and Charles's dynamic use of hymnody to communicate
his theology is enticing to incorporate in this project, the overlap between
John and Charles's theologies is so great that this path has not been chosen
for this study.[14]

Were this study able to include the careful analysis and comparison of
Edwards's theology of conversion, it would certainly be stronger. Why, then,
has Edwards been discarded in this study? Simply put, a proper study of
Edwards would require attention to too many differences. Edwards was
not a minister in the Church of England (like Wesley and Whitefield); he
was a Congregationalist. Edwards was not born in England (like Wesley
and Whitefield); he was from Connecticut. Edwards was not educated
at Oxford (like Wesley and Whitefield); he was educated at Yale. While
broadly Calvinistic like Whitefield, Edwards's soteriology did not neatly
align with general Calvinistic understandings (the mature Whitefield's theology aligned closely with general Calvinism of his day).[15] Edwards traveled
infrequently and never crossed the Atlantic, unlike the almost unbeliev-
able amount of travel by horse and crossing of the Atlantic undertaken by

---

14. It is hoped that others may pursue a careful analysis of Charles Wesley's theology
of conversion.

15. McDermott argues that Edwards's soteriology and view of conversion were against
the grain of traditional Reformational and Calvinistic views. For instance, McDermott claims
that Edwards taught that conversion can come after a person is already regenerate, that
justification is only complete at death, that sinners are made holy in the act of regeneration,
and that a person can become a "saint before conversion." Gerald R. McDermott, "A Possibility
of Reconciliation: Jonathan Edwards and the Salvation of Non-Christians," in *Edwards in Our
Time: Jonathan Edwards and the Shaping of American Religion*, ed. Sang Hyun Lee and Allen C.
Guelzo (Grand Rapids: Eerdmans, 1999), 187–89.

Wesley and Whitefield.[16] While Edwards never met Wesley, Edwards did meet and hosted Whitefield in his pulpit.[17] The missional ethos of Edwards was quite different from that of Wesley and Whitefield. Edwards "was a revival preacher to a people that was already intensely religious."[18] Wesley and, in particular Whitefield, were known to seek out those who were far from being intensely religious, such as the coal workers in the colliers of England. Hughes Oliphant Old nuances this claim: "Edwards may not have been too well suited to be a missionary. He was a pastor, to be sure, and he did manifest a real pastoral concern for the Indians to whom he had been sent, but he was above all a theologian who spoke to theologians."[19] In sum, of the three leading figures of early evangelicalism (John Wesley, George Whitefield, and Jonathan Edwards), Edwards has enough dissimilarity from the other two that for the limited scope of this study, only Wesley and Whitefield have been examined.[20] It is hoped that the findings of this study can be utilized by Edwards scholars to further the understanding of early evangelical theologies of conversion.[21]

---

16. Old, *The Reading and Preaching of the Scriptures in the Worship of the Christian Church*, 5:248.

17. Edwards and Whitefield's friendship sometimes is exaggerated: "Whitefield and Edwards long knew of each other by reputation, though the two were never close friends or working associates." John E. Smith, Harry S. Stout, and Kenneth P. Minkena, eds., *A Jonathan Edwards Reader* (New Haven, CT: Yale University Press, 2003), xxxv.

18. Old, *The Reading and Preaching of the Scriptures in the Worship of the Christian Church*, 5:253.

19. Old, *Reading and Preaching of the Scriptures*, 5:283.

20. There may be a further argument that, of the three figures, Edwards influenced the early evangelical movement the least, but that claim has not yet been demonstrated.

21. It is anticipated that several of the conclusions of this study align with Edwards's theology of conversion. For instance, Cherry claims that Edwards believed that regenerative conversion was immediate and instantaneous. This study will show that Wesley and Whitefield also held to instantaneous conversion. See Conrad Cherry, *The Theology of Jonathan Edwards: A Reappraisal* (Garden City, NY: Doubleday, 1990), 66–67. Additionally, Strobel argues that Edwards understood conversion as a single moment, but one in which "there is also a gradual work of grace postconversion in sanctification." See Kyle Strobel, "By Word and Spirit: Jonathan Edwards on Redemption, Justification, and Regeneration," in *Jonathan Edwards and Justification*, ed. Josh Moody (Wheaton, IL: Crossway, 2012), 66; see also Oliver D. Crisp and Kyle Strobel, *Jonathan Edwards: An Introduction to His Thought* (Grand Rapids: Eerdmans, 2018), 146–69. This study will show that Wesley and Whitefield were also committed to "ongoing conversion."

3. ARGUMENT

John Wesley once said that he did not use the word "conversion" often.[22] But he actually did, and four motifs emerge which are central to his understanding of conversion. First, Wesley understood conversion to be a personal experience turning *from* and *to* one state to another in the journey toward holiness. Wesley understood conversion to be experiential in nature despite frequent attacks on Wesley in which he was labeled as an enthusiast.[23] Second, for Wesley conversion is always preceded by a profound experience with personal sinfulness. This experience was described as being convinced, convicted, or awakened. Third, and most notably, for the mature Wesley the actual moment of conversion is instantaneous. The fourth area of discussion of Wesley's theology is that conversion is always, for him, followed by continued evidence which shows an individual to be a genuine convert. Conversion is a theological concept describing experience, and Wesley expected experience to mirror reality if one was justified and regenerated: the genuine convert would have the internal witness of the Spirit and external works which gave evidence of his or her instantaneous conversion.

Wesley's four-fold primary understanding of conversion reveals three attendant topics which further help to unpack the theology of conversion with which Wesley worked. The first attendant theme of Wesley's theology of conversion is the relationship between baptism and conversion. Wesley took several decades to work out the full implications of his theology of conversion in his understanding and practice of baptism. In the end, Wesley believed that one could "sin away" the benefits of his or her baptism, and thus, a subsequent conversion was needed for an individual to be regenerated. The second attendant theme of Wesley's theology of conversion is the relationship between assurance of salvation and conversion. Wesley's understanding of assurance went through four phases in which he concluded that one could be a genuine convert and potentially never experience assurance of salvation. The third, and final, attendant theme of Wesley's theology of conversion addresses Wesley's *ordo salutis*,

---

22. Wesley, *The Appeals to Men of Reason and Religion and Certain Related Open Letters*, 11:368.

23. Chapter two will explain why enthusiasm was often a pejorative term in Wesley and Whitefield's era.

or more properly in Wesley's understanding, how Wesley's *via salutis* conceptualized conversion. Wesley's overarching soteriological schema has four primary features (that which comes before conversion, that which happens in the moment of instantaneous conversion, that which follows conversion, and the possibility of backsliding or reversal through the *via salutis*) that provide the foundational theological framework from which emerges the overarching conceptualization of conversion in terms of inaugurated teleology.

Whitefield's discussions of conversion also cohere around four primary motifs. First, Whitefield understood conversion to be the experience of turning *from* self-righteousness and *to* the righteousness of Christ through the power of the Holy Spirit. Whitefield believed that conversion is an experience which was a profound work of the Holy Spirit. Second, Whitefield understood that people become either convinced, convicted, or awakened, or perhaps a combination of each of these, in regard to their need for conversion to Christ. Third, instantaneous conversion is an essential motif of Whitefield's theology of conversion and pinpoints the moment when an individual experiences salvation and is regenerated. Fourth, Whitefield's theology of conversion requires an ongoing component of continued evidence that does not merit salvation but marks a genuine conversion.

Whitefield's theology of conversion, like Wesley, includes three attendant themes. First, Whitefield's view of conversion influenced his understanding of baptism as an office of Christ that imparts preparatory grace requiring a later spiritual regeneration, which was a baptism in the *nature* of the Spirit. Second, Whitefield believed that assurance of salvation was available to every genuine believer, but that assurance was not required for an individual to be a genuine convert. The third, and final, theme is Whitefield's *ordo salutis* and his theology of conversion regarding grace, election, faith, repentance, regeneration, new birth, justification, sanctification, and glorification.

The primary contours of Wesley and Whitefield's theologies of conversion share many characteristics. This book presents nine common espoused synoptic statements from Wesley and Whitefield's operant theologies of conversion. Central to these theses is the foundational understanding of conversion as the experience of turning to God in terms of inaugurated teleology. This inaugurated teleological framework further aids unpacking areas of discontinuity in Wesley and Whitefield over conversion. Wesley and Whitefield disagreed on issues related to election, foreknowledge, predestination, irresistible grace, imputation, perseverance, and Christian perfection. Each of these issues will be examined and shown to be secondary in nature on the topic of conversion because Wesley and Whitefield based the core of these concepts in the hidden decrees, which are logically prior to the experience of conversion (with the exception of the timing of Christian perfection, which for Wesley, via his own unique definition, was possible before glorification, but otherwise, for Wesley and Whitefield, was a realization of the teleological aspect of conversion after death). It will be concluded that, in relation to questions of the *arché* of conversion, Wesley and Whitefield are divided, but in relation to questions of the *telos* of conversion there is a deep unity.

2

—

JOHN WESLEY'S CONVERSION THEOLOGY MOTIFS

The argument of this book is that Wesley and Whitefield's theologies of conversion are best understood in terms of inaugurated teleology with an emphasis on the *telos* of salvation rather than the *arché* of salvation. This chapter shows what is meant theologically regarding conversion as inauguration and *telos*. Four primary theological motifs of conversion emerge which are present in Wesley's operant theology of conversion. These four motifs form the four sections of the chapter, as follows: (1) conversion as an experience turning *from* and *to*; (2) preceding conversion: being convinced, convicted, and awakened; (3) instantaneous conversion; and (4) continued evidence. It is from the analysis of the four operant motifs in each section that the espoused synoptic statements of conversion (to be presented below) emerge.

1. CONVERSION AS AN EXPERIENCE TURNING "FROM" AND "TO"

Wesley's 1753 dictionary entry captures the basic essence of his view of conversion: "Conversion: 'a thorough change of heart and life from sin to holiness; a turning.' "[1] For Wesley, the very nature of conversion means to convert *from* one state *to* another. Wesley describes five common prior states *from* which people convert to Christianity: heathenism, gentilism, Judaism, deism, and "popery." Wesley's theology of conversion is described as an experience of turning from one belief or path to another belief or path. The primary prior state of conversion in Wesley's writing is "converting

---

1. Wesley, *The Complete English Dictionary Explaining Most of Those Hard Words, Which Are Found in the Best English Writers*. No pages are listed, only the alphabetical list of words.

from" heathenism. Heathenism, as will be shown, is both a geographic reference and a reference to one who does not truly have saving faith. In this
formulation, we will see that John Wesley considered himself a "heathen"
before his Aldersgate experience in his own understanding of heathenism.
Conversion requires a prior state from which one turns, and conversion is
the turn itself, which happens at the instant of conversion. From Wesley's
basic definition of conversion, one of the synoptic espoused statements of
the theology of conversion for Wesley is introduced: conversion is a turning
from self and *to* Christ (synoptic statement 3). Another synoptic statement
will be introduced in this section: conversion is the experiential correlate
of salvation (synoptic statement 2).

1.1. EXPERIENCE

Conversion is not only a turn *from* and *to*, conversion is an *experiential* and
felt change. Wesley's Aldersgate experience was a *felt* experience. Wesley
wrote: "I *felt* my heart strangely warmed. I *felt* I did trust in Christ, Christ
alone for salvation: And an assurance was *given me*, that he had taken away
my sins, even *mine*, and *saved me* from the law of sin and death."[2] Wesley's
Aldersgate experience was a subjective moment that attested to the objective reality of God's work of salvation in Wesley's life. Wesley believed
experience to be an essential element of Methodist doctrine, and is, thus,
essential to an espoused theology of conversion for Wesley. Wesley's insistence upon the role of experience in doctrine is accentuated when the
climate of theological rejection of enthusiasm in Wesley's era is considered. Wesley's reliance upon experience as an epistemological event sets
a foundation to understand how Wesley conceived of conversion as being
experiential in nature. As it will be shown below and as one of the synoptic
statements of the espoused theology of conversion in chapter six, conversion is the experiential correlate of salvation.

Wesley believed that the objective work of God is perceptible. While
justification is accomplished objectively and fully by the work of God
alone,[3] Wesley taught that the appropriation of justification in the life of

---

2. Wesley, *Journals and Diaries*, 18:250. Italics added.

3. Wesley described justification, in its simplest sense, as "that great work which God
does *for us*, in forgiving our sins." Wesley, *Sermons*, 2:187. Italics in original.

a Christian is perceptible through experience. Wesley wrote: "The notification of justification to be as perceptible as the sun at noon-day."[4] Not only was justification perceptible; Wesley wrote a letter to his mother, Susanna, telling her that regeneration must, also, be perceptible, otherwise the Christian life would be full of fear and trembling rather than joy.[5] Thus, Wesley encouraged the use of the senses as a tool to discern the veracity of God's objective work in the life of the Christian believer. For Wesley, experience was more than a feeling. As Runyon writes, "Wesley ultimately understood religious experience as an epistemological event between the Divine and the human participant."[6] Since conversion is a *turn* that is experienced, conversion is an experiential indicator of the objective work of God, namely God's ongoing work of salvation. Wesley taught that salvation hinged on experience; more specifically, salvation hinged upon "perceptible inspiration."[7] He wrote, "None is a *true Christian* till he experiences [perceptible inspiration]."[8] Wesley taught, therefore, that God's work of justification, regeneration, and salvation are all perceptible through the human capacity of experience.

Experience, or more precisely perceptible inspiration, is a primary issue in Wesley's doctrine. Wesley went so far as to call perceptible inspiration "the main doctrine of the Methodists."[9] Wesley's ministry was constantly concerned with the intersection between God's objective work and the subjective work of human experience. Wesley sought experience not only for himself but for all who encountered his ministry. Experience was

---

4. Wesley to John Smith, March 22, 1748, in *Letters*, ed. Frank Baker and Ted A. Campbell, The Bicentennial Edition of the Works of John Wesley (Nashville: Abingdon Press, 1980), 26:292.

5. *Letters*, 25:170.

6. Theodore Runyon, "The Importance of Experience for Faith," in *Aldersgate Reconsidered*, ed. Randy L. Maddox (Nashville: Kingswood Books, 1990), 94. In Runyon's monograph, he distinguished between experience, feeling, and emotions in Wesley's thought. Runyon's most important observation is that experience is the combination of feeling plus interpretation. See *The New Creation: John Wesley's Theology Today* (Nashville: Abingdon Press, 1998), 152.

7. Wesley to John Smith, December 30, 1745, in *Letters*, 26:182. The sermon, *The Witness of Our Own Spirit*, echoes Wesley's thought regarding God's work of salvation from the vantage of individual experience. Wesley wrote: "No man is a partaker of Christ until he can clearly testify, 'The life which I now live … I live by faith in the Son of God' in him who is now revealed in my heart." Wesley, *Sermons*, 1:304.

8. Wesley to John Smith, in *Letters*, 26:182. Italics in original.

9. Wesley to John Smith, in *Letters*, 26:182.

front and center in Wesley's formal publication of his *Sermons*. Sermons 10–12, *The Witness of the Spirit I* (sermon 10), *The Witness of the Spirit II* (sermon 11), and *The Witness of Our Own Spirit* (sermon 12) present Wesley's understanding of experience.[10] Wesley elevated, and even required, experience, enabled by divinely inspired perception, as a foundational concept of his entire theology.[11] William J. Abraham summarizes Wesley's perspective on experience well: "Wesley was fascinated by the reality of religious experience in part because he thought that it implicitly supplied the crucial evidence for the truth of the Christian faith."[12] Conversion is a *turn* which is *felt*, and experience is not merely intellectual: conversion, like all truly perceptible inspiration for Wesley, must be confirmed by the outworking of spiritual fruit.[13]

In the eighteenth century, substantive claims regarding a personal experience with God, including Wesley's focus on conversion, were subject to swift criticism. "Enthusiasm" is the claim to have a supernatural experience with God. Enthusiasm was a charge leveled early and often against Wesley and the Methodists. Albert Outler wrote in his introduction to Wesley's sermon *The Nature of Enthusiasm*: "The Methodists, then, were obvious targets of scorn with their claims of assurance and their irregular ways of worship."[14] Wesley presented his basic understanding of enthusiasm in *The Nature of Enthusiasm* and traced the understanding of the term from its Greek origin, which means "in God."[15] Wesley penned that the

---

10. The primary topic expounded in these sermons is assurance, but these sermons illustrate Wesley's view of experience more broadly. For example, in the sermon *The Witness of the Spirit I*, Wesley explained, "The Spirit of God does give a believer such a testimony of adoption that while it is present to the soul he can no more doubt the reality of his sonship than he can doubt the shining of the sun while he stands in the full blaze of his beams." Wesley, *Sermons*, 1:276.

11. While experience was central to Wesley's theology, he felt the need to clarify that experience was not adequate to determine doctrine, but that doctrine should be founded on Scripture. Wesley argued: "Experience is sufficient to confirm a doctrine which is grounded on Scripture." Wesley, *Sermons*, 1:297.

12. William J. Abraham, "The Epistemology of Conversion," in *Conversion in the Wesleyan Tradition*, ed. Kenneth J. Collins and John H. Tyson (Nashville: Abingdon Press, 2001), 182.

13. For more on Wesley and experience, see Ted A. Campbell, *Wesleyan Beliefs: Formal and Popular Expressions of the Core Beliefs of Wesleyan Communities* (Nashville: Kingswood Books, 2010), 72–73; Maddox, *Responsible Grace*, 44–46; Donald A. Thorsen, "Experimental Method in the Practical Theology of John Wesley," *Wesleyan Theological Journal* 24 (1989): 117–41, esp. 122.

14. Wesley, *Sermons*, 2:44.

15. Wesley, *Sermons*, 2:48.

biblical prophets and apostles were filled with enthusiasm, being led and inspired by the Spirit of God.[16] Wesley addressed the popular understanding of enthusiasm in his day which was extremely negative. He acknowledged that in his day enthusiasm was normally understood as "a religious madness arising from some falsely imagined influence or inspiration of God."[17] In a letter from January 17, 1739, Wesley wrote about two people he called enthusiasts: "They think themselves inspired by God, and are not. But false, imaginary inspiration is enthusiasm. That theirs is only imaginary inspiration appears hence: it contradicts the law and the testimony."[18] Wesley was well aware of the dangers and error of enthusiasm. He believed, however, there was a proper mode of enthusiasm, which was the biblical understanding of enthusiasm—enthusiasm from the Spirit, in keeping with Scripture.

For Wesley, the topic of conversion must engage the topic of enthusiasm since enthusiasm relates to what an individual is able to truly perceive regarding God. A person who claims an instantaneous conversion experience could be accused of being an enthusiast. The same accusation could be brought to those who claim to have a felt assurance. These are exactly the types of questions Dr. George Lavington, Bishop of Exeter, brought against Wesley in his work *The Enthusiasm of Methodists and Papists Compar'd.*[19] Lavington's letter began a series of open letters to Lavington from Wesley, with the first being *A Letter to the Author of "The Enthusiasm of Methodists and Papists Compared."* Wesley recounted that Lavington wrote that Wesley "represent[s] conversion as sudden and instantaneous," which Wesley did not deny.[20] Wesley continued to account for other references to his belief in instantaneous conversion, correcting Lavington on other associated points, but without any comment needed on the instantaneous aspect. Wesley believed in the instantaneous experience of conversion, even if it brought with it the unpopular label of "enthusiast."

---

16. Wesley, *Sermons,* 2:48.

17. Wesley, *Sermons,* 2:50.

18. Wesley, *Journals and Diaries,* 19:31–32.

19. George Lavington, *The Enthusiasm of Methodists and Papists Compar'd* (London: Knapton, 1749).

20. Wesley, *The Appeals to Men of Reason and Religion and Certain Related Open Letters,* 11:368.

Despite a climate that shunned enthusiasm, Wesley's theology operated comfortably, and necessarily, in the category of experience. As stated,
Wesley defined conversion as a thorough change of heart and life *from* sin
to holiness; conversion is a turning. This change and turn is *experiential*,
felt, and perceptible. Having discussed the experiential change brought
about in conversion, it is now necessary to consider the pre-conversion
states *from* which one experienced this felt and perceptible turn.

1.2. PRE-CONVERSION STATES

Wesley's operant material on conversion reveals frequent dependence on
the *from* and *to* motif. Wesley's most frequent pre-conversion state, the
state *from* which one turns, is heathenism. Four other pre-conversion states
emerge in Wesley's corpus, but to a lesser extent, with these being gentilism, Judaism, deism, and "popery."[21] While the less frequent pre-conversion
states tend to highlight theological categories, the much more frequent
category of heathenism can be summarized as simply being non-Christian. Thus, when Wesley spoke of conversion as a thorough turning *from*
sin, he was not only talking about individual sins; Wesley's extensive usage
of conversion was a turning *from* a non-Christian and sinful orientation.

1.2.1. Heathenism

The most frequent pre-conversion state Wesley described was that of being
a "heathen." An early example of this usage emerges in a letter from Wesley
to his brother Samuel on October 15, 1735. John wrote, "For assure yourself, dear brother, you are even now called to the converting of heathens
as well as I."[22] Owing to Wesley's frequency of discussing conversion and
heathens, it is important to understand precisely what Wesley meant by
the term "heathen." Wesley's discussion of heathens falls in two categories, both of which align with the idea of being a foreigner. The first category is an external heathenism similar to the cultural and geographical
attributes of a foreigner. The second category is an internal heathenism

---

21. The following section on pre-conversion states will draw frequently upon labels and
categories which make this author anxious and uncomfortable, for example, "popery." While
we are tempted to make judgments about Wesley's labels and categories today, this study
aims to present Wesley in his own terms as a person of his time and using his terminology.

22. Wesley, *Letters*, 25:444.

where one is a foreigner internally, or spiritually, to the proper mode of faith and salvation.

In the Wesley corpus, over 400 occurrences of the word "heathen" appear, including over 100 occurrences in his published sermons. Wesley presented a rather rough understanding of heathens by surveying the world geographically. Wesley began his description geographically via Africa, with Egyptians who worshiped birds, beasts, and "creeping things."[23] He continued further south to what he called "Negroland"; he criticizes a lack of virtue, justice, and truth in Africans.[24] He then echoed Deuteronomy 12:8, Judges 21:25, and other passages, saying that in these places, "every man does what is right in his own eyes."[25] After this, Wesley described America where the natives "seem to breathe a purer air and to be in general men of a stronger understanding and a less savage temper."[26] Although the general description of America might be considered a brief nod of kindness, perhaps because of his personal involvement with Indians in America, Wesley went on to state that the Indians had no laws, lived in ill-contrived huts inferior to "English dog-kennels," lacked proper clothing, and ate poor food.[27] Wesley differentiated the northern and southern Indians, with the northerners being "idolaters of the lowest kind."[28] Wesley described the southern Indians as having no laws and no religion.[29] He wrote that these conditions led to violent behavior such as shooting neighbors and scalping them alive, being gluttons, drunkards, thieves, liars, and murderers of their fathers, mothers, children, and unborn children, and more.[30] Wesley continued his survey by describing Asia, where he had nicer things to say about their learning and integrity.[31] Yet, Wesley quickly criticized the Asian

---

23. Wesley, *Treatises I*, 12:176.

24. Wesley, *Treatises I*, 12:177–78. As stated above, Wesley's terminology is left untouched to present his writing in its original form.

25. Wesley, *Treatises I*, 12:178.

26. Wesley, *Treatises I*, 12:178.

27. Wesley, *Treatises I*, 12:179.

28. "Indians" are properly called "Native Americans" in the modern North American description today. However, Wesley's usage of "Indians" has been retained in order to avoid confusion with Wesley's direct quotations.

29. Wesley, *Treatises I*, 12:180.

30. Wesley, *Treatises I*, 12:180.

31. Wesley, *Treatises I*, 12:182.

alphabet, of which he said, "To keep an alphabet of thirty hundred letters could never be reconciled to common sense."[32] He even went on to critique how Asians ate their food.[33] Wesley noted Asian idolatry as those who worshiped Confucius and the souls of their ancestors.[34] After a few brief comments on some European heathens, Wesley concluded by saying that heathens make up "very near two-thirds of mankind."[35] Wesley returned to a geographic, and bluntly pejorative, understanding of "heathens" in his sermon *The General Spread of the Gospel*. Wesley preached: "Many nations have been discovered—numberless islands, particularly in the South Seas, large and well inhabited. But, by whom? By heathens of the basest sort, many of them inferior to the beast of the field."[36] Furthermore, Wesley viewed heathens just a step down from "Mahometans." Wesley wrote: "A little, and but a little, above the heathens in religion are the Mahometans."[37] To summarize, the first category of heathens in Wesley's works describes an external heathen nature based in geographic, ethnic, and cultural categories; religious beliefs may be implied but are not a primary focus. Wesley did discuss conversion from this category of external heathenism, but when he discussed conversion from heathenism, he primarily had in mind the second category, to which we now turn.

The second category of heathenism Wesley discussed was an internal heathenism, in which one was a foreigner spiritually to true faith and salvation. Wesley addressed heathens in *Sermon 1: Salvation by Faith*. This sermon describes the "faith of a heathen" and equivocated a heathen as a "Greek or Roman, therefore, yea, a Scythian or Indian."[38] Wesley explained that one could believe in the being and attributes of God, and in Christian virtue, reward, and punishment, and still be considered a heathen.[39] In the sermon, *The Almost Christian*, Wesley said that heathens could share in the

32. Wesley, *Treatises I*, 12:182.
33. Wesley, *Treatises I*, 12:182.
34. Wesley, *Treatises I*, 12:183.
35. Wesley, *Treatises I*, 12:185.
36. Wesley, *Sermons*, 2:486.
37. Wesley, *Sermons*, 2:486.
38. Wesley, *Sermons*, 1:119.
39. Wesley, *Sermons*, 1:119.

virtue of honesty.[40] Furthermore, Wesley addressed "the heathen, baptized or unbaptized" all in the same phrase.[41] In other places, Wesley spoke of the internal knowledge of the "heathen."[42] For instance, in Wesley's letter to John Taylor in *The Doctrine of Original Sin, Part 1*, Wesley traced the origins of knowledge and virtue and in doing so provided a survey of three sources: heathens, "Mahometans," and Christians.[43] Therefore, a heathen could be one who believed in God and virtue, and even be baptized.

More could be said of the 400-plus references to heathens in Wesley's writings, but space does not suffice here. It is sufficient to understand that, for Wesley, the first sense of being a heathen could be understood in a worldly and even geographical sense, with a full and harsh critique of their culture, manners, and beliefs. In the second sense, Wesley believed that a heathen could be an individual who believed in God and virtue, and even one who had partaken in Christian baptism. Wesley's view of heathenism is relevant for his theology of conversion because, in his writings, heathenism is the most frequent state from which one converts. While Wesley understands the first sense of heathenism in an external sense, the theological understanding of conversion falls within the second sense, an internal heathenism. An example that is illustrative of the intersection between Wesley's conception of conversion and his understanding of heathenism is Wesley's own self-understanding.

Returning to John Wesley's letter to his brother Samuel in which he spoke of converting heathens, it is significant that John continued in his letter to say that "Christianity is not a negation, or an external thing, but a new heart, a mind conformed to that of Christ, 'faith working by love.' "[44] Wesley is saying that a heathen is one who does not have a mind conformed to Christ, does not have faith working by love, and does not have a new heart. Wesley's letter was written in October 1735, over two years before his Aldersgate moment. If Wesley did have a "conversion" moment

---

40. Wesley, *Sermons*, 1:131–32.

41. *The Spirit of Bondage and Adoption*, in Wesley, *Sermons*, 1:263.

42. Outler commented that Wesley's use of heathen for "baptized or unbaptized" was a "strange usage." This idea will be further developed below. *The Spirit of Bondage and Adoption*, in Wesley, *Sermons*, 1:263n136.

43. Wesley, *Doctrinal and Controversial Treatises I*, 12:175–85.

44. Wesley, *Letters*, 25:444.

at Aldersgate, what did he convert "from"? It may be that he, in retrospect, would have seen himself as one who was baptized, believed in God, and assented to virtue, but did not possess the requisite genuine faith which brought about conversion. In other words, he could well have classified himself as a "heathen." It may be that Wesley was properly a heathen by his understanding. Indeed, Wesley could have been preaching retrospectively to himself in a 1746 sermon, *The Spirit of Bondage and Adoption*: "Have you heaven in your heart? Have you the Spirit of adoption, ever crying, 'Abba, Father'? ... overwhelmed with sorrow and fear? Or are you a stranger to this whole affair, and cannot imagine what I mean? Heathen, pull off your mask. Thou hast never put on Christ."[45] Wesley may have been preaching to a version of himself a decade earlier.

Identifying pre-Aldersgate Wesley conceptually as a heathen becomes clearer by looking at his journal entry upon returning from Georgia on January 24, 1738. Wesley wrote: "I went to America to convert the Indians; but Oh! who shall convert me?" As stated above, the Indians were a prime example of heathens in Wesley's mind, but he saw himself as needing the same conversion the Indians and heathens needed: he too belonged to the category of heathen requiring conversion, even as an Anglican minister. There is another allusion combining geographically and culturally distant heathens and Christianized heathens in Wesley's account of the ministry of George Whitefield in the colliers of Kingswood. Wesley wrote that the people in the colliers of Kingswood were famous for "neither fearing God nor regarding man, so ignorant of things of God that they seemed but one remove from the beasts that perish."[46] Wesley continued to write that many had taunted Whitefield, saying: "If [Whitefield] will convert heathens, why does not he go to the colliers of Kingswood?"[47] In effect, the people equated the heathens Whitefield had converted afar, likely an allusion to Whitefield's preaching and ministry to Indians in America, with those in a particularly rough group in Christianized England.[48] Later in his

---

45. Wesley, *Sermons*, 1:264.

46. Wesley, *Journals and Diaries*, 19:124.

47. Wesley, *Journals and Diaries*, 19:124.

48. Wesley recorded that Whitefield did go to Kingswood and that the "scene is already changed ... peace and love are there ... and hardly is 'their voice heard in the streets' [unless] singing praise unto God their Saviour." *Journals and Diaries*, 19:125.

life, Wesley continued to think of a Christianized nation as heathen, as he did in a short letter to Duncan McAllum on July 14, 1778. Wesley encouraged young Duncan not to go to Africa as a missionary but to stay and "convert the heathen in Scotland."[49] Similarly, late in his life, Wesley continued to describe people such as the Native Americans as heathen. In his letter to Francis Asbury on November 25, 1787, Wesley wrote "that [Asbury] would first stir up the hearts of some of his children to make the conversion of the heathens also a matter of solemn prayer!"[50] Therefore, Wesley spoke often of "converting from" heathenism. Wesley may have understood himself to be a heathen before his Aldersgate experience. As Wesley aged, his clear-cut reflections back to Aldersgate changed their hue, as his errata in 1774 added that "I am not sure of this" to his entry: "I who went to America to convert others, was never myself converted to God."[51] But, by his admission, Wesley had self-identified as a changed person, a person changed *from* being a heathen.

1.2.2. Gentilism, Judaism, Deism, and Popery[52]

Wesley's most repeated "convert from" state is heathenism. However, there is another, less frequent state, from which one can convert; this state is broadly defined as theological conversion. Theological conversion includes four prior states in Wesley's corpus, conversion from gentilism, Judaism, deism, and popery.

Wesley made at least three references to Jewish converts in his sermons.[53] Wesley's other references to Jewish conversion occur in his *Notes*

---

49. Wesley, *The Letters of John Wesley*, 6:316.

50. Wesley, *The Letters of John Wesley*, 8:24.

51. Wesley, *Journals and Diaries*, 18:214. See note "h" for the errata. Two significant contributions regarding Wesley's Aldersgate experience include Randy L. Maddox, *Aldersgate Reconsidered* (Nashville: Kingswood Books, 1990), and Kenneth J. Collins, "Other Thoughts on Aldersgate: Has the Conversionist Paradigm Collapsed?," *Methodist History* 30, no. 1 (October 1, 1991), 10–25.

52. Throughout this study, my aim is to present Wesley in his own terms and as a man of his day, despite my anxiousness and discomfort using Wesley's terms such as "popery."

53. Wesley described the Jewish converts in the Galatian church in his sermon *The Great Privilege of those that are Born of God*, in *Sermons*, 1:440. In the sermon *The Mystery of Iniquity* Wesley described the audience of the epistle of James being the converted Jews who were scattered abroad; *Sermons*, 2:459. Conversely, Wesley spoke of the unconverted Jews who are known for their wisdom, spirit, and fashions of the age; *Sermons*, 3:127. As per the notes above regarding Wesley's language, Wesley's language and comments regarding Jewish people

on the Old Testament and New Testament. As a whole, the *Notes* comments anticipated a day when some Jews will convert to Christianity upon the coming of Jesus Christ.[54] Similarly, Wesley also discussed the conversion of the gentiles frequently.[55] Conversion from deism and "popery" can be understood as a conversion from one theology to a new one. Wesley's preface to *The Doctrine of Original Sin: According to Scripture, Reason, and Experience* discussed that, from the deist perspective, one "can't see that we have much need for Jesus Christ ... I can't see that we have much need of Christianity."[56] Wesley continued by stating that for a deist there was no need for Jesus, or for Christianity, in that there was no "sickness" that needed healing.[57] Wesley made a clear distinction between deism and Christianity. A person could "convert from" deism to Christianity, but this conversion was a theological conversion which Wesley observed.[58] Similarly, "popery" was another theological position Wesley spoke of to "convert from." Wesley outlined his position on the Roman Catholic Church in his tract, *Popery Calmly Considered.*[59] While the details are not necessary to rehearse in this section, Wesley was clear that a conversion *from* "popery" was needed.[60] Each of the four theological conversions was a position from which one could be said to "convert from." These four positions work within Wesley's definition of conversion as a turn "from and to." Wesley called

---

are presented in his own voice, despite the challenges of language and sensitivity that are appropriate in a post-Shoah context.

54. See Wesley, *Explanatory Notes upon the Old Testament*, Deut 32:43; Pss 67; 85:10; Isa 49:12; 65:1; 66:12; Jer 3:18; 32:40; 49:6; Ezek 37:25; Hos 14:5; Mic 5:4; Wesley, *Explanatory Notes upon the New Testament*, Acts 8:32; 18:27; 21:21; Rom 11:16, 18, 25.

55. Wesley, *Explanatory Notes upon the Old Testament*, Gen 9:27; 10:5; Pss 47:9; 67; 68; 85:10; 87:7; Isa 12:1; 49:12; 65:1; Jer 12:16.

56. Wesley, *Doctrinal and Controversial Treatises I*, 12:157–58.

57. Wesley, *Treatises I*, 12:158.

58. For examples of Wesley's discussion of conversion from deism, see Wesley, *Journals and Diaries*, 18:182, 20:293; Wesley, *Letters*, 26:177; Wesley, *The Letters of John Wesley*, 3:357, 6:298; Wesley, *The Works of John Wesley*, 9:494.

59. Following the comments above, Wesley's language regarding Roman Catholicism is retained in order to present him in his own terms.

60. See Wesley, *Journals and Diaries*, 18:182, 19:209, 22:26; Wesley, *The Appeals to Men of Reason and Religion and Certain Related Open Letters*, 11:420, 423; Wesley, *The Letters of John Wesley*, 5:23, 121; Wesley, *The Works of John Wesley*, 10:140–58, 161, 167.

upon gentiles and Jews to move to a primary identification with and allegiance to Christianity. Similarly, Wesley called deists and "papists" to turn their theology to what he understood to be genuine Christianity. Wesley felt that these conversions were necessary in order for one to turn *from* sin and *to* holiness. These changes would come upon a profound experience, the experience of instantaneous conversion, which is where we now turn our attention.

2. PRECEDING CONVERSION: CONVINCED, CONVICTED, AWAKENED

Within the Wesley corpus, a particular set of phrases surrounds many of Wesley's discussions of conversion. The form of these phrases differs from time to time and as Wesley aged, but they generally follow a simple form: first being convinced, convicted, or awakened, then being converted. This section analyzes, therefore, Wesley's usage of this form, seeking to further understand Wesley's theology of conversion. It is evident that both "convincing" and "conviction" (which Wesley used synonymously) have four characteristics. First, both include the sense of being deeply convinced of sin, being cut to the heart, and feeling the wrath of God. Second, this pre-converting work could include a visible manifestation such as crying and tears. Third, convincing and convicting are a work of the grace of God given by the power of God. Fourth, convincing and convicting are steps leading toward conversion, though these experiences do not automatically lead to conversion. Similarly, Wesley's use of the word "awakened" describes the same pre-converting work of convincing and conviction, but "awakened" is used to emphasize the preaching of the law as a preparative step before delivering the gospel and calling for conversion. This section closes by highlighting two aspects which accompany convincing, convicting, and awakening: visible manifestations in response to personal sinfulness and the capacity of children to be convinced, convicted, and awakened. These two aspects are highlighted to, once again, illustrate Wesley's insistence that pre-converting experiences are expressions of the grace and work of God. This section relates to the current chapter to show that Wesley's four primary operant conversion motifs work together in a way which is sequential and inseparable. Instantaneous conversion and continued conversion do not occur in Wesley's operant instances of conversion without the pre-converting work of convincing, convicting, and awakening.[61]

2.1. CONVINCED, CONVICTED

John Wesley taught that conversion was preceded by "convincing." Convincing, in Wesley's thought, is an experience with personal sinfulness that is brought about by the grace of God as a step leading, ideally, toward conversion. Wesley's operant instances of "convincing" contribute to the formulation of the espoused conversion theology of Wesley, notably, the common synoptic principles that conversion is both initiated and sustained by the grace of God and foreshadowed by a deep sense of sinfulness. My analysis of Wesley's writing shows that "convincing" includes at least three dynamics related to conversion. First, convincing is an experience with personal sinfulness, at times manifested visibly. Second, convincing is an act of the grace of God. Third, convincing is an action which leads toward, but does not always end in, conversion. In the few instances when Wesley spoke of being convicted in the context of conversion,[62] similar to conviction, he meant the work of God that brought a sense of sinfulness that led one toward conversion.

Wesley taught that people were convinced through personal sinfulness; this is the first dynamic of his understanding of convincing. In *A Plain Account of Christian Perfection*, Wesley explained: "More and more sinners were convinced; while some were almost daily converted to God, and others enabled to love him 'with all their heart.'"[63] Though this quotation could be understood to say that sinners are those who were convinced, converted, and enabled to love, the grammar leads us to read the subjects and

---

61. In my efforts to catalogue key words and phrases in the Wesley corpus, 86% of the occurrences of this form were found in the journals, letters, diaries, and documents written to individuals. Only 6% were found in the sermons and 8% in the Old and New Testament explanatory notes. Thus, the form, "convinced," "convicted," or "awakened" (followed often by conversion), exists largely in the anecdotal and narrative writing of Wesley, in his letters, journals, and engagement with others. The form can be found in his sermons and explanatory notes on the Bible, and these will be discussed. But it is important to observe that the form rarely appears in the public theology of his sermons. The existence of this form shows that conversion did not stand alone as an isolated experience; rather, conversion included an experiential preliminary stage.

62. My analysis shows five instances of "convicting" along with "conversion" in this sense.

63. Wesley, *Doctrinal and Controversial Treatises II*, 13:179.

verbs together: sinners/convinced, some/converted, others/enabled to love. These pairings tell us that the convinced are sinners and the convincing has to do with their sin. Later in Wesley's life the connection between "convincing" and "sinning" became more explicit. Wesley wrote a letter to Lady Huntington on August 14, 1771, mentioning "converting as well as convincing sinners."[64] Wesley's sermon *On the Death of George Whitefield*, explained that through Whitefield's ministry, "many were deeply convinced of their lost state."[65] With increasing frequency in Wesley's ministry, those who were converted first experienced a "convincing" which highlighted their sinfulness. Convincing could be an emotional experience of sinfulness which was "felt." It was an experience of the heart, accompanied by tears, crying, and feeling the "wrath of God."[66]

The second and third dynamics of convincing are intertwined: God's grace leads the sinner toward conversion through convincing. The dual dynamic of convincing as a leading-grace is exemplified in a letter from Wesley to John Fletcher on March 22, 1771. Wesley wrote: "The Lord's rewarding no work and accepting of none but so far as they proceed from His preventing, convincing, and converting grace through the Beloved."[67] Here, Wesley showed a progression through which the convert proceeds: first through preventing (that is, prevenient) grace, then convincing grace, then converting grace.[68] This progression tells us the order in which Wesley expected convincing to happen. It is also important to understand convincing as a grace, which may not be the first description one might imagine to designate what we have already learned brings the "wrath of God." A journal entry on May 13, 1789 has a similar progression. Wesley recalled: "Many

---

64. Wesley, *The Letters of John Wesley*, 5:275. For similar examples, see Wesley, *The Methodist Societies: History, Nature, and Design*, 9:399; Wesley, *Journals and Diaries*, 21:342, 22:335, 444; Wesley, *The Letters of John Wesley*, 6:279; Wesley, *The Works of John Wesley*, 10:424. A particular engaging example is Wesley's mention of the work in Northampton and Jonathan Edwards; see Wesley, *Sermons*, 3:596.

65. Wesley, *Sermons*, 2:335.

66. Wesley, *Journals and Diaries*, 21:381.

67. Wesley, *The Letters of John Wesley*, 5:231. For an example of Wesley's use of conviction as a work of God, see *The Letters of John Wesley*, 4:133, 5:99; *The Appeals to Men of Reason and Religion and Certain Related Open Letters*, 11:496; *Journals and Diaries*, 21:427.

68. Prevenient grace, synonymous with "preventing grace," are from the Latin meaning "come before." For more on this concept in Wesley, see chapter three, section 1.3., and in Whitefield, see chapter five, section 3.1.

in every place have been deeply convinced, many converted to God, and
some perfected in love."[69] These progressions reveal a four-fold sequence:
preventing grace, convincing grace (regarding sin and the wrath to come),
converting grace, and, finally, being perfected in love. At each step of this
progression is an action of God's grace leading the convinced sinner toward
conversion.[70]

While it has become clear, therefore, that convincing is an experience of personal sinfulness brought about by the grace of God leading
one to be converted, Wesley did not presume that convincing always led
one to be converted. Some did move quickly from convincing to conversion;[71] however, being convinced of sin did not always result in conversion,[72] even when deeply persuaded of their lost state as sinners, cut to the
heart, feeling the wrath of God, and manifesting crying and tears. Wesley
believed that convincing was truly a grace given by the power of God as
a step toward conversion, though convincing did not automatically lead
to conversion.[73]

2.2 AWAKENED

Wesley utilized a third term to describe a critical experience before conversion: being "awakened" prior to conversion. Wesley's use of "awakening"
is similar to his use of convincing and conviction; awakening is also an
experience with personal sinfulness that leads toward conversion.[74] Wesley
spoke of being awakened when he was emphasizing the law of God as an
instrumental cause of convincing and conviction. To be awakened is the

---

69. Wesley, *Journals and Diaries*, 24:133.

70. Convincing is a work of grace by the power of God. A journal entry on September
23, 1759, is illustrative. Wesley discussed field preaching and noted that not only did a great
number attend, but also that the "converting as well as convincing power of God is eminently
present." Wesley, *Journals and Diaries*, 21:230.

71. On July 29, 1762, Wesley recorded in his journal several accounts of those who were
"both convinced and converted in the same hour." Wesley, *Journals and Diaries*, 21:381.

72. Wesley, *Journals and Diaries*, 22:329–30.

73. See, also, the entire section of hymns under the heading "convincing" in Wesley, *A
Collection of Hymns for the Use of the People Called Methodists*, 188–200.

74. In a journal entry on June 5, 1772, Wesley wrote: "many of whom were ... both convicted of sin (without any previous awakening) and converted to God." Thus, Wesley could
speak of being convicted and awakened synonymously. Wesley, *Journals and Diaries*, 22:335.
Similar examples of the form awakened or converted can be found in *Journals and Diaries*,
22:443, 23:141, 196.

experience of being "cut to the heart," primarily through the preaching of the law by Wesley and his associates.

Wesley spoke of awakening in the scheme of the convicting aspect of the three uses of the law.[75] Early in his ministry, Wesley said that an awakening via the law was needed before the reception of the gospel. Wesley wrote: "[Preaching the gospel] does not answer the very first end of the law, namely, the convincing men of sin, the awakening those who are still asleep on the brink of hell."[76] Similar to Calvin's first use of the three uses of the law, Wesley understood awakening as a preparative stage before the presentation of the gospel. The preaching of the law is the preaching of God's righteous commands for humanity. Wesley utilized the preaching of the law prior to his gospel proclamation to bring about an awakening that would help lead people toward conversion. Even before Aldersgate, Wesley recognized the awakening power of the law which would lead to his conversion. In an January 18, 1780 letter to Thomas Taylor, Wesley reflected back on the origins of the Methodist movement. Wesley recalled: "It pleased God by me to awaken, first my brother, and then a few others; who severally desired of me as a favor that I would direct them in all things. After my return from Georgia many were both awakened and converted to God."[77] Wesley identified Charles as being awakened prior to conversion, along with many others. Thus, for Wesley, awakening comes before the reception of the gospel, and that conversion comes upon the preaching of the gospel.[78]

---

75. Calvin described the first use of the law in a way which most closely resembles awakening. Calvin wrote: "The first part is this ... [the law] warns, informs, convicts, and lastly condemns, every man of his own righteousness." John Calvin, *Calvin: Institutes of the Christian Religion*, trans. Ford Lewis Battles (Louisville, KY: Westminster John Knox Press, 2001), 2.7.6 (1:354). Campbell described awakening as "the moment when a person recognizes her or his fearful state in relation to God and thus passes from the 'natural' to the 'legal' state." Campbell, *Wesleyan Beliefs*, 78. See also Maddox, *Responsible Grace*, 100–101; Kenneth J. Collins, *The Theology of John Wesley: Holy Love and the Shape of Grace* (Nashville: Abingdon Press, 2007), 10–11.

76. *The Law Established through Faith*, in Wesley, *Sermons*, 2:22–23.

77. Wesley, *The Letters of John Wesley*, 6:375.

78. Randy Maddox wrote that early in Wesley's ministry Wesley preached a particularly intense and prolonged call for awakening, so much so that Wesley was charged with brain-washing and using "the fear of damnation as the main motive for conversion." Maddox believes that the intense, awakening preaching of the law early in Wesley's career (1739-1744) brought the side effect of extraordinary behavior such as outcries, convulsions, and trances. Maddox notes that Wesley's focus shifted away from this approach as he matured. See Maddox, *Responsible Grace*, 160–61.

2.3. OTHER ASPECTS PRECEDING CONVERSION

Wesley included two associated experiential dynamics that emerged in instances of convicting, convincing, and awakening. First, in the midst of convicting, convincing, and awakening, it was not uncommon for Wesley to observe in his audiences (especially early in his career) instances of physical manifestations brought upon by the revelation of personal sinfulness. The physical manifestations were deemed to be from God's Spirit. Second, children could also experience convicting, convincing, and awakening as they were being led to convert; intellectual capacity or maturity were not prerequisites for pre-conversion experiences. These two observations thicken Wesley's insistence that the experiences people underwent prior to their conversion were brought upon by God's work of grace.

Wesley believed that physical manifestations could be indicative of God's pre-converting work. People in the midst of conviction and conversion appear as mad to those who are without God, those who are not Christians. Emotional responses to the conviction of sin on the mind, heart, and soul are alien to those who are without God. Thus, Wesley did not see anything improper with these manifestations. In *A Further Appeal to Men of Reason and Religion, Part I*, Wesley described those who were "driven mad" and "crying." Wesley wrote: "[People with manifestations are] occasioned either by those who are convinced of sin, or those who are inwardly converted to God."[79] In one of his most public sermons, *On the Death of George Whitefield*, Wesley highlighted one of Whitefield's dynamic preaching occasions. Wesley recounted: "Many were deeply convinced of their lost state; many truly converted to God. In some places thousands cried out aloud; many as in the agonies of death; others were wringing their hands; others lying on the ground; others sinking in to the arms of their friends; almost all lifting their eyes, and calling for mercy."[80] Wesley's recollection could be dismissed as gratuitous eulogizing, but the public nature of both this sermon and the many thousands who experienced Whitefield's sermon and its effects limit how far an accusation of exaggeration could have been

---

79. Wesley, *The Appeals to Men of Reason and Religion and Certain Related Open Letters*, 11:199.

80. Wesley, *Sermons*, 2:335. Later on the same page, Wesley recounted a time when Whitefield preached. Wesley wrote: "As almost as soon as he began, crying, weeping, and wailing were to be heard on every side. Many sunk down to the ground, cut to the heart; and many were filled with divine consolation."

taken. Thus, some who were convicted and converted experienced significant physical manifestations. Wesley believed miracles and other "unusual" behavior, such as physical manifestations, were not far from the convincing and converting power of God.[81]

Wesley taught that convincing and converting were not limited to adults only; children were also included. Children can be convinced, convicted, and awakened to their sin just as ably as adults. Convincing and conversion were not limited to those with adult intellectual capacities, but were, instead, works owing to the power of God.[82] It is important to recognize the many ways Wesley credited God as the one working in those being led to conversion in these pre-conversion experiences. God is the one who convicted people through the law. God is the one who brought manifestations upon those who felt the weight of their sin. And, on the topic of the awakening of children, Wesley believed that God did not require full intellectual capacity or maturation of children in order to lead them toward conversion. Since this section considers Wesley's observations on God's pre-conversion work, this chapter now moves to reflect upon Wesley's view of the inauguration of conversion: instantaneous conversion.

3. INSTANTANEOUS CONVERSION

John Wesley's theology of instantaneous conversion has received more attention than perhaps any other topic in the scope of this study. The abundant interest is due to the lasting influence of Wesley's Aldersgate experience on May 24, 1738. Typically, if people know one thing about John Wesley, it has something to do with Aldersgate and Wesley's heart being "strangely warmed." Indeed, Aldersgate is a landmark event in Wesley's life and any examination of Wesley's theology of conversion must attend to Wesley's Aldersgate experience. This study does not aim to produce a historical account and analysis of Aldersgate itself; abundant and excellent scholarly analysis already exists on this topic.[83] Instead, this section

---

81. The "power of God" is another phrase that accompanies the form we are examining; see Wesley, *Journals and Diaries*, 21:230; Wesley, *The Letters of John Wesley*, 4:151.

82. Wesley wrote in his journal on April 1, 1788: "Sinners, men, women, and children are still convinced and converted to God." Wesley, *Journals and Diaries*, 24:74.

83. The most thorough analysis of Aldersgate is in the recent PhD thesis: Mark K. Olson, "Exegeting Aldersgate: John Wesley's Interpretation of 24 May 1738" (PhD diss., University of Manchester, 2016). See also Maddox, *Aldersgate Reconsidered*; Collins, "Other Thoughts

considers the issue of how Wesley *understood* instantaneous conversion *theologically* throughout his life. The analysis concludes that a significant shift took place in Wesley's theology of conversion during the timeframe surrounding Aldersgate which yielded Wesley's normative and enduring belief: instantaneous conversion comes immediately at the onset of genuine faith.[84]

Three observations will be made regarding instantaneous conversion in the theology of John Wesley. First, prior to Aldersgate, Wesley viewed conversion in two parts: an initial conversion brought upon through baptism, and a full conversion best understood as Christian perfection. Second, leading up to Aldersgate and following, Wesley held that the normative mode of conversion was an experiential instantaneous conversion inaugurated by responding in faith to Christ. This second observation provides one statement of Wesley's espoused theology of conversion: conversion happens instantaneously by faith (synoptic statement 5). Third, in the decades after Aldersgate, Wesley may have become more comfortable with exceptions to the experience of instantaneous conversion and recognizing genuine conversion without a sudden experience. Another synoptic statement of Wesley's operant theology of conversion arises in this third observation: conversion is instantaneous but is not always recognizable by the true convert (synoptic statement 6). This section concludes by observing that his theology's lasting legacy lies in his understanding of conversion as instantaneous.

3.1. PRE-ALDERSGATE WESLEY: INITIAL CONVERSION AT
BAPTISM AND FULL CONVERSION UPON CHRISTIAN PERFECTION

The first era of Wesley's understanding of instantaneous conversion begins with a traditional Church of England understanding of instantaneous conversion at baptism.[85] Upon Wesley's exposure to the theology of Richard

---

on Aldersgate: Has the Conversionist Paradigm Collapsed?"; John H. Tyson, "John Wesley's Conversion at Aldersgate," in *Conversion in the Wesleyan Tradition*, ed. Kenneth J. Collins and John H. Tyson (Nashville: Abingdon Press, 2001).

84. In this section references to "Aldersgate" designate the time period surrounding Aldersgate, primarily the months leading up to Aldersgate, not just May 24, 1738. Specific dates will be mentioned when relevant.

85. The relationship between conversion and baptism will be looked at in further detail in chapter three, section one.

Lucas and, then, more prominently, William Law, Wesley understood the benefits of baptism could be sinned away. The attainment of the experience of instantaneous conversion came via the realization of a radical threshold: Christian perfection. Toward the end of this first era, Wesley became disillusioned with Law's radical demands for perfection as the threshold of conversion. However, Wesley agreed with Law that the benefits of baptism could be sinned away, but Wesley knew that the attainment of Christian perfection could not be the point of instantaneous conversion. The threshold of instantaneous conversion must be something else. The question of when instantaneous conversion occurs will lead us into the next era, Wesley's Aldersgate experience, but in order to understand that era, it is essential to comprehend Wesley's understanding of instantaneous conversion, baptism, and Christian perfection in the first era. The first era is observed in three phases: first, Wesley's foundational phase established by the principle documents of the Church of England; second, the transition to a phase whereby Christian perfection was to be sought by being "fully converted"; third, the phase introduced by Law in which the benefits of baptism could be sinned away and conversion came through the attainment of Christian perfection.

The first phase of this era is the time period when Wesley understood baptism as conversion. Wesley was brought up in the Church of England context which was theologically bounded by the doctrine of the *Thirty-Nine Articles*, the *Book of Common Prayer*, and the *Edwardian Homilies*—all of which spoke of baptism and regeneration.[86] Before his Aldersgate-era transition, Wesley saw baptism as conversion to Christianity. In other words, if a person was baptized, they had been regenerated, and thus, converted to Christianity. Wesley's intent to reach the unconverted "heathen" highlights Wesley's early view of conversion.[87] Wesley was influenced not only by his church's foundational documents on baptism and conversion; he was also influenced by his father's writing on the subject. In 1700, Wesley's father published an extensive work on baptism. Samuel Wesley wrote: "If any of our Ministers goes among the Heathens, and converts them, he would

---

86. See chapter three, section one for further details.

87. See the letters to Richard Morgan on March 15, 1734, and Samuel Wesley on October 15, 1735: Wesley, *Letters*, 25:379, 444. See, also, the diary entry on July 12, 1737: Wesley, *Journals and Diaries*, 18:527.

certainly baptize Infants."[88] Following in the footsteps of his father and his Church of England heritage, Wesley initially believed conversion to occur at baptism.

The second phase of Wesley's pre-Aldersgate theology of conversion was when Wesley added the nuance that people could be "fully" converted as they attained Christian perfection. Christian perfection, in this era, was the entire sanctification of a person in which one is led "in to all truth and into all holiness."[89] Conversion was more of an attitude and temper of the soul which could be attained when one was in a state where one did not drive the Holy Spirit away from oneself, with full conversion manifest expressly in entire sanctification. In a letter to Reverend John Burton on October 10, 1735, Wesley said that he had received a saving knowledge of the gospel of Christ, but that he still needed to be converted himself. Wesley wrote: "If I only be converted myself."[90] The editor of the critical edition of Wesley's earliest letters, Frank Baker, inserted the adverb "fully": "If I only be fully converted myself."[91] Baker gave a clue to what Wesley meant since the rest of the passage described the struggle to live a holy life, including the desire to attain "Christian perfection." Thus, in this instance, Wesley was speaking of conversion as an attempt at complete holiness, not in a salvific sense.[92] Concerning Christian perfection, Wesley's teaching shifted over time, particularly before 1738. Maddox argues: "[Wesley] championed pursuit of recovered holiness through spiritual disciplines, typically describing the goal to which one aspired via these means as 'perfection' or 'perfect love.' ... It is also clear in Wesley's early writings that his aspirations towards holiness were driven by a desire for assurance that he was in a state of acceptance with God (that is, justification)."[93] In other words,

---

88. Samuel Wesley, *The Pious Communicant Rightly Prepar'd* (London: Charles Harper, 1700), 227; see also 229. Chapter three, section one, discusses Wesley's view of baptism in further depth.

89. See Wesley's 1732 sermon, *On Grieving the Holy Spirit*; Wesley, *The Works of John Wesley*, 7:485. See the note on Wesley's use of this sermon in Wesley, *Sermons*, 4:531.

90. Wesley, *Journals and Diaries*, 25:441.

91. Wesley, *Journals and Diaries*, 25:441n8.

92. Note that this letter was written three days before Wesley departed for Georgia and gives an important snapshot of Wesley's theology immediately before he encountered the Moravians on the boat to Georgia which would become the pathway to his post-Aldersgate view of conversion.

93. Maddox, *Responsible Grace*, 180–81.

Wesley pushed toward Christian perfection in his efforts to be justified; this is what Wesley likely meant when he told Burton that he wanted to "be [fully] converted himself."[94]

The second phase of Wesley's pre-Aldersgate theology of conversion and the inclusion of the concept of Christian perfection was influenced by several authors, but most importantly by the writing of Richard Lucas.[95] Wesley read Richard Lucas's *Religious Perfection* in March 1730.[96] Lucas understood baptism and conversion as the beginning of the Christian life, with Christian perfection as the consummation of conversion; conversion was related to infancy, perfection to "manhood."[97] In Lucas's theology, conversion was not constrained only to the beginning of faith. Lucas wrote: "We must not stop in faith, till it be made perfect in love. We much meditate divine truths ... till all our other desires and passions be converted into, and swallowed up of love; till God becomes the center of our souls."[98] For Lucas, the interior desires and passions experience conversion, and to become perfect in love requires full conversion. Thus, Wesley's theology of instantaneous conversion was shaped by Lucas's teaching which extended conversion past a one-time occurrence.

Wesley began to see baptism as an initial conversion which needed maturation. The maturation of conversion blurs the instantaneousness of conversion. In the first phase, the moment of baptism was simply the isolated moment of instantaneous conversion. In the second phase, Christian perfection was understood as the moment of full conversion. The second phase provided an initial conversion (baptism) and a full conversion (Christian perfection) with a period of maturation between the two, thus blurring a simple understanding of instantaneous conversion.

---

94. Wesley, *Journals and Diaries*, 25:441n8.

95. The eastern fathers influenced Wesley's theology of Christian perfection, but their direct influence came later. It was Lucas, Law, and others who first attracted Wesley to the doctrine of Christian perfection. See Runyon, *The New Creation*, 91; Ted A. Campbell, *John Wesley and Christian Antiquity: Religious Vision and Cultural Change* (Nashville: Kingswood Books, 1991), 45, 65–67. I am indebted to Mark K. Olson for pointing me to primary sources that influenced Wesley's early view of Christian perfection.

96. Richard P. Heitzenrater, "John Wesley and the Oxford Methodists" (PhD diss., Duke University, 1972), 511.

97. Richard Lucas, *Religious Perfection, or, a Third Part of the Enquiry after Happiness* (London: S. Smith and B. Walford, 1704), 2.

98. Lucas, *Religious Perfection*, 359–60.

Wesley's deep engagement with the theology of William Law would distinguish these moments with greater clarity, which brings us to the third,
and final, phase of Wesley's pre-Aldersgate era regarding his understanding of instantaneous conversion.

  Wesley read Lucas and Law in nearly the same time period (Lucas first
in March 1730, then Law in December 1730); while read in chronologically
proximity, Law's influence became dominant and the most influential voice
in the third phase of Wesley's pre-Aldersgate era of understanding instantaneous conversion.[99] Law's *Christian Perfection* (published in 1726 and read
by Wesley in November 1732) and *Serious Call* (published 1729, Wesley read
in December 1730) made few direct references to conversion.[100] However,
what Law lacked in specific terminology regarding conversion, he more
than made up for when he displayed his theology of the new birth and
being born of God. To understand Law's view of the new birth, it is cru-
cially important to observe Law's understanding of post-baptismal sin.
Law wrote:

> Did we enough consider this, we should find, that whenever we
> yield ourselves up to the pleasures, profits, and honours of this life,
> that we turn apostate, break our covenant with God, and go back
> from the express conditions, on which we were admitted into the

---

99. For Wesley's reflections on Law's influence in this period, see Wesley, *Journals and
Diaries*, 18:244–45; Wesley, *Letters*, 25:540–41.

100. The dates of Wesley's reading come from Wesley's Oxford diary. See Heitzenrater,
"John Wesley and the Oxford Methodists," 510. Wesley's recollection of exactly when he first
read Law's works is a story all on its own. One source of confusion stems from Wesley's letter
to John Newton on May 14, 1765, where Wesley said he read Law in 1727. The issue was sorted
out by Frank Baker in the Wesleyan Historical Society proceedings, later responded to by
Fredrick Hunter, and Baker responded to Hunter. In the opinion of the author of this study,
Baker's arguments are stronger and, thus, place Wesley's reading of *Serious Call* in December
1730 and *Christian Perfection* in November 1732. The chronology is important to understand
Wesley's theological development and in this study places Law after Lucas. See Wesley, *Letters*,
27:428; Frank Baker, "John Wesley's Introduction to William Law," *Wesley Historical Society* 36,
no. 3 (1969): 78–82; Fredrick Hunter, "John Wesley's Introduction to William Law (Response),"
Wesley Historical Society 37, no. 5 (1970): 143–50; Frank Baker, "John Wesley's Introduction to
William Law: A Reconsideration," *Wesley Historical Society* 37, no. 6 (1970): 173–77. See also
Wesley, *Doctrinal and Controversial Treatises II*, 11–12. Law hints at a connection between conversion and holiness. Law wrote: "[A good preacher] will make converts to holiness; he will
be heard with reverence on the Sunday, not so much for what he says, as for what he says
and does all the week." The conversion Law spoke of related more to the authenticity of
the ministry than an explicit theological statement on conversion. William Law, *A Practical
Treatise Upon Christian Perfection* (London: William and John Innys, 1726), 312.

communion of Christ's church. If we consult either the life or doctrines of our Saviour, we shall find that Christianity is a covenant,
that contains the terms of changing and resigning this world, for
another, that is to come.[101]

According to the *Book of Common Prayer* one entered the church at baptism. The baptismal rubric and the Edwardian Homilies presented the
seeds which could be developed into a doctrine of the "sinning away" of
regeneration and the benefits of one's baptism; Law made this possibility
explicit. Law's response to breaking the baptismal covenant was to propose
the need for active pursuit of the new birth: "That Christianity requires
a change of nature, a new life perfectly devoted to God, is plain from the
Spirit and tenor of the Gospel ... another birth that brings us into a condition altogether as new, as when we first saw the light."[102] Therefore, Law
taught the ubiquitous need for all to experience the pursuit of being born
again (after the "sinning away" of baptism).[103] Law made clear to Wesley
the need for the new birth. Indeed, Wesley, as with many in the evangelical
revival, are indebted to Law's insights and built upon the clarity which Law
brought to this topic. Yet, the *means* which Law taught to acquire the new
birth eventually became a major point of departure for Wesley's theology.

As shown above, Lucas introduced Wesley to the maturation of conversion which came "fully" upon the attainment of Christian perfection.
Law's view of "sinning away" baptism interrupted the continuity of Lucas's
view of conversion. For Law, conversion was no longer initially found in
baptism and then matured through life; instead, the benefits of baptism
were lost through sin and the new birth was needed (again)—continuity
was lost, and a new beginning was needed. Wesley first read *A Serious Call*
and learned from Law that salvation came through striving for perfection,
Law wrote: "The salvation of our souls is set forth in Scripture as a thing
of difficulty, that requires all our diligence, that is to be worked out with
fear and trembling. ... And that many will miss of their salvation, who

---

101. Law, *Treatise Upon Christian Perfection*, 43.
102. Law, *Treatise Upon Christian Perfection*, 45.
103. See also Collins, *The Theology of John Wesley*, 234.

seem to have taken some pains to obtain it."[104] Law continued: "It seems plain, that our salvation depends upon the sincerity and perfection of our endeavours to obtain it."[105] Law went on to recommend voluntary poverty and chastity for those who sought perfection.[106] A Serious Call indeed was a serious call for everyone, baptized or unbaptized, to seek earnestly the means of grace for the salvation of their souls with its zenith being Christian perfection. Notably, A Serious Call did not make clear if perfection was required for salvation.

It is important to point out that Wesley read Christian Perfection after reading A Serious Call. This order intensified the difficulties of Wesley's experience in light of his emerging theology of conversion. Law had written these two books in the reverse order (that is, Christian Perfection was first). By reading A Serious Call first, Wesley was introduced initially to how one could push toward perfection. It was twenty-three months later when Wesley read Christian Perfection, which set out the telos of Christian perfection more clearly. Christian Perfection could be accused of teaching that Christian perfection was the point of instantaneous conversion. Law wrote:

> Thus is he that is born of God, purity and holiness is his only aim, and he is more incapable of having any sinful intensions, than the miser is incapable of generous experience. ... This it is to be born of God, when we have a temper and mind so entirely devoted to purity and holiness, that it may be said of us in a just sense, that we cannot commit sin. When holiness is such a habit in our minds, so directs and forms our designs, as covetousness and ambition directs and governs the actions of such men, as are governed by no other principles, then are we alive in God, and living members of the mystical body of his Son Jesus Christ.[107]

Law's A Serious Call slightly softens the requirement of perfection as the threshold of salvation and conversion. By reading the two works in

104. William Law, A Serious Call to a Devout and Holy Life (London: William Innys, 1729), 30.
105. Law, A Serious Call, 32.
106. Law, A Serious Call, 134, 482.
107. Law, Treatise Upon Christian Perfection, 49–50.

reverse order Wesley instead can be seen to exacerbate the requirement for absolute perfection as a requirement for conversion.

The examination of Wesley's life after he read Law and before Aldersgate shows the enormous influence of Law's theology on Wesley and his associates as they pursued the means of grace extensively as the means to attain the new birth which they were convinced they so needed.[108] Essentially, they were striving for Christian perfection as a converting experience. They understood Law's teaching on *full* conversion as the *only* conversion. The letters between Wesley and Law in the two weeks before Aldersgate show the tremendous frustration Wesley had built up toward Law as Wesley felt misled by Law regarding how to acquire the new birth.[109] Wesley accused Law of teaching works-based justification, pushing Wesley to the point of death via the means of grace.[110] Wesley even inferred that Law was not saved.[111]

The first era of Wesley's understanding of instantaneous conversion, thus, comes to a close with Wesley holding three precepts concerning instantaneous conversion. First, Wesley believed that conversion was attained through the new birth and was necessary to be saved. Second, the new birth came instantaneously upon baptism, but was sinned away,

---

108. A further analysis could be pursued which examines the main ideas related to conversion in all of the critical texts Wesley first read in his Oxford years. This would include Lucas's *Perfection* (read in March 1730), Law's *Serious Call* (read in December 1730), Scupoli's *Spiritual Combat* (read in August 1732), Scougal's *Life of God in the Soul of Man* (read in August 1732), Francke's *Christ the Sum and Substance of All the Holy Scriptures* (read in September 1732), Law's *Christian Perfection* (read in November 1732), Francke's *Nicodemus, or a Treatise Against the Fear of Man* (read in November 1733), and Francke's *Pietas Hallensis* (read in May 1734). Space does not allow a full treatment but the primary contribution has been presented (for example, Lucas and Law). The role of Scougal will be discussed further in chapter six. One key point that deserves attention is that the introduction of *Busskampf* (repentance struggle) via Francke has been overplayed by some scholars. See D. Bruce Hindmarsh, *The Evangelical Conversion Narrative: Spiritual Autobiography in Early Modern England* (Oxford: Oxford University Press, 2005), 58–59; Roger E. Olson and Christian T. Collins Winn, *Reclaiming Pietism: Retrieving an Evangelical Tradition* (Grand Rapids: Eerdmans, 2015), 52–54; Douglas H Shantz, *A Companion to German Pietism, 1660-1800* (Leiden: Brill, 2015), 302.

109. The proximity of the letters to Aldersgate is significant (all in 1738); see Wesley to Law on May 14, Law to Wesley on May 19, Wesley to Law on May 20, Law to Wesley on May 22. Wesley, *Letters*, 25:540–50.

110. Wesley wrote: "Under this heavy yoke I might have groaned till death had not an holy man to whom God lately directed me, upon my complaining thereof, answered at once." The man Wesley spoke of was surely Peter Böhler. Wesley, *Letters*, 25:541.

111. Wesley, *Letters*, 25:542.

and could be re-attained instantaneously through Christian perfection. Third, Wesley was entirely frustrated in his efforts to understand how one could attain salvation through the rigorous path of Christian perfection. However, when Wesley encountered the Moravians, his eyes were opened to the potential of a conversion at the *beginning* of the pursuit of Christian perfection, not upon the acquisition of Christian perfection. This beginning came through faith. This section now turns its attention to the second era of Wesley's theology of instantaneous conversion.

3.2. NORMATIVE CONVERSION IN POST-ALDERSGATE WESLEY: INSTANTANEOUS CONVERSION UPON GENUINE FAITH

If the first era of Wesley's view of instantaneous conversion concluded with the disassociation of instantaneous conversion from the attainment of Christian perfection, the second era of Wesley's view of instantaneous conversion is Wesley's normative and enduring view: instantaneous conversion arrives upon the onset of genuine faith, and not, as Wesley previously thought, upon the attainment of Christian perfection. It will be shown that Spangenberg, and then Böhler, helped guide Wesley in the evolution of his theology. Following the formative period with these men, Wesley quickly settled into his normative view of instantaneous conversion commencing upon genuine faith. From this discussion emerges one of the synoptic statements of Wesley's espoused theology of conversion: conversion arrives by faith in an instant. It is this instant, brought upon by faith, that is the inauguration of conversion which is described as inaugurated teleology.

A major turning point from the first era to the second era in Wesley's theology of conversion came on July 31, 1737, in a series of questions Wesley asked which were answered by the Moravian leader, August Spangenberg.[112] Wesley wrote thirty-one questions to Spangenberg, with the first three concerning the nature of conversion. Wesley's first three questions were:[113]

---

112. This was a dynamic time for Wesley; it was hardly a week later, on August 7, 1737, when Wesley repelled Mrs. Sophy Williamson [Hopkey] from taking the Eucharist, which became the catalyst of Wesley's disgraceful departure from America on December 22 and return to England.

113. Wesley, *Journals and Diaries*, 18:531.

1. What do you mean by conversion?

2. Is [conversion] wrought at once, or by degrees?

3. Ought we so to expect the Holy Ghost to convert either our own or our neighbour's souls as to neglect any outward means?

This was the same Spangenberg who asked Wesley, the day after his first step in America, if Wesley knew that Jesus had saved him. Wesley's answer was, famously, "I do," but Wesley added in his journal: "But I fear they were vain words."[114] Wesley's relationship with Spangenberg from day one became an exploration of the meaning of salvation.

The evidence before July 31, 1737, shows that Wesley thought of conversion in two senses: first, converting the heathen, or in other words, bringing people into the church, usually accompanied by baptism; second, full conversion, meaning a tipping point where one attains Christian perfection and singleness of intention, free from temptation. Wesley's questions to Spangenberg present Wesley's reflection on the nature of the faith of the Moravians. What had begun with Wesley's fascination with the Moravians' lack of fear on the voyage to America had culminated in Wesley's questions regarding conversion. Spangenberg spoke of an experience which was available at the beginning of faith which gave a person confidence of their relationship with God. Prior to Wesley's engagement with the Moravians, Wesley understood initial conversion being at baptism but "full" conversion as only available to those fully perfected in faith.

What Spangenberg sparked in Wesley, Peter Böhler fanned into flame. Wesley and Böhler met on February 7, 1738, upon Wesley's first week back in England. Almost immediately Böhler began challenging Wesley's philosophy.[115] Soon thereafter, on March 5, 1738, Wesley wrote: "I was ... clearly convinced of unbelief, of the want of 'that faith whereby alone we are saved,' with the full, Christian salvation."[116] This is when Böhler instructed Wesley to preach faith "till you have it."[117] A sudden change in

---

114. Journal entry on February 8, 1736; Wesley, *Journals and Diaries*, 18:146.

115. On February 18, 1738, Böhler said to Wesley: "My brother, my brother, that philosophy of yours must be purged away." Wesley, *Journals and Diaries*, 18:226.

116. Wesley, *Journals and Diaries*, 18:228.

117. Wesley, *Journals and Diaries*, 18:228.

Wesley's theology may be observed because the next day Wesley offered Christ to a man named Clifford in prison who was sentenced to death (despite Wesley's previously self-professed disbelief in deathbed repentance).[118] Having tracked Wesley's early view of conversion, we have seen that, prior to Aldersgate, Wesley understood full conversion only as the *end result* of a struggle toward Christian perfection, hence a possible reason for Wesley's reluctance for deathbed repentance. In other words, deathbed repentance could have only indicated the *beginning* and not the *end result* of the struggle toward converting Christian perfection. Another likely reason for Wesley's reluctance concerning deathbed repentance would have been the genuineness of authentic faith in the midst of impending death. Wesley was now able to call people to turn to Christ, through a "moment" dependent not upon perfected intention, per the teaching of Law, but upon the grace of God and response of faith at the *beginning* of their struggle toward Christian perfection.

Wesley had come to the conclusion that authentic faith was available at the beginning of turning to Christ.[119] Yet, Wesley wrote: "I could not comprehend what [Böhler] spoke of *an instantaneous work*. I could not understand how this faith should be given in a moment; how a man could *at once* be thus turned from darkness to light, from sin and misery to righteousness and joy in the Holy Ghost."[120] Wesley's question to Spangenberg nine months earlier (whether conversion is wrought at once, or by degrees) had now come to a head. Wesley had adjusted his understanding of the order of saving faith from the the moment of perfection to the moment of genuine faith; but, he questioned the onset and speed of genuine faith and, hence, raised the question of the instantaneousness of conversion.

Wesley's journal described how he searched the book of Acts and could hardly find anything but instances of instantaneous conversions, less St. Paul's "three days in the pangs of new birth."[121] Wesley hypothesized that instantaneous conversion was a feature of the early church and was now different. However, the following day Wesley encountered several people

---

118. Wesley, *Journals and Diaries*, 18:228.

119. On April 22, 1738, Wesley wrote: "I had now no objection to what [Böhler] said of the nature of faith." Wesley, *Journals and Diaries*, 18:234.

120. Wesley, *Journals and Diaries*, 18:234. Italics in the original.

121. Wesley, *Journals and Diaries*, 18:234.

who spoke of the instantaneous work of conversion in their lives.[122] A few days later, on April 26, 1738, Wesley heard two individuals share their experiences: "that God can (at least, if he does not always) give that faith whereof cometh salvation in a moment, as lightning falling from heaven."[123] It seemed everywhere Wesley turned in Scripture and his community, Wesley encountered evidence of God's instantaneous work to convert.

In 1742, Wesley wrote *The Principles of a Methodist* in response to a long pamphlet critical of Methodism by Josiah Tucker. In *The Principles of a Methodist*, Wesley discussed instantaneous conversion and how he formed his view of conversion.[124] *The Principles of a Methodist* clarified Wesley's view (by citing Wesley's journal of August 1738) by bringing into the discussion the concept of assurance of faith. Wesley distinguished here between *conversion* and *full assurance*. In the section "Of the assurances of justification" in *The Principles* Wesley wrote: "I believe that conversion (meaning thereby justification) is an instantaneous work, and that the moment a man has living faith in Christ he is converted or justified. ... I believe, the moment a man is justified he has peace with God."[125] Since Wesley here equated

---

122. Wesley, *Journals and Diaries*, 18:234.

123. Wesley, *Journals and Diaries*, 18:235.

124. *The Principles of a Methodist* stated that the evidence from Scripture and experience convinced Wesley of instantaneous conversion, not Böhler. Yet, Wesley's comments do not appear to give enough credit to Böhler. Wesley appears to understate the influence of the Moravians and his theological development during his Georgian endeavour in the paragraph before his comments regarding Böhler. Wesley wrote: "For I came back [from America] with the same notions I went." *The Principles of a Methodist* was written in 1742, which was a time when Wesley was distancing himself from the Moravians and their teaching; thus, Wesley's comments need to be understood in this context. See Wesley, *The Methodist Societies: History, Nature, and Design*, 9:57–58. Along these lines, Davies commented in his introduction as an editor of the critical edition of this work that the Moravians "perhaps influenced [Wesley] more than he is willing to concede." Rupert E. Davies, "Introduction," in *The Methodist Societies: History, Nature, and Design*, The Bicentennial Edition of the Works of John Wesley, vol. 9 (Nashville: Abingdon Press, 1989), 48. Davies's corrective is vital because in *The Principles of a Methodist* Wesley is caught in the middle of correcting Tucker's assessment of Wesley's Methodism as a byproduct of William Law's *A Serious Call* with the influences of Count von Zinzendorf and Peter Böhler. What Wesley was trying to do was to state what Wesley believed, not what Zinzendorf or Böhler believed, nor Tucker's portrait of Methodism. In effect, *The Principles of a Methodist* captured Wesley's own early post-Aldersgate thoughts regarding instantaneous conversion. See Wesley, *The Methodist Societies: History, Nature, and Design*, 9:57–61.

125. Wesley, *The Methodist Societies: History, Nature, and Design*, 9:60–61. It is important to note here that in this passage Wesley equated justification with conversion, something which will be discussed further in this chapter and in the next chapter.

justification and instantaneous conversion, we can say that Wesley believed that upon instantaneous conversion one had peace with God, which was a sense of assurance. Wesley differentiated himself from those who thought that peace with God, which was an experience of assurance, came "long after" justification. In other words, Wesley was arguing against a silent instantaneous conversion which could go undetected, or un-experienced. As this study claims, experience is critical to Wesley's theology of conversion. Against Wesley's pre-Aldersgate era conversion theology, an individual should not strive in their good works as if they were blinded or being kept from the truth of knowing whether or not they were saved. Wesley now believed that full conversion was not synonymous with Christian perfection; instantaneous conversion was the *experience* of justification at the outset of the Christian life.[126]

In a 1745 letter responding to John Smith, Wesley presented his primary post-Aldersgate understanding of conversion as an immediate and instantaneous act. Smith had been in dialogue with Wesley and written concerning how some miracles such as the forty, fifty, or hundredfold growth of a field of wheat advance in "slow and imperceptible degrees," while other supernatural activity such as the miracle of the five loaves satisfied five thousand hungry people quickly.[127] Wesley stated: "I am induced to believe that God's ordinary way of converting sinners to himself is by 'suddenly inspiring them with an immediate testimony of his love, easily distinguishable from fancy.' "[128] Additionally, Wesley said that God had worked instantaneously in all whom Wesley had known, less "perhaps three or four persons."[129] Wesley did not explain what he meant by the three or four people who did not experience conversion in this manner, but this may be Wesley admitting that some undergo a more extended experience, and not an instantaneous conversion.[130] Wesley made clear that the normative, essentially homogeneous, mode of conversion was instantaneous. Indeed, six months later, in *The Principles of a Methodist Farther Explained,*

---

126. Wesley, *The Methodist Societies: History, Nature, and Design,* 9:60–61.

127. Wesley, *Letters,* 26:168–69.

128. Wesley, *Letters,* 26:179.

129. Wesley, *Letters,* 26:179.

130. For more on the exceptions to Wesley's normative view of conversion, see the next subsection in this chapter.

Wesley spoke of the three thousand who were converted in the midst of one sermon (that is, Acts 2:41). Conversion was not the culmination of holiness; conversion was available in a moment (and, like faith, independent from personal holiness).[131]

The 1750 letter from Wesley to Dr. Lavington, *A Letter to the Author of "The Enthusiasm of the Methodists,"* continued to make clear the instantaneous nature of conversion contra conversion via perfection. Wesley wrote: "A man is usually converted long before he is a perfect man."[132] Saint Paul's experience provided a very helpful case to understand the instantaneous nature of conversion for Wesley. In a letter to Reverend Potter, Vicar of Reymerston, dated November 4, 1758, Wesley responded to Potter's claim of the "instantaneous impulse in the sudden conversion of St. Paul."[133] Wesley wrote: "It is true 'a great light suddenly shone round about him'; but this light did not convert him."[134] Wesley described how Paul was for three days without sight and food, "and probably during the whole time God was gradually working in his heart, till he 'arose, and, being baptized, washed away his sins, and was filled with the Holy Ghost.'"[135] In Wesley's note on Acts 26:17, one of the passages where Paul described his conversion, Wesley commented: "For his apostleship, as well as his conversion, commenced at this moment."[136] The note on Acts 26:17 confirms that Wesley placed Paul's proper conversion three days after the Damascus road experience. The three-day gap between Jesus' appearance to Paul and Paul's baptism, washing away of sins, and filling by the Holy Ghost, map to Wesley's morphology of awakening preceding actual instantaneous conversion. Thus, the enduring and normative view of Wesley was that conversion commenced instantaneously upon genuine faith in the believer.

Wesley's conception of initial faith commencing instantaneous conversion and full, mature faith arriving at a state of Christian perfection can be envisioned in the term *inaugurated teleology*. Inaugurated teleology captures both the beginning and the end of the aim of conversion.

---

131. Wesley, *The Methodist Societies: History, Nature, and Design*, 9:232.

132. Wesley, *The Appeals to Men of Reason and Religion and Certain Related Open Letters*, 11:369.

133. Wesley, *The Letters of John Wesley*, 4:42.

134. Wesley, *The Letters of John Wesley*, 4:42.

135. Wesley, *The Letters of John Wesley*, 4:42.

136. Wesley, *Explanatory Notes upon the New Testament*, Acts 26:17.

Inauguration is an appropriate explanation of the subjective experience of instantaneous conversion. Inauguration, in this formulation, is an inauguration brought upon by God, similar to the prevenient grace of God that allows a faithful response; inauguration is a subjective experience in the life of the believer. Yet, the inauguration is only the beginning, since conversion has a *telos*, that being Christian perfection. Instantaneous conversion as inaugurated teleology maintains the aim and end of conversion while requiring a punctiliar beginning. The full fleshing out of conversion as inaugurated teleology will happen through the course of this book, but it is introduced now due to the full establishment of Wesley's normative understanding of instantaneous conversion.

To summarize Wesley's view of conversion after Aldersgate, Wesley came to believe that conversion was an instantaneous experience inaugurated by the giving of true faith as a gift of God at the beginning of the journey toward Christian perfection (inaugurated teleology). Wesley gained his enduring view of instantaneous conversion due to formative interactions with Spangenberg and Böhler, both of whom helped Wesley understand instantaneous conversion commencing upon the beginning of faith rather than the outcome of a mature faith (evidenced by Christian perfection). While a clear moment of instantaneous conversion was normative in Wesley's theology, later in his life Wesley's theology of conversion enlarged to include those who did not have a clear moment of instantaneous conversion, which is the final era to be examined in this section.

3.3. NON-NORMATIVE CONVERSION IN POST-ALDERSGATE WESLEY: NON-INSTANTANEOUS CONVERSION

Although the previous discussion has shown Wesley's normative and enduring understanding of instantaneous conversion as an experience which occurs in a moment at the onset of genuine faith, a careful study of Wesley reveals that he may also have understood God to work outside this normative mode of instantaneous conversion, though the evidence is scarce. Wesley hinted at non-instantaneous conversion in 1745, but the issue did not re-emerge explicitly until late in his ministry and life through his correspondence with Mary Cooke in 1785. What is at stake in this discussion is the normativity of instantaneous conversion in Wesley's theology. This subsection will examine Wesley's correspondence with Cooke, the recent debate over instantaneous and non-instantaneous conversion in Wesley's theology, and suggest that, while the evidence may be scant, Wesley's theology of God's irresistibility in conversion provides a possible explanation of non-normative non-instantaneous conversion in Wesley's theology. Simply put: Wesley believed that God can work in unusual ways, including the unusual occurrence of non-instantaneous conversion. Wesley wrote a letter on December 30, 1745, which hints at a non-instantaneous conversion view after Aldersgate. Wesley wrote:

> I am induced to believe that God's ordinary way of converting sinners to himself is, by "suddenly inspiring them with an immediate testimony of his love, easily distinguishable from fancy." I am assured thus he hath wrought in all I have known, (except, perhaps, three or four persons,) of whom I have reasonable ground to believe that they are really turned from the power of Satan to God.[137]

In this letter, Wesley reaffirms his view of instantaneous conversion, except for "three or four persons."[138] Wesley did not clarify what he meant by this comment regarding the three or four persons, but attention to later comments, discussed below, reveals more information on this topic. To be clear, Wesley did not invent a new theology of instantaneous conversion in 1745. Wesley maintained his view that conversion and Christian perfection were instantaneous after 1745.[139] Thus, in 1745, Wesley hinted at, but did not make clear, a variability in the way that God converts; the ordinary way was suddenly (instantly), but some were genuinely turned to God in a way that was not sudden. (Wesley implies the non-suddenness in the quote above; it is not explicit.) Wesley did not address the topic of non-instantaneous conversion explicitly for another forty years.

On September 10, 1785, Wesley initiated a correspondence with Mary Cooke. Wesley and Cooke had been at a gathering together, and Wesley

---

137. Wesley, *Letters*, 26:179.

138. Wesley, *Letters*, 26:179.

139. See the letters on December 28, 1770, November 15, 1775, June 21, 1784, April 9, 1785, December 5, 1789. Wesley, *The Letters of John Wesley*, 5:214–15, 6:189–90, 7:222, 267–68, 8:189–90. See also the 1785 sermon *On Working Out Our Own Salvation* where Wesley reasserted justification and perfection as instantaneous while gradual growth led up to justification and perfection as well. Wesley, *Sermons*, 3:203–4.

requested that she send him some poetry she had written.[140] Wesley's simple request for copies of poetry began a series of twenty-three known letters that would move quickly beyond the topic of poetry and delve deeply into the topic of instantaneous conversion, full sanctification, and experience. This correspondence, while not convincingly clear, would show that Wesley believed that the experience of instantaneous conversion would vary from person to person, but that instantaneous conversion itself (not the *experience* of it) was still instantaneous.[141] Cooke's first response to Wesley indicated that when writing poetry she would be overcome by questions such as "Is this [writing poetry] the one thing needful?" and "What must I do to be saved?"[142] Cooke could not concentrate on her poetry because of these pressing spiritual questions. Wesley's response was: "You know well that one thing, and one only, is needful for you upon earth— to ensure a better portion, to recover the favour and image of God. The former by His grace you have recovered; you have tasted of the love of God. See that you cast it not away."[143] Wesley continued in the letter to implore her to seek full sanctification which comes "by the power of the Highest overshadowing you in a moment, in the twinkling of an eye, so as utterly to abolish sin and to renew you in His whole image!"[144] Thus, Wesley still held to the instantaneous moment of full sanctification. He also assumed Cooke to have been justified, though he does not explain why.[145] Had the correspondence ended at this point, their letters would not be notable for the discussion of instantaneous conversion. However, Cooke's response to Wesley brings to the fore the topic of non-instantaneous conversion. Cooke responded:

---

140. Wesley, *The Letters of John Wesley*, 7:288.

141. Wesley, *The Letters of John Wesley*, 7:288, 292–93, 298, 303–4, 318, 341, 357, 377–78, 8:8, 28. The Bridwell collection at Perkins School of Theology, Southern Methodist University, holds the collection of Cooke's letters to Wesley. Mary Cooke, "Mr Wesley Letterbook: Cooke and Clarke Family Documents and Images at Bridwell Library," accessed December 22, 2016, digitalcollections.smu.edu/cdm/ref/collection/cooke/id/446.

142. Cooke, "Mr Wesley Letterbook," 1.

143. Wesley, *The Letters of John Wesley*, 7:293.

144. Wesley, *The Letters of John Wesley*, 7:293.

145. Perhaps Wesley implied that Cooke was justified because of their time together in person or another reason that is not captured in these letters. All that can be established is that Wesley presumed Cooke to be justified.

I never knew the time that the Spirit of God witnessed with my spirit that I was born of Him, that my sins were blotted out, and I was accepted of God in Christ. I feel that I have tasted of his love; but is it not rather a visit of encouragement, than an evidence of liberty? ... Was any person to ask me, do you believe you are reconciled to God? I would reply: I cannot [illegible word] any person to any particular moment when God spoke peace to my soul as his adopted child, enabling me to say "Abba Father" yet have I in a measure partaken of the fruit of the Spirit.[146]

Cooke stated that she could not recall the moment when she felt that she had been born again and accepted by God. Cooke admitted that she had a "measure" of the fruit of the Spirit and had "tasted" of God's love; but, she lacked a specific moment when she had been converted. Cooke appears to struggle because she did not have a testimony of instantaneous conversion. Cooke went on to plead: "Dear Sir, will you candidly and simply tell me what you think of my case? explain me to myself; and plainly speak your sentiments: My inexperience needs an interpreter: I want, and wish for one to tell me truly what my feelings mean."[147] Wesley responded by writing a letter to Mary Cooke on October 30, 1785, which indicated an alternative approach to his normative view of instantaneous conversion. Wesley wrote:[148]

There is an irreconcilable variability in the operations of the Holy Spirit on [human] souls, more especially as to the manner of justification. Many find him rushing in upon them like a torrent, while they experience "The o'erwhelming power of saving grace." ... But in others he works in a very different way: "He deigns his influence to infuse; Sweet, refreshing, as the silent dews." It has pleased him to work the latter way in you from the beginning; and it is not improbable he will continue (as he has begun) to work in a gentle

---

146. Cooke, "Mr Wesley Letterbook," 2.

147. Cooke, "Mr Wesley Letterbook," 2.

148. In this letter, Wesley continues to believe that Cooke had, indeed, experienced justification. Wesley wrote: "I can make no doubt of your having a measure of faith." Wesley, *The Letters of John Wesley*, 7:298.

and almost insensible manner. Let him take his own way: He is wiser than you; he will do all things well.[149]

In contrast to Wesley's normative view of instantaneous conversion, in his letter to Cooke he describes the variability of God's work, including in justification. Not only does Wesley attend to the explicit theological topic of justification, he also comments on the role of experience: some experience God's work as a rushing torrent (for example, instantaneously), others experience God's work in a gentle and insensible manner (for example, gradually). In other words, Wesley makes room in his theology for a variability of experience concerning justification and, thus, conversion. Cooke's response to Wesley was a heart-wrenching letter of her struggle to come to terms with her wandering and sinful desires.[150] Cooke was not comforted by Wesley's allowance for a variability in God's timing. Wesley and Cooke's letters continued for several months, over the course of which an emphasis emerged regarding the topic of full sanctification.[151] At no point did Wesley actually state that conversion was not instantaneous; in other words, Wesley always believed that conversion was always instantaneous. However, Wesley did allow for a variability of experience and perceptibility of instantaneous conversion.

A recent debate between Maddox and Collins on the instantaneousness of justification relates to the analysis of non-normative instantaneous conversion. Maddox believes that Wesley taught justification can be gradual, while Collins believes that Wesley taught justification can only be instantaneous. Since justification marks the moment of instantaneous conversion, their debate addresses the normativity of instantaneous conversion in Wesley's theology.[152] Maddox recognizes that Wesley's mature theology included the possibility of a *degree* of justification. Maddox makes it clear that he was aware of the challenges which a theology of partial justification

---

149. Wesley, *The Letters of John Wesley*, 7:298.

150. Cooke, "Mr Wesley Letterbook," 3.

151. The conversation between Cooke and Wesley settled into a discussion on full sanctification (full salvation); for example, Cooke wrote: "When you were describing the preparatives for a full salvation my heart cried out, These are what I want; Lord, give them now to me!" Cooke, "Mr Wesley Letterbook," 10–11.

152. For more on the relationship between justification and conversion, see chapter three, section three.

would bring. He writes: "The late Wesley maintained that one who has the faith of a servant is—*in a degree*—accepted by God. ... I would be the first to admit that the late Wesley's understanding of the servant of God appears problematic when judged in terms of the Protestant soteriological principle of adoption, regeneration, and justification occur both simultaneously and instantly."[153] Maddox's view that Wesley made an allowance for a "gradual justification" may logically entail the possibility of a "gradual conversion." Ken Collins responds to Maddox, saying: "Maddox's language of 'degrees of justification' confuses the issues of *acceptance* and *justification* by faith in Jesus Christ. Again, can one be a little bit justified by faith?"[154] Both Maddox and Collins agree that Wesley taught that the instantaneous work of God in justification and conversion was normative in Wesley's theology and indicative of Western soteriology. However, Maddox understands the exception of gradual justification as indicative of Wesley's Eastern influence.[155] Maddox appears to embrace the variability of God's work, not just in the context of experience (as explored above), but also in the context of God's justifying action—effectively creating an unusual and non-normative category of non-instantaneous conversion.

If, as Maddox claims, Wesley did allow for a gradual justification, Wesley did not make the same allowance for perfection. While Cooke could not identify a conversion moment, Wesley did not allow for the same lack of specificity to occur regarding her long-awaited full sanctification.[156] Wesley's insistence upon instantaneous full sanctification hinders the strength of the Eastern non-instantaneous justification argument. Maddox argues that Wesley's advice to Cooke related to justification but could also be related to sanctification, and Maddox cites two sources to support his view.[157] Yet, the two sources do not explicitly describe full

---

153. Randy L. Maddox, "Continuing the Conversation," *Methodist History* 30, no. 4 (July 1992): 237–38. Italics in the original.

154. Kenneth J. Collins, "A Reply to Randy Maddox," *Methodist History* 31, no. 1 (October 1992): 53. Italics in the original.

155. Maddox did not formally reply to Collins's questions. In my personal correspondence with Randy Maddox, he told me that he is content to let other people handle the issue. It appears that the theological conflict is rooted in the differences between Western and Eastern soteriology, primarily juridical versus the therapeutic approaches.

156. Wesley, *The Letters of John Wesley*, 7:292–93.

157. Maddox, *Responsible Grace*, 155–56.

Christian perfection: they appear to relate to the gradual growth in sanctification which Wesley always recommended. Wesley often paired the first moment of instantaneousness (justification and conversion) with the second (perfection), and, thus, makes Maddox's view of Wesley's advice to Cooke difficult to understand. In other words, Wesley understood a symmetry and consistency of instantaneous conversion with instantaneous full sanctification. As another exhibit from the mature Wesley, he wrote a letter several years later to Sarah Rutter on December 5, 1789, which stated: "Gradual sanctification may increase from the time you was justified; but full deliverance from sin, I believe, is always instantaneous—at least, I never yet knew an exception."[158] Wesley never wavered on his insistence of instantaneous full deliverance from sin (in Christian perfection); thus, the symmetrical correlation maintains instantaneous conversion, against Maddox's view, even in the mature Wesley.

What may be suggested, in the case of Cooke, but cannot be proven, therefore, is that the tone of Wesley's ongoing personal correspondence with Cooke was so delicate, gentle, and warm,[159] that Wesley, especially in his old age, was more concerned pastorally to care for Cooke's Christian growth rather than to debate the recollection of her conversion experience.[160] It may also be possible that Wesley had in mind the category of assurance rather than conversion and justification. Since we lack other examples of this kind, Wesley's correspondence with Cooke may be an exceptional, and not instructive, case for Wesley's theology of conversion.[161] However, an associated soteriological category, irresistibility, may speak into the possibility of Wesley's theology of conversion containing a non-instantaneous aspect.

---

158. Wesley, *The Letters of John Wesley*, 8:190.

159. On April 17, 1788 Mary Cooke married Adam Clarke. In a letter from Wesley to Clarke on June 26, 1788, Wesley describes Mary as "my dear Molly," thus showing Wesley's warmth and gentleness toward her. Wesley, *The Letters of John Wesley*, 8:68.

160. More information on Mary Cooke and John Wesley can be found at Page A. Thomas, "The Wesley Center Online: John Wesley: Spiritual Advisor To Young Women As He Speaks Through His Letters," accessed December 22, 2016, wesley.nnu.edu/?id=4723.

161. One similar example may be the letter from Wesley to Lady Maxwell on July 5, 1765, but it is not convincingly clear that Wesley was discussing conversion, perfection, or assurance. See Wesley, *Letters*, 27:438–39.

Wesley's theology of irresistibility shows the variability with which Wesley believed God could act; this divine variability provides possible support for the possibility of a non-instantaneous conversion per Wesley's 1745 and 1785 comments discussed above. Wesley had much to say about God's irresistible influence on individuals. On the one hand, Wesley denied God's continual irresistible work, due to what he saw as its lack of support from Scripture and its logical connection to the doctrine of reprobation and antinomianism.[162] On the other hand, Wesley allowed for divine irresistibility to break through at the moment of conversion and perfection.

Wesley never denied the sovereignty of God. In *Predestination Calmly Considered* (1752) Wesley wrote: "Perhaps you will say, 'But there are other attributes of God, namely, his sovereignty, unchangeableness, and faithfulness. I hope you do not deny these.' I answer, No; by no means."[163] In 1774, Wesley distinguished between God as Creator and Governor in *Thoughts upon God's Sovereignty*.[164] In other words, God maintains his freedom over creation but utilizes his divine freedom in creation to limit divine control over the individual redemption of individuals. In this sense, Wesley understood God as all-sovereign yet not responsible for the rejection of the gospel by individuals. Though Wesley understood humans as free agents, he believed that God may step in and act irresistibly as God saw fit. Wesley wrote: "Whatever, therefore, it hath pleased God to do of his sovereign pleasure as Creator of heaven and earth; and whatever his mercy may do on particular occasions over and above what justice requires, the general rule stands firm as the pillars of heaven: 'The Judge of all the earth' will 'do right.' "[165] Thus, God may step into human free agency to do "whatever his mercy may do on particular occasions." Wesley applied this point specifically to irresistibility in conversion: "It may be allowed that God acts as Sovereign in convincing some souls of sin; arresting them in their mid career, by his resistless power. It also seems, that, at the moment of our conversion, he acts irresistibly."[166] These comments were made in 1774. Wesley

---

162. See Wesley, *Explanatory Notes upon the New Testament*, Acts 26:19, Rev 3:15; *Sermons*, 3:547; Wesley, *Doctrinal and Controversial Treatises II*, 13:258, 404.

163. Wesley, *Doctrinal and Controversial Treatises II*, 13:293.

164. Wesley, *Doctrinal and Controversial Treatises II*, 13:548–50.

165. Wesley, *Doctrinal and Controversial Treatises II*, 13:550.

166. Wesley, *Doctrinal and Controversial Treatises II*, 13:549–50.

made similar comments thirty-two years earlier near the peak of his controversies with Whitefield. Wesley's journal on August 24, 1742, recorded:
"That the grace which brings faith, and thereby salvation into the soul, is
irresistible at that moment ... I do not deny, That, in those eminently styled
'the elect' (if such there be), the grace of God is so far irresistible that they
cannot but believe and be finally saved. But I cannot believe, That all those
must be damned in whom it does not thus irresistibly work."[167] In other
words, Wesley was saying that, in some cases, God may assert divine power
over human freedom to convert. It is this divine variability, or perhaps
non-normative behavior, in a specific moment that provides a paradigm
in which non-instantaneous conversion, per Maddox's analysis, may exist
in Wesley's theology.

Therefore, while there may be a few instances in the mature Wesley for
non-instantaneous conversion (such as his correspondence with Cooke),
the evidence for non-instantaneous conversion is scant and not entirely
convincing. Non-instantaneous conversion may be an example of Wesley
choosing to emphasize Eastern emphases in his soteriology, per Maddox,
as a therapeutic and gradual soteriological work. Wesley's belief that divine
sovereignty could override human responsibility provides a possible paradigm for non-normative non-instantaneous conversion. Or, it may be that
non-instantaneous conversion was simply an instance of Wesley's pastoral accommodation (in the Cooke example). In sum, the normative mode
for the initiation of conversion in Wesley's theology is instantaneous and
the evidence for non-instantaneous conversion is not entirely convincing,
but is tenable via a non-normative paradigm through Wesley's theology of
irresistibility or if an Eastern emphasis, as explained above, is prioritized.

Instantaneous conversion in Wesley's post-Aldersgate era led to his
enduring belief that conversion begins instantaneously upon the onset
of genuine faith. From this analysis, a synoptic statement can be made in
service of offering an espoused theology of Wesley on conversion: conversion arrives by faith in an instant. Conversion is best understood as
being instantaneous, though it may not always be recognizable on behalf
of the true convert. Therefore, conversion begins instantaneously, but

---

167. Wesley, *Journals and Diaries*, 19:332–33.

the beginning of conversion is not the end of conversion. Conversion must continue, with evidence of good works along the way, toward its end: perfection.

4. CONTINUED EVIDENCE

The inauguration of conversion is not the end of conversion. The end of conversion is perfection which is evidenced by good works. In order to demonstrate the requirement of continued evidence on the path toward the *telos* of conversion (perfection), the framework of good works and conversion in the schema of inaugurated teleology will be looked at in its entirety. Notably, Wesley believed that prior to instantaneous conversion, all acts of obedience were depraved and fallen. But, after instantaneous conversion, genuine good works were possible and necessary to evidence genuine Christian conversion. In this section emerges one of the synoptic statements of the espoused theology of conversion that Wesley held: conversion is marked by ongoing good works.

4.1. CONVERSION AS INAUGURATED TELEOLOGY:
A BEGINNING WITH AN END

The previous section considered conversion as inaugurated teleology in Wesley's theology, with a focus on the inauguration, the instantaneous beginning. This section gives an overview of the progress of conversion, which is the journey toward the end of conversion: perfection. Along this journey, good works emerge. Inward and outward good works before and after instantaneous conversion were categorically different in Wesley's theology; before instantaneous conversion, all works were poisoned by the fallen nature. Wesley wrote in his sermon, *Self-denial*: "Our nature is altogether corrupt, in every power and faculty. And our will, depraved equally with the rest, is wholly bent to indulge our natural corruption."[168] The consequences of the fallen nature impinge the positive potential of good works prior to conversion in Wesley's theology.[169] In 1745, Wesley acquired Richard Baxter's *Aphorisms of Justification* and found it so agreeable that

---

168. Wesley, *Sermons*, 2:242.

169. See Collins's comments regarding Wesley's view of human depravity being "fully in the footprints" of Augustine, Luther, and Calvin. Collins, *The Theology of John Wesley*, 71–73.

Wesley published it in an abridged edition as *An Extract of "Aphorisms of Justification."* This work stated: "Actual obedience goeth not before the first moment of justification."[170] In other words, the nature of obedience and good works before the experience of instantaneous conversion is that they are corrupt and depraved.

Though obedience and good works prior to instantaneous conversion are corrupt, upon the experience of instantaneous conversion they are possible, necessary, and indicative of the journey toward the end of conversion: perfection. Wesley wrote: "Perseverance in faithful obedience doth, both in nature and time, go before our complete and final justification, and that as a part of the condition of obtaining it."[171] Instantaneous conversion enables the capacity to engage in genuinely good works; faithful, actual, obedience comes after conversion and leads up to final justification. In the quote above, Wesley called faithful obedience part of the *condition* of obtaining final justification. Thus, faithful obedience, or continued evidence of genuine conversion, is not only possible but is necessary for salvation. Wesley's *Sermon on the Mount XII* juxtaposed wicked and good works before and after authentic conversion as a test of a true prophet; a true prophet would lead people to convert, and these converts would show evidence of having the mind of Christ and walk as Christ walked. Wesley wrote: "[Good works after conversion in their hearers are] a manifest proof that those are true prophets, teachers sent of God."[172] In 1756, Wesley responded to James Hervey. Hervey had claimed that, per 1 John 3:7, the one who does righteousness is righteous and "manifests the truth of his conversion."[173] Wesley responded that righteousness could only come through faith working by love.[174] In other words, Wesley was saying that true righteous deeds were only possible as a fruit of genuine faith and genuine conversion. The following year, in his detailed exposition of the *Doctrine of Original Sin*, Wesley showed that the "new man," the "convert," had four characteristics: first, he is created for good works; second, he is renewed with original righteousness restored; third, he is re-stamped

---

170. Wesley, *Doctrinal and Controversial Treatises I*, 12:88.

171. Wesley, *Doctrinal and Controversial Treatises I*, 12:88.

172. Wesley, *Sermons*, 680.

173. Wesley, *Doctrinal and Controversial Treatises II*, 13:327.

174. Wesley, *Doctrinal and Controversial Treatises II*, 13:327.

with the image and likeness of God; fourth, the "new man" consists of righteousness and holiness.[175] Nearly a decade later Wesley still spoke of the instantaneous nature of perfection while not discounting the "constant gradual" change as well.[176]

In addition to the possibility of genuine obedience and good works after instantaneous conversion, Wesley described the moment of instantaneous conversion as the threshold of sanctification leading toward the experience of instantaneous perfection. Wesley's landmark sermon, *The Scripture Way of Salvation*, made clear that gradual growth follows from the new birth (which is virtually synonymous with instantaneous conversion). Wesley wrote: "From the time of our being 'born again' the gradual work of sanctification takes place."[177] Late in Wesley's ministry, Wesley preached the sermon, *The Mystery of Iniquity*. In this sermon, Wesley described the audience of the epistle of James as the "converted Jews" who were dealing with the issue of faith without works. Wesley described faith without works as "wisdom from beneath" and James' message as instruction for the converted about the form of godliness to which they must adhere.[178] Wesley echoed the idea of gradual growth after instantaneous conversion in his sermon, *On God's Vineyard*. Wesley wrote: "Regeneration ... is only the threshold of sanctification—the first entrance upon it. And as in the natural birth, a man is born at once, and then grows larger and stronger by degrees, so in the spiritual birth a man is born at once, and then gradually increases in spiritual stature and strength."[179] This increase had not only been inaugurated, this increase has an end: perfection. However, the end (perfection) need not come immediately. Wesley's letter to Lavington, *A Letter to the Author of "The Enthusiasm of the Methodists,"* distinguished between conversion and being a perfect man. Wesley wrote: "A man is usually converted long before he is a perfect man."[180] Wesley gave the Ephesian church as his proof; he noted that they *were* converted but had not come to

175. Wesley, *Doctrinal and Controversial Treatises I*, 12:419.

176. Wesley to Dorothy Furly, December 15, 1763, in Wesley, *Letters*, 27:346.

177. Wesley, *Sermons*, 2:160.

178. Wesley, *Sermons*, 2:459.

179. Wesley, *Sermons*, 3:507.

180. Wesley, *The Appeals to Men of Reason and Religion and Certain Related Open Letters*, 11:369.

"the measure of the stature of the fullness of Christ."[181] While conversion, in Wesley's understanding, required continued evidence, continued evidence need not be perfect, full, and complete. Perfection was not expected to prove true conversion. A tree did not need fruit on every inch of every branch to reveal what kind of tree it was.

The above evidence shows that Wesley expected a convert to grow in their sanctification as a sign of continued evidence after their instantaneous beginning. Growth in sanctification after instantaneous conversion did not end upon Christian perfection. In Wesley's theology, perfection is not the completion or full attainment of Christian maturity; it includes ever-increasing growth in Christlikeness. Maddox and Chilcote wrote in their editorial introduction to a recent reproduction of *Christian Perfection*: "In his mature writings Wesley affirmed that attainment of Christian perfection was ultimately an *instantaneous gift* of God's grace, received in faith. But he also emphasized growth in grace, nurtured through the means of grace, both preceding and following this attainment."[182] Growth in holiness was a normative expectation upon the inauguration of conversion and even continuing to perfection.[183]

4.2. EVIDENCE OF CONVERSION REQUIRED

Along the path toward perfection, good works were expected to evidence genuine conversion. Put negatively, if a person claimed to be converted and lacked good works, their conversion would be doubted. Wesley wrote: "We are to entertain his [the Holy Spirit's] divine presence; so as not either to drive him from us, or to disappoint him of the gracious ends for which his abode with us is designed; which is not the amusement of our understanding, but the conversion and entire sanctification of our hearts and lives."[184] Wesley described the end for which humans were designed, which is conversion and entire sanctification of heart (internal) and life (external); but, Wesley admits that the Holy Spirit can be driven upon the

---

181. Eph 4:13.

182. Wesley, *A Plain Account of Christian Perfection*, 27. Italics in the original.

183. I write of "to (and beyond) perfection" in order to capture the concept of perfection as something that can become realized and, yet, still be increased.

184. Wesley, *The Works of John Wesley*, 7:485. See the note on the authorship and abridgement of this sermon, Wesley, *Sermons*, 4:531.

non-entertainment, or nurture, of God's presence. A true convert and one seeking entire sanctification must not do anything which may disappoint the Holy Spirit, so as not to "drive him from us."[185]

The true convert was expected to show outward holiness in their actions and works. Wesley distinguished between the instantaneous beginning of faith (instantaneous conversion) and the subsequent continuance, increase, and growth of faith in Wesley's letter to John Smith on September 28, 1745.[186] Similarly, in another letter to John Smith on March 22, 1748, Wesley spoke about the expectation of outward works for true converts. Wesley wrote that if people are converted, "they are converted from all manner of wickedness 'to a sober, righteous, and godly life.' Such an uniform practice is true outward holiness. And where this is undeniably found, we ought to believe, there is holiness of heart, seeing the tree is known by its fruits."[187] Thus, Wesley expected uniformity of holiness in genuine converts. In a sermon preached not long after his letter to Smith, Wesley's 1750 sermon *Upon the Lord's Sermon on the Mount, Discourse XII*, discussed the verse "Ye Shall know them by their fruits." Wesley asked the following questions of supposed converts: "Have these the mind of Christ? And do they walk as he also walked? And was it by hearing these men [the Apostles] that they began to do so?"[188] Wesley bluntly asked if supposed converts lived liked Jesus lived as a way to ascertain a genuine conversion.

Wesley believed that, after an instantaneous beginning, the new Christian was capable of growing in Christian holiness, in sanctification. A genuine convert would show the fruit of their restored nature by good works. In many ways, the continued growth a genuine convert showed in their life was an example of Wesley's fundamental understanding of conversion, which was a turning "from" self and "to" the righteousness of Christ. Conversion was not a one-time occurrence, but a present tense and necessary "maintaining" of conversion, a "keeping" of the new direction and re-orientation brought upon by the initial converting turn to Christ.

---

185. Wesley, *The Works of John Wesley*, 7:485.
186. Wesley, *Letters*, 26:158–59.
187. Wesley, *Letters*, 26:290.
188. Wesley, *Sermons*, 1:680.

Having established Wesley's view of continuing conversion, the four primary motifs of Wesley's theology of conversion will be concluded.

5. CONCLUSION

This chapter has examined the four primary motifs in Wesley's teaching on conversion. The first section showed that Wesley understood conversion to be a turning *from* self and *to* Christ (synoptic statement 3). Conversion is the experiential parallel of salvation (synoptic statement 2). The second section showed that Wesley believed that conversion is initiated and sustained by the grace of God (synoptic statement 1). Additionally, conversion is foreshadowed by a deep sense of sinfulness (synoptic statement 4) through the pre-converting work of convincing, convicting, and awakening. Wesley was clear that not all who had convincing, convicting, and awaking experiences would undergo the next experience, as outlined in section three: the inauguration of conversion through instantaneous conversion. Section three showed that Wesley believed that conversion arrives by faith in an instant (synoptic statement 5). Wesley further taught that conversion is instantaneous but is not always recognizable on behalf of the true convert (synoptic statement 6). The fourth section showed that instantaneous conversion was not the end point, or *telos*, of his view of conversion. The *telos* of Christian conversion is the full sanctification of the believer, also known as Christian perfection. Further, section four showed that genuine conversion must show evidence of good works (synoptic statement 7). Amid this analysis, seven of the nine synoptic statements which articulate the espoused theology of conversion of Wesley have emerged. Wesley's formulation of conversion brings up an assortment of questions related to baptism, the assurance of salvation, and the *ordo salutis*, each of which will be examined in the next chapter.

3

—

JOHN WESLEY'S CONVERSION THEOLOGY ATTENDANT THEMES

The previous chapter presented the four primary motifs of John Wesley's theology of conversion. In the current chapter we investigate the attendant themes which arise from the preceding analysis. The attendant themes arise frequently in Wesley's writing on conversion, which is no surprise since Wesley's theology of conversion had practical and theological implications for Christian practice and doctrine. This chapter will address three attendant themes which can be posed as questions: How did Wesley view baptism (specifically baptismal regeneration) in light of conversion? What was the role of assurance in conversion? Where does conversion fit in Wesley's *via/ordo salutis*? These three attendant themes consider topics which thicken the articulation of the espoused account of Wesley's theology of conversion in chapter two, but are attendant because they are not primary for Wesley in a dominant sense in his own operant articulation of conversion. Our study of Wesley's theology of conversion will conclude at the end of this chapter but will be revisited in chapter six where Wesley's and Whitefield's theologies of conversion will be compared to establish a robust understanding of early evangelical theologies of conversion.

1. CONVERSION AND BAPTISM

As a minister of the Church of England, Wesley believed in and practiced infant baptism throughout his life.[1] The Church of England taught that regeneration (and thus conversion) came upon the rite of baptism, be

---

1. For several examples, see Wesley, *Journals and Diaries*, 18:157, 19:32, 20:217, 334, 435, 21:132, 172.

it infant or adult.[2] Yet, the Church of England embedded nascent seeds within their theology for the "sinning away" of the benefits of baptism. Chapter two showed that Wesley's engagement with William Law brought the issue of sinning away the benefits of baptism to the fore, with Wesley's Aldersgate narrative explicitly stating Wesley's self-understanding as one who had sinned away the benefits of his baptism. Wesley's enduring ministry demanded that one not rest in his or her baptism. Wesley preached that each individual can experience the new birth, which came through conversion via justifying faith.[3] An important attendant topic remains: Wesley's

---

2. The teaching of the Church of England in Wesley's era was anchored in three primary sources: the *Book of Common Prayer*, the *Thirty-Nine Articles*, and the *Edwardian Homilies*. Oden sustains the primacy of these three sources in his book *Doctrinal Standards in the Wesleyan Tradition* and adds that the *Book of Common Prayer* and the *Edwardian Homilies* were "probably more persistently influential than the *Thirty-Nine Articles*." Oden's analysis is based on frequency of use and theological dependence in Wesley's writings. Thomas C. Oden, *Doctrinal Standards in the Wesleyan Tradition* (Nashville: Abingdon Press, 2008), 33. The *Book of Common Prayer*'s "publik baptism of such as are of riper years" mirrors the infant service in its aim to bring people to "be regenerate and born anew of Water and of the Holy Ghost." The "riper years" service is largely identical to the infant service except that in place of godparents, the baptismal candidate answers for themself emphasizing the renunciation of the devil and all his works, belief in God's holy word, and obedience to keep the commandments. Upon these commitments one is declared regenerate and born again. The preface to the *Book of Common Prayer* discusses the growth of Anabaptism and claims that this growth was an opportunity "for the baptizing of Natives in our Plantations, and others converted to the Faith." The collect on Good Friday implores that the sinner "should be converted and live." While not made explicit, the *Book of Common Prayer* makes a connection between baptism, the beginning of the Christian life, and conversion. Church of England, *Book of Common Prayer, 1662 Edition* (Cambridge: Cambridge University Press, 2005), vii, 279, 283–87. The *Thirty-Nine Articles* do not discuss conversion directly. Article twenty-three, entitled "Of Baptism," however, teaches that baptism "is also a sign of regeneration or new birth." As will be seen in section three of the current chapter, regeneration and the new birth align logically with instantaneous conversion in Wesley's theology. Article thirty-five mandates the reading of the *Edwardian Homilies*, and it is in these homilies that we find further connection between baptism and conversion. *Book of Common Prayer, 1662 Edition*, 623, 626. The homily "A Sermon of the Salvation of Mankind by only Christ our Saviour from Sin and Death Everlasting, in three Parts" explicitly discussed the relationship between conversion and baptism. The first page of this sermon described that when infants are baptized they are cleansed of their sin, but when they sin again after baptism, they are in need of conversion once again. The sermon stated: "And they which in act or deed do sin after their baptism, when they convert and turn again to God unfeignly, they are likewise washed by this sacrifice from their sins, in such sort that there remaineth not any spot of sin that shall be imputed to their damnation." Therefore, the *Edwardian Homilies* contained a theological model for the sinning away of the salvation gained instantaneously through baptism and the need for a conversion which fully, and instantly, washes them of their sins. Church of England, *The Two Books of Homilies* (Oxford: Oxford University Press, 1859), 24; see also 186, 187, 190, 191, 366.

3. As a prime example of the requirement of justifying faith, see Wesley's sermon *The Marks of the New Birth*. Wesley preached: "Lean no more on the staff of that broken reed, that

view of baptism, especially his continued insistence of infant baptism, in light of his enduring emphasis on conversion through justifying faith.[4]

This section will show that Wesley's theology of conversion took decades to emerge fully in his baptismal theology and practice of baptism. By the time of Wesley's publication of the 1784 *Sunday Service*, Wesley made clear that regeneration could be chronologically separate from the actual act of baptism, but that baptism always gives a person entrance into the benefits of the church. For Wesley, regeneration activates by genuine faith; regeneration is not activated directly by baptism. Genuine faith could come before or after baptism through conversion. In the case of infants, Wesley's view of prevenient grace understood infants to be saved before their salvation was sinned away at a later date.[5] In this section a synoptic statement of the espoused theology of conversion for Wesley will emerge: baptism marks one's entrance to the church but is not chronologically tied to conversion.[6]

1.1. WESLEY'S FOUNDATIONAL STATEMENTS
REGARDING CONVERSION AND BAPTISM

As a Church of England priest, Wesley fulfilled his ministerial duty by regularly baptizing infants and adults, as can be seen from his diary and journal entries.[7] Wesley adhered to the *Book of Common Prayer* rites for baptizing infants and adults. Wesley's theology of conversion also

---

ye were born again in baptism." Wesley, *Sermons*, 1:430.

4. The practice of baptism in the Church of England was distanced, on one hand, from Roman Catholic *ex opera operato*, and on the other hand, Zwinglian concepts that characterize baptism as a badge and token. Baptism in the Church of England was not an objective act of the church for the baptized person (Roman Catholic); neither was baptism merely a sign without any special promise of grace (Zwingli). Instead, baptism in the Church of England is generally thought of as an effectual sign of grace by which God works invisibly within a person. Thomas Pownall Boultbee, *A Commentary on the Thirty-Nine Articles: Forming an Introduction to the Theology of the Church of England* (London: Longmans, 1877), 228; Lee Gatiss, "The Anglican Doctrine of Baptism," *Foundations: An International Journal of Evangelical Theology* 63 (Autumn 2012): 82–84.

5. Borgen's analysis largely mirrors the findings of this section. Ole E. Borgen, *John Wesley on the Sacraments: A Definitive Study of John Wesley's Theology of Worship* (Grand Rapids: Francis Asbury Press, 1985), 151–82.

6. See, especially, section 1.4. in this chapter.

7. For several examples, see Wesley, *Journals and Diaries*, 18:157, 19:32, 20:217, 334, 435, 21:132, 172.

influenced his views on baptism, as will be seen in the foundational statements leading up to his landmark sermon on the new birth.

In 1751, Wesley published an extract of William Wall's *Thoughts Upon
Infant-Baptism*. This work put forth two reasons supporting infant baptism.
First, the author correlated infant baptism, and baptism in general, with
scriptural support regarding circumcision.[8] Through baptism, a young
person was introduced to the church. Wesley explained: "Children should
be admitted into the visible church by the Christian door of entrance; that
is, baptism."[9] Wesley hoped that, like circumcision, infant baptism would
give identification to the young person as they grew up:

> It is granted that [children] neither could then [in the New
> Testament era], nor can now, understand the blessings nor the
> duties; yet they might receive the seal of circumcision, or of bap-
> tism, as a bond laid upon them in their infancy to fulfil the obliga-
> tions and the duties of riper years, and as an encouragement to wait
> and hope for their blessings. This was the case of Jewish infants;
> and why may not Christians be favoured with it also?[10]

The extract argued that faith and repentance were not conditions for baptism just as they were not conditions for circumcision.[11]

The second reason *Thoughts Upon Infant-Baptism* gave to support infant
baptism was its practice throughout church history. The author cited quotations from Justin Martyr, Irenaeus, Clement, Origen, Eusebius, Cyprian,
and Ambrose in support of infant baptism.[12] Tertullian is cited as the only
source in the first four hundred years of the church who advised a delayed
baptism.[13] The document also claimed that no one in the next seven hundred years of church history advised against infant baptism.[14] Further, the
document claimed that no one had spoken against infant baptism until

---

8. The obvious problem that circumcision only applied to men and not women is not dealt
with in this treatise. See Wesley, *Thoughts Upon Infant-Baptism (Extracted from a Late Writer)*, 5.

9. Wesley, *Thoughts Upon Infant-Baptism*, 5.

10. Wesley, *Thoughts Upon Infant-Baptism*, 6.

11. Wesley, *Thoughts Upon Infant-Baptism*, 7.

12. Wesley, *Thoughts Upon Infant-Baptism*, 10–18.

13. Wesley, *Thoughts Upon Infant-Baptism*, 18.

14. Wesley, *Thoughts Upon Infant-Baptism*, 18.

about 200 years before *Thoughts upon Infant-Baptism* was written, that is, around the time of the Reformation.[15]

Thoughts Upon Infant-Baptism added little to the theological understanding of baptism. The document mostly defended the *practice* of infant baptism. However, one minor point was made regarding regeneration. The treatise claims that Irenaeus's use of the word "regenerated" is synonymous with the word "baptizing."[16] Wesley never showed support for this idea anywhere else in his writing: Wesley's comment is simply a historical observation and nothing more.

Wesley adhered to infant baptism due to its affinity to circumcision and support in church tradition. Wesley's thoughts, however, on the purpose of godparents in the baptismal rite contrasted with church tradition. In August 1752, Wesley published a short work titled *Serious Thoughts Concerning Godfathers and Godmothers.*[17] In this work, Wesley dealt with three critiques of the practice of baptismal sponsors. First, baptismal sponsors were not found in Scripture; on this point Wesley agreed.[18] Second, baptismal sponsors were usually chosen rashly; on this point, Wesley also agreed and stated that sponsors were usually chosen rashly and for merely sentimental reasons, rather than because they were potentially godly influences for the child.[19] Third, the pledge the sponsors took was impossible to perform.[20] It is the third issue, however, on which Wesley dwelt the most and which has the most relevance for conversion. Wesley explained that when the sponsor was initially addressed the priest said: " 'This infant must for his part promise.' It is [the infant who] promises in these words not they [the sponsors]."[21] In other words, the wording of the rite made the "promise" explicitly *from* the infant and not the sponsors; the sponsors did not make a promise *for* the infant, nor could they. Wesley engaged the obvious question of why sponsors responded to pledges that did not apply to themselves. Wesley wrote: "I believe the compilers of our Liturgy inserted

---

15. Wesley, *Thoughts Upon Infant-Baptism*, 20.

16. Wesley, *Thoughts Upon Infant-Baptism*, 11.

17. Wesley, *The Works of John Wesley*, 10:506–9.

18. Wesley, *The Works of John Wesley*, 10:507.

19. Wesley, *The Works of John Wesley*, 10:507.

20. Wesley, *The Works of John Wesley*, 10:508.

21. Wesley, *The Works of John Wesley*, 10:508.

them [the sponsors] because they were used in all the ancient Liturgies."[22] Essentially, Wesley isolated the sole role of the sponsors as being a good influence on the life of the young person, a point which foreshadowed Wesley's elimination of sponsors in the 1784 *Sunday Service*. More important for our study of conversion, Wesley *insisted* upon the requirement of personal faith as the initiation of conversion. Wesley denied that the baptismal service released the infant from future personal responsibility to convert.

In 1756, Wesley published an abridged version of his father's earlier work on baptism.[23] Outler described the elder Wesley's work as a "squared-toed summary of what was already essentially commonplace in central Anglican sacramental theology."[24] A few features deserve highlighting. John Wesley's abridgement stated that in baptism one is regenerated. It also stated: "Baptism doth now save us, if we live answerable thereto; if we repent, believe, and obey the gospel: Supposing this, as it admits us into the Church here, so into glory hereafter."[25] The instruction in the *Book of Common Prayer* to the baptized, whether infant or adult, was to personally act upon their promises in order to benefit from them; the qualifying clause of "*if*" shows the responsibility of the baptized after their baptism (for example, "*if* we live answerable," "*if* we repent, believe, and obey"). One final feature to be highlighted was that this work adhered to the theology of inherited sin and guilt, which, as we will see, Wesley disavowed publicly twenty years later.[26]

By 1756, Wesley's views on conversion and regeneration failed to work their way into his practice or teaching on baptism. Wesley still followed the status quo of his church. Yet, Wesley emphasized two dynamics in the baptismal rites which highlighted the need for conversion: first, sponsors did not actually answer *for* the infant (the infant must, eventually, answer for herself or himself); second, the benefits of baptism required continued faithfulness and holiness for their benefits to be continued. Outler's

---

22. Wesley, *The Works of John Wesley*, 10:508.

23. Wesley, *The Works of John Wesley*, 10:188–201; Samuel Wesley, *The Pious Communicant Rightly Prepar'd*.

24. Albert C. Outler, *John Wesley* (Oxford: Oxford University Press, 1964), 317.

25. John Wesley, *The Works of John Wesley*, 10:192.

26. Wesley's abridgement stated: "It has already been proved, that this original stain cleaves to every child of man; and that hereby they are children of wrath, and liable to eternal damnation." Wesley, *The Works of John Wesley*, 10:193.

comments on Wesley's abridgement of his father's work help transition us into the landmark sermon Wesley was to deliver a few years later. Outler wrote: "One ought, however, to compare this essay on baptism (with its mild allowance of the doctrine of baptismal regeneration) with the sermon on 'The New Birth' where the stress falls heavily on conversion as a conscious adult experience of regeneration. The point is that Wesley held to both ideas."[27] It is to this sermon we now turn.

1.2. BAPTISM IS NOT THE NEW BIRTH: WESLEY'S SERMON THE NEW BIRTH (1760)

Wesley published the collection, *Sermons on Several Occasions*, in 1760. The collection included the sermon *The New Birth*. It is possible that Wesley preached much of the content of this sermon before 1760. Outler described this sermon as the "distillate of more than sixty oral sermons on John 3:7."[28] Outler continued: "We may see here a rough measure of the importance of the point about 'conversion' as perceived by Wesley and his people. 'The New Birth' is Wesley's conscious effort to provide them with a formal statement of the issue."[29] This sermon is a landmark sermon regarding Wesley's theology of conversion in relation to baptism. Outler's designation of the sermon as a formal statement regarding conversion is appropriate because it annexed the new birth theologically from baptism.

In *The New Birth*, Wesley clarified that baptism and the new birth were not the same things. Wesley wrote: "Baptism is not the new birth."[30] Wesley distinguished between the new birth and baptism using the metaphor of signage. Wesley wrote: "Baptism, the sign, is spoken of as distinct from regeneration, the thing signified."[31] Thus, just as a road sign may indicate a town down the road, the road sign is not the city itself. Using the language of a "sign" to describe baptism did not betray Wesley's commitment to the Church of England. The *Book of Common Prayer* catechism states:

---

27. Outler, *John Wesley*, 318.
28. Wesley, *Sermons*, 2:186.
29. Wesley, *Sermons*, 2:186.
30. Wesley, *Sermons*, 2:196.
31. Wesley, *Sermons*, 2:196.

Question: What meanest thou by this word Sacrament?

Answer: I mean an outward and visible sign of an inward and spiritual grace given to us.[32]

Wesley went beyond the figurative inward and outward metaphor and
pushed the sign in a chronological direction. Wesley wrote: "[The new
birth] does not always accompany baptism; they do not constantly go
together."[33] Thus, while baptism and regeneration go together, logically
speaking it is not required that regeneration happens simultaneously with
the act of baptism. Further, it is possible to be baptized and to not be regenerated. Maddox writes: "[Wesley's] purpose was not to reject the possibility
of regeneration, but to avoid the impression of its inevitability—apart from
our responsiveness."[34] *The New Birth* is a landmark sermon for Wesley's
theology of conversion because this sermon showed that Wesley understood regeneration to be required for salvation, while not chronologically
requiring regeneration to occur at baptism.[35]

1.3. ORIGINAL SIN CANCELED BY PREVENIENT GRACE (1776)

After Wesley's chronological separation of baptism and regeneration, the
next critical theological move related to conversion is that Wesley stated
that original sin is canceled by prevenient grace. In a letter to John Mason
on November 21, 1776, Wesley wrote:

---

32. Church of England, *Book of Common Prayer, 1662 Edition*, 294.

33. Wesley, *Sermons*, 2:197.

34. Maddox, *Responsible Grace*, 224.

35. Campbell shows an interesting possible parallel in the potential chronological separation between baptism and the realization of its benefits in the Westminster Confession of
Faith (WCF). The WCF states that it would be a sin to avoid baptism; "yet, grace and salvation
are not so inseparably annexed unto it, as that no person can be regenerated or saved without it, or that all that are baptized are undoubtedly regenerated." Thus, the WCF does not
demand baptism for salvation, and it also does not guarantee salvation for all who were baptized. Campbell also shows logic parallel to Wesley in the WCF that baptism and regeneration
are not chronologically linked. The WCF states: "The efficacy of baptism is not tied to that
moment of time wherein it is administered." See Ted A. Campbell, "Conversion and Baptism
in Wesleyan Spirituality," in *Conversion in the Wesleyan Tradition*, ed. Kenneth J. Collins and
John H. Tyson (Nashville: Abingdon Press, 2001), 167–69; Westminster Confession of Faith
28.5–6, in John H. Leith, *Creeds of the Churches: A Reader in Christian Doctrine, from the Bible to
the Present* (Atlanta: John Knox Press, 1982), 224–25.

No man living is without some preventing grace, and every degree of grace is a degree of life. That "by the offence of one, judgment came upon all men" (all born into the world) "unto condemnation," is an undoubted truth; and affects every infant, as well as every adult person. But it is equally true, that, "by the righteousness of one, the free gift came upon all men" (all born into the world, infant or adult) "unto justification." Therefore no infant ever was or ever will be "sent to hell for the guilt of Adam's sin," seeing it is cancelled by the righteousness of Christ as soon as they are sent into the world.[36]

To those unfamiliar with Wesley's view of prevenient grace, the canceling of original sin may sound Pelagian. Maddox clarifies: "Wesley understood Prevenient Grace to be God's initial move toward restored relationship with fallen humanity. As a first dimension, this involved God's merciful removal of any inherited guilt, by virtue of Christ."[37] In other words, inherited guilt existed, but was removed by God's grace. Thus, baptism does not serve as a neutralizer of inherited guilt. Wesley's 1756 abridgement of his father's work taught that a key benefit of baptism was to wash away inherited guilt,[38] but at this point of Wesley's life his theology had worked out fuller implications of his theology of prevenient grace and conversion to come to the conclusion that inherited guilt was canceled by the righteousness of Christ and not in the moment of baptism.

Wesley's theological moves in 1760 and 1776, therefore, effectively qualified the ongoing benefits of infant baptism and set the stage for Wesley to present publicly his mature view of baptism in light of his theology of the new birth and understanding of conversion. The occasion for the presentation of Wesley's mature view on baptism would come upon the growth of the Methodist movement in America and American independence, with the obvious need for a prayer book which did not require daily morning and evening prayers for the monarchy of England.[39]

---

36. Wesley, *The Letters of John Wesley*, 6:239–40.
37. Maddox, *Responsible Grace*, 90.
38. Wesley, *The Works of John Wesley*, 10:193.
39. See Church of England, *Book of Common Prayer, 1662 Edition*, 14–15, 25.

1.4. WATERSHED MOMENT: SUNDAY SERVICE (1784)

The publication of *The Sunday Service of the Methodists in North America* in 1784 provided the opportunity for Wesley to incorporate his updated theology of conversion in the form of a ministerial instruction book, including his mature thoughts on baptism. In the 1784 *Sunday Service* Wesley retained the language of regeneration before actual baptism but omitted the language of regeneration after the actual baptism. In other words, Wesley was willing to announce the possibility of regeneration at baptism but specifically did not make an assumptive declaratory statement regarding the regenerative state of the one who had been baptized.

Wesley's updated understanding of regeneration and baptism may be most easily understood by comparing directly the contents of the 1662 *Book of Common Prayer* with the 1784 *Sunday Service*. The figure below shows how the sections compare between the two documents:[40]

INFANT BAPTISM		ADULT BAPTISM (RIPER YEARS)	
1662 BCP	1784 SERVICE	1662 BCP	1784 SERVICE
Introductory Rubrics	*Introductory Rubrics*[41]	Introductory Rubrics	*Introductory Rubrics*
Opening Address	Opening Address	Opening Address	Opening Address
1st Opening Prayer	1st Opening Prayer	1st Opening Prayer	1st Opening Prayer
2nd Opening Prayer	2nd Opening Prayer	2nd Opening Prayer	2nd Opening Prayer
The Gospel	The Gospel	The Gospel	The Gospel
Exhortation on Gospel	[Omitted]	Exhortation on Gospel	[Omitted]
Prayer of the Spirit	Prayer of the Spirit	Prayer of the Spirit	Prayer of the Spirit

40. This analysis is built upon the research found in Charles R. Hohenstein, "The Revisions of the Rites of Baptism in the Methodist Episcopal Church, 1784–1939" (PhD diss., University of Notre Dame, 1990), 299–300.

41. In the sections which were not omitted the wording is identical except for the sections which are in *italic*.

Address to the Sponsors	[Omitted]	Address to the Candidates	Address to the Candidates
Renunciation of Satan	[Omitted]	Renunciation of Satan	Renunciation of Satan
Profession of Faith	[Omitted]	Profession of Faith	Profession of Faith
Prayer for Candidates	Prayer for Candidates	Prayer for Candidates	Prayer for Candidates
The Baptism	*The Baptism*	The Baptism	*The Baptism*
The Signation	The Signation [omitted in some copies]	The Signation	[Omitted]
Invitation to Prayer	*Invitation to Prayer*	Invitation to Prayer	*Invitation to Prayer*
The Lord's Prayer	The Lord's Prayer	The Lord's Prayer	The Lord's Prayer
Prayer of Thanksgiving	*Prayer of Thanksgiving*	Prayer of Thanksgiving	*Prayer of Thanksgiving*
Charge to Sponsors	[Omitted]	Charge to Sponsors	[Omitted]
Concluding Rubrics	[Omitted]	Charge to the Candidates	[Omitted]
---	---	Concluding Rubrics	[Omitted]

The comparison above shows that some sections were omitted in the *Sunday Service*, most obviously the sections related to sponsors, which is not surprising considering Wesley's comments related to sponsors in *Serious Thoughts Concerning Godfathers and Godmothers* (1752), as discussed above.[42] Again, regarding conversion, the omission of sponsors showed the requirement of a personal appropriation of faith. Another section omitted was the concluding rubric from the 1662 *Book of Common Prayer* rite of infant baptism; its significance will be discussed below.

---

42. See section 1.1. in this chapter.

The sections which were changed (in italics) are noticeably *after* the actual baptism in the service, with the exception of the introductory rubric, which was essentially deleted. The post-baptismal changes to the infant and adult services are critical to Wesley's presentation of his theology of conversion shown through his baptismal beliefs. In order to compare carefully the changes Wesley made, see the texts below:

Invitation Prayer (After Baptism)

INFANT		ADULT	
1662 BCP	1784 SERVICE	1662 BCP	1784 SERVICE
Seeing now, dearly beloved brethren, that this Child is	Seeing now, dearly beloved brethren, that this Child is	Seeing now, dearly beloved brethren, that these Persons are	Seeing now, dearly beloved brethren, that these Persons are
regenerate and grafted	*grafted*	*regenerate and grafted*	*grafted*
into the body of Christ's Church, let us give thanks unto Almighty God for these benefits, and with one accord make our prayers unto him, that this Child may lead the rest of his life according to this beginning.	into the body of Christ's Church, let us give thanks unto Almighty God for these benefits, and with one accord make our prayers unto him, that this Child may lead the rest of his life according to this beginning.	into the body of Christ's Church; let us give thanks unto Almighty God for these benefits, and with one accord make our prayers unto him, that they may lead the rest of their life according to this beginning.	into the body of Christ's Church; let us give thanks unto Almighty God for these benefits, and with one accord make our prayers unto him, that they may lead the rest of their life according to this beginning.

Thanksgiving Prayer (After Baptism)

INFANT		ADULT	
1662 BCP	1784 SERVICE	1662 BCP	1784 SERVICE
We yield thee hearty thanks, most merciful Father, that it hath	We yield thee hearty thanks, most merciful Father, that it hath	We yield thee humble thanks, O heavenly Father, that thou	We yield thee humble thanks, O heavenly Father, that thou

pleased thee to *regenerate this Infant with thy Holy Spirit,* to receive him for thine own Child by adoption, and to incorporate him into thy holy Church. And humbly we beseech thee to grant, that he, being dead unto sin, and living unto righteousness, and being buried with Christ in his death, may crucify the old man, and utterly abolish the whole body of sin; And that as he is made partaker of the death of thy Son, he may also be partaker of his resurrection; so that finally, with the residue of thy holy Church, he may be an inheritor of thine everlasting kingdom, through Christ our Lord. Amen.

pleased thee to receive this Infant for thine own Child by adoption, and to incorporate him into thy holy Church. And humbly we beseech thee to grant, that he, being dead unto sin, and living unto righteousness, and being buried with Christ in his death, may crucify the old man, and utterly abolish the whole body of sin; and that, as he is made partaker of the death of thy Son, he may also be partaker of his resurrection; so that finally, with the residue of thy holy Church, he may be an inheritor of thine everlasting kingdom, through Christ our Lord. Amen.

hast vouchsafed to call us to the knowledge of thy grace, and faith in thee; Increase this knowledge, and confirm this faith in us evermore. Give thy Holy Spirit to these Persons; that *now being born again,* and made heirs of everlasting salvation, through our Lord Jesus Christ, they may continue thy servants, and attain thy promises, through the same Lord Jesus Christ thy Son; who liveth and reigneth with thee, in the unity of the same Holy Spirit, everlastingly. Amen.

hast vouchsafed to call us to the knowledge of thy grace, and faith in thee; Increase this knowledge, and confirm this faith in us evermore. Give thy Holy Spirit to these Persons; that *being born again,* and made heirs of everlasting salvation, through our Lord Jesus Christ, they may continue thy servants, and attain thy promises, through the same Lord Jesus Christ thy Son; who liveth and reigneth with thee, in the unity of the same Holy Spirit, everlastingly. Amen.

In the invitation prayer, it is clear that Wesley omitted the word "regenerate" in his 1784 *Sunday Service* from both the infant and adult baptismal service.[43] In the following comparison, we are able to see that Wesley removed the reference to regeneration in his 1784 *Sunday Service* infant thanksgiving prayer. The 1784 adult thanksgiving prayer removed the word "now" from "now being born again," which, especially given the other edits, is understood as removing the assumptive present-tense condition of being "born again" spoken of in the thanksgiving prayer. Barton comments: "[Wesley] found both conversion and the necessity of baptism in the Bible, so he held both. But conversion was the stronger doctrine. At every point in the prayer book, baptismal regeneration was altered to prevent its intrusion as a doctrine of assured salvation."[44] The 1784 *Sunday Service* was, thus, a watershed moment for Wesley's theology of conversion since it allowed him to work out fully the implications of his conversion theology back into, what would become, the Methodist prayer book. Baptism brought benefits, but regeneration, and thus conversion, were not implied as assumed to happen for every person in the moment of the actual baptism based on an analysis of the language of the prayer book. From the preceding analysis one of the synoptic statements of the espoused theology of conversion emerges for Wesley: baptism marks one's entrance to the church but is not chronologically tied to conversion.

1.5. SYNTHESIS: BAPTISM AS ADMITTANCE INTO THE BENEFITS OF THE CHURCH

Based on the above evidence, several conclusions can be stated regarding the mature Wesley's view of baptism in light of his theology of conversion. For anyone who was baptized, they received at least two benefits: entry into the benefits of the church (for example, admission to communion)

---

43. There was an additional update to the Sunday Service in 1786 which replaced the word "grafted" with the word "admitted." The difference between being admitted rather than grafted into the body of Christ is debatable, but being "grafted" may denote a permanency which "admittance" may not imply, and thus emphasize even further the requirement of the newly baptized to remain co-operant with God's grace in their life. However, it is unclear if the 1786 edition was from the pen of Wesley or Thomas Coke. See Hohenstein, "The Revisions of the Rites of Baptism in the Methodist Episcopal Church, 1784–1939," 57–58; J. Hamby Barton, "The Two Version of the First Edition of John Wesley's 'The Sunday Service of the Methodists in North America,'" *Methodist History* 23, no. 3 (April 1985): 153–62.

44. Barton, "The Two Versions of the First Edition of John Wesley's 'The Sunday Service of the Methodists in North America,'" 159–60.

and the pronouncement of the contract for justification, which came, in Wesley's view, through genuine faith.

Adults who had already converted were already justified and regenerated upon their conversion; so, for the converted adult, their baptism introduced them formally into the church and its benefits.[45] English writes: "[Baptism] is the ceremony of initiation into the visible church. Furthermore, the person who receives baptism may thereby give testimony to the faith that is within him."[46] In the case of the already converted adult, their salvation did not hinge on their subsequent baptism, but they were called to be baptized as their entrance into the church and in obedience to Jesus' command.[47]

For adults who were baptized but did not have genuine saving faith, baptism was still the entrance into the benefits of the church, yet their baptism did not save them; their baptism was a signpost for them to follow forward into faith. Maddox writes: "While the grace of baptism is *sufficient* for initiating Christian life, it becomes *efficient* only as we responsively participate."[48] Baptized people should not rest in their baptism, but as their baptism instructs them to do, they should turn to Christ in faith.

In the case of infants who were baptized, Wesley never explicitly denied the possibility of their salvation. Since, in 1776, Wesley made it clear that original sin was canceled by prevenient grace,[49] it is possible that redemption of infants was complete unless they "sinned it away." In this case, Wesley maintained a sacramental salvific exception for infants who had not come to an age of accountability. Furthermore, by not attributing the "response" to the godparents, Wesley made the sacrament of infant baptism an entirely direct sacrament, not based upon anyone else's fidelity. English writes: "In Wesley's hands, then, the baptism of infants becomes an occasion on which two things are done. The child is received into the Church, the sphere in which saving grace is particularly active,

---

45. Wesley taught that baptism was not required for salvation. See Wesley, *Explanatory Notes upon the New Testament*, John 3:5, Acts 10:47.

46. John C. English, "The Sacrament of Baptism according to the Sunday Service of 1784," *Methodist History* 5, no. 2 (1967): 15.

47. In Wesley's sermon *Of the Church* (1785) he taught that even those who received the baptism of the Holy Spirit should be baptized in the church. See Wesley, *Sermons*, 3:49–50.

48. Maddox, *Responsible Grace*, 222.

49. See section 1.3. in this chapter.

and prayer is made that God in his good time will justify the child."[50] We
may go a step further than English and say that, in Wesley's theology, prevenient grace before active sin determines that the infant was properly
justified by Christ himself through prevenient grace. To restate Wesley's
own words: "No infant ever was or ever will be 'sent to hell for the guilt of
Adam's sin,' seeing it is canceled by the righteousness of Christ as soon as
they are sent into the world."[51]

Another synthetic observation is required. Most of the analysis of baptism has been thought of as teleological; in other words, projecting the
future benefits of the baptismal candidate. It may be helpful to begin with
the end in mind when considering the implications of Wesley's theology
of conversion related to baptism. Runyon writes: "The key to this seeming
contradiction [the requirement of baptism and conversion] is found in
Wesley's view that the sacrament is a means, not an end. Baptism, whether
of an infant or an adult, is the foundation, the beginning, but not the end
of a process."[52] Runyon's explanation of Wesley's apparent contradiction
between infant baptism and requirement for subsequent conversion captures Wesley's passion for the *telos* of humanity.

We have seen that Wesley's theology of conversion took decades to work
out in the context of baptism. The primary conclusion of this section is,
therefore, one of the synoptic statements of the espoused theology of conversion for Wesley: baptism marks one's entrance to the church but is not
chronologically tied to conversion (synoptic statement 8). Questions about
the relationship between baptism and conversion are not only theological; they are practical inquiries posed by those concerned about the experience of living the faithful Christian life. We now turn our attention to

---

50. English, "The Sacrament of Baptism according to the Sunday Service of 1784," 15.

51. Wesley, *The Letters of John Wesley*, 6:239–40. However, while Wesley's support of infant
salvation is clear, what is not initially clear is why Wesley removed the 1662 concluding
rubric of the infant baptismal service which stated that baptized children were "undoubtedly
saved" before they committed actual sin. Two reasons may be stated. First, the 1662 private
baptism of infants did not include the "undoubtedly saved" rubric, so the explicit inclusion
or exclusion of a statement did not necessarily imply the denial of infant salvation. Second,
one of Wesley's aims in the 1784 *Sunday Service* was brevity; for example, the opening rubric is
almost entirely eliminated. Thus, by omitting the "undoubtedly saved" rubric, Wesley was not
denying its truthfulness. See Church of England, *Book of Common Prayer, 1662 Edition*, 271, 278.

52. Runyon, *The New Creation*, 140.

another question regarding the intersection of Christian experience and the theology of conversion.

2. CONVERSION AND ASSURANCE

Assurance of salvation is a natural attendant theme in Wesley's theology of conversion, not in the least part due to the climatic section of Wesley's Aldersgate account. Wesley wrote: "About a quarter before nine, while [the reader of Luther's Preface to the Epistle of Romans] was describing the change which God works in the heart through faith in Christ, I felt my heart strangely warmed. I felt I did trust in Christ, Christ alone for salvation, and an assurance was given me that he had taken away *my* sins, even *mine*, and saved *me* from the law of sin and death."[53] At least two things happened when Wesley's heart was warmed: a felt salvation, and an assurance of salvation. Assurance of salvation is, thus, a natural and required attendant theme to buttress the primary themes of the espousal of Wesley's theology of conversion because of its literary and theological proximity to the most famous words Wesley ever penned—which address directly the topics of salvation and assurance.

While Wesley's Aldersgate account brings the topic of assurance to the fore, it is of critical importance to recognize that Aldersgate occurred in the midst of Wesley's developing understanding of assurance and does not represent his lasting and mature outlook on the topic of assurance of salvation.[54] It will be possible to see, therefore, that Wesley's conception of assurance and conversion underwent four distinct transitions which ended with his mature view, which is that assurance of salvation is available but not required for a genuine convert (synoptic statement 9). First, beginning in 1725, Wesley understood conversion as an ascent to truth. Second, beginning around 1735, Wesley understood the need for the witness

---

53. Wesley, *Journals and Diaries*, 18:250. Italics in the original.

54. Collins wrote: "Wesley's teaching on assurance underwent more modifications and was sustained by more nuances than any other single element in his doctrine of salvation." Kenneth J. Collins, *The Scripture Way of Salvation: The Heart of John Wesley's Theology* (Nashville: Abingdon Press, 1997), 136. I concur with Maddox that the best analysis of the contours of Wesley's theology of assurance over the course of his life are found in Richard P. Heitzenrater, "Great Expectations: Aldersgate and the Evidences of Genuine Christianity," in *Aldersgate Reconsidered*, ed. Randy L. Maddox (Nashville: Kingswood Books, 1990), 49–91. See Maddox, *Responsible Grace*, 124.

of the Holy Spirit to give assurance of a true conversion. Third, at the height of Wesley's positive interactions with the English Moravians, Wesley understood conversion to occur when one had full assurance of one's faith as indicated by a lack of fear and doubt. Fourth, beginning in 1747, Wesley understood that full assurance was not required for salvation; thus, full assurance was not required for conversion.

2.1. ASSURANCE AVAILABLE: RATIONAL AND PRACTICAL ASSENT TO TRUTH (1725)

The early Wesley began a quest for assurance of salvation as an antidote to fear and trembling; Wesley understood assurance to come through rational and practical assent to the truth which God revealed. At first, Wesley believed that assurance of salvation came when a person truly assented to and practiced the truth of the gospel. Wesley's early correspondence with his mother showed his interest in the relationship between assurance and salvation. On June 18, 1725, John Wesley wrote: "If we can never have any certainty of our being in a state of salvation, good reason it is that every moment should be spent, not in joy, but in fear and trembling."[55] Later in their correspondence, on November 22, 1725, Wesley concluded: "Saving faith ... is an assent to what God has revealed, because he has revealed it, and not because the truth of it may be evinced by reason."[56] Maddox summarizes Wesley's understanding of salvation in this era as follows: "God's pardon [for Wesley] would be based on the rational credibility both of the divine revelation promising it and of our conformity to the conditions of that promise."[57] Wesley, thus, sought the assurance of salvation, because without assurance fear and trembling resulted; however, since assurance was attained by rational assent and the difficult task of conformity to God's laws, assurance was elusive.

It is understandable that Wesley did not find his early understanding of assurance satisfying. Essentially, he believed that the strength of one's assurance corresponded with the strength of one's capacity to avoid sin inwardly and outwardly. In Wesley's Aldersgate narrative he recalled that

---

55. Wesley, *Letters*, 25:170.
56. Wesley, *Letters*, 25:188.
57. Maddox, *Responsible Grace*, 124.

prior to 1725 he had stressed the outward means of holiness, but after 1725 realized the need for inward holiness. Wesley wrote: "I cannot well tell what I hoped to be saved by now, when I was continually sinning against the little light I had."[58] Wesley did not find his search for assurance successful because he could not sustain a holy life. In this era of Wesley's life, it is unclear how Wesley would have thought about the relationship between conversion and assurance; though, it is likely, per the analysis of the complicated relationship between conversion and baptism (as shown in chapter two, section 4.1. and earlier in the present chapter, chapter three, section 1.1.), that in the era of 1725–1734 Wesley would have understood conversion to have occurred at baptism and for assurance of salvation to be relatively unrelated to conversion.

2.2. ASSURANCE REQUIRED: THE WITNESS OF THE SPIRIT (1735)

In 1735, Wesley's view on assurance and conversion evolved to not only include rational and practical assent to God, but to include also the requirement of the inward witness of the Spirit. This change occurred upon a landmark event for Wesley's understanding of assurance of salvation: his father's death. The elder Wesley stated on his deathbed: "The inner witness, son, the inner witness … that is the proof, the strongest proof of Christianity."[59] John Wesley commented regarding his father's words: "I cannot therefore doubt but the Spirit of God bore an inward witness with his spirit that he was a child of God."[60] At that time, in 1735, John Wesley commented that he did not understand his father regarding the assurance that could come from the inner witness of the Spirit.[61]

After 1735 Wesley continued to seek assurance of his salvation. Shortly after the death of Wesley's father, John Wesley set off for Georgia and began his engagement with the Moravians. In terms of Wesley's assurance of salvation, Maddox summarized: "By early 1738 Wesley was convinced that assurance of salvation was a provision available to Christians through the activity of the Holy Spirit in their lives. He became equally convinced that

---

58. Wesley, *Journals and Diaries*, 18:243.
59. Wesley, *Letters*, 26:289.
60. Wesley, *Letters*, 26:289.
61. Wesley, *Letters*, 26:289.

he did not yet have this assurance."[62] Wesley's efforts to attain the witness of the Spirit rested on his endless pursuit of the means of grace. Thus, Wesley did not have assurance because, once again, as in 1725, his view of assurance was rooted in good works. What one can see in light of this, therefore, is that the connection between assurance and conversion is not entirely clear for Wesley in this era, because Wesley could not reconcile his theology of assurance with his experience, namely his experience of his own imperfection.

2.3. ASSURANCE REQUIRED: THE LACK OF ALL FEAR AND DOUBT (1738)

Wesley's search for assurance entered a new era when he came to understand the beginning of conversion to start with genuine faith, i.e. instantaneous conversion. Wesley's requirements for assurance were still in place (the assent to truth and the witness of the Spirit), yet these were available at the onset of true faith and not as the result of a faith accomplished by the means of grace. On February 1, 1738, Wesley wrote: "I want that faith which none can have without knowing that he hath it. ... For whosoever hath it is 'freed from sin' ... He is freed from fear ... He is freed from doubt ... which 'Spirit itself beareth witness with his spirit, that he is a child of God.' "[63] Wesley believed that he received this gift of faith at Aldersgate. He wrote: "I felt I did trust in Christ, Christ alone for salvation, and an assurance was given me that he had taken away *my* sins, even *mine*, and saved *me* from the law of sin and death."[64] What Wesley wanted on February 1, 1738, he received on May 24, 1738, at Aldersgate: faith accompanied by personal assurance of salvation. Yet, Wesley's journal showed that the very next day after Aldersgate, Wesley began experiencing increasing fear and doubt once again.[65]

---

62. Maddox, *Responsible Grace*, 125. See also Runyon, *The New Creation*, 59–60; Arthur S. Yates, *The Doctrine of Assurance: With Special Reference to John Wesley*, reprint edition (Eugene, OR: Wipf & Stock, 2015), 12–15; Wesley, *Journals and Diaries*, 18:247–48.

63. Wesley, *Journals and Diaries*, 18:216.

64. Wesley, *Journals and Diaries*, 18:250. Italics in the original.

65. Perhaps the most depressing self-assessment of Wesley's post-Aldersgate failings is found in his journal on January 4, 1739. Wesley, *Journals and Diaries*, 19:29–31.

Over the next decade, Wesley began to reflect upon his own personal experience while continuing to preach that true faith and assurance excluded doubt, fear, and sorrow. For instance, Wesley's attack on Whitefield's teaching in Wesley's sermon *Free Grace* (1739) was an example of Wesley's public teaching on assurance during that time. Wesley wrote regarding the necessity of assurance accompanying true faith: "That assurance of faith which these enjoy [those with an uninterrupted witness of the Spirit] excludes all doubt and fear."[66] However, his public statements were not aligned with his personal experience. Indeed, Maddox argues: "Wesley was [privately] distinguishing between saving faith and the full assurance of faith."[67] For instance, a comparison of the 1744, 1745, and 1747 *Minutes* shows a transition in Wesley's public teaching on assurance. The 1744 *Minutes* recorded:

> Q. 5. Have all true Christians this faith? May not a man be justified and not know it?
>
> A. That all true Christians have such a faith as implies an assurance of God's love appears from [then a list of Scriptures].[68]

The 1744 *Minutes* state that all true Christians (via faith) have an assurance of God's love. The 1745 *Minutes* of August 2 recorded a modified answer to a similar question which casts some flexibility on the requirement of absolute assurance:

> Q. 1. Is an assurance of God's love absolutely necessary to our being in his favour? Or may there possibly be some exempt cases?
>
> A. We dare not positively say, there are not.
>
> Q. 2. Is such an assurance absolutely necessary to inward and outward holiness?

---

66. Wesley, *Sermons*, 3:550.

67. Maddox, *Responsible Grace*, 126.

68. Wesley, *The Methodist Societies: The Minutes of Conference*, 10:127.

A. To inward, we apprehend it is; to outward holiness, we incline
to think it is not.[69]

The 1747 *Minutes* have several pages of questions and answers about
biblical examples of people who appeared to have and not have assurance
of their salvation. The *Minutes* also include questions and answers regarding assurance of salvation of specific members of the Methodist societies.
These questions and answers culminate in the statement that there may
be some "exempt cases" of people who do not have assurance of salvation
but who are saved.[70] An evaluation of the *Minutes* of 1744–1747 shows a transition and relaxation of the expectation of assurance of salvation accompanying genuine conversion. In other words, for approximately a decade
after Aldersgate, Wesley was increasingly attempting to understand his
own experience, the experiences of others, and the implications of his new
understanding of faith and instantaneous conversion.[71]

The beginning of this era (1738) was inaugurated by Wesley's attainment of assurance through his lack of fear and doubt (for example, what
he observed in the Moravians while crossing the Atlantic). The end of this
era (as evidenced in the 1745 *Minutes*) shows that Wesley reduced the centrality of assurance as an essential Christian experience. Wesley's theology of assurance, thus, underwent a massive change from 1738 to 1745, as
did his theology of conversion. Wesley's initial thoughts on conversion
following Aldersgate were closely linked to his sense of assurance. Thus,
initially, assurance of conversion was linked to assurance of salvation,
which was based upon lacking fear and doubt. It was not until 1747 that
Wesley's mature view of assurance provided a clearer understanding of
the relationship between conversion and assurance.

---

69. Wesley, *The Methodist Societies: The Minutes of Conference*, 10:149–50. See Collins, *The
Scripture Way of Salvation*, 137–38; Maddox, *Responsible Grace*, 315n52.

70. Wesley, *The Methodist Societies: The Minutes of Conference*, 10:192–94.

71. The most thorough treatment of Wesley's views of assurance in this era is found in
Heitzenrater, "Great Expectations: Aldersgate and the Evidences of Genuine Christianity,"
67–83.

2.4. ASSURANCE NOT REQUIRED: BUT AVAILABLE (1747)

In 1747, Wesley finally settled his view on assurance and concluded that assurance of salvation is available but not required for a genuine convert. In a letter to his brother Charles on July 31, 1747, John Wesley delineated between justifying faith and the sense of pardon. He wrote: "I cannot allow that justifying faith is such an assurance."[72] With this statement, John Wesley made clear that authentic justifying faith, such as that which he received at Aldersgate, did not always require a constant sense of assurance.

Further details regarding Wesley's mature view of assurance are explained in a letter from March 28, 1767, which Wesley wrote to Dr. Thomas Rutherford. Wesley stated:

> I believe a few, but very few, Christians have an assurance from God of everlasting salvation; and that is the thing which the Apostle terms the plerophory or full assurance of hope. I believe more have such an assurance of being now in the favour of God as excludes all doubt and fear. And this, if I do not mistake, the Apostle means by the plerophory or full assurance of faith. I believe the consciousness of being in the favour of God (which I do not term plerophory or full assurance, since it is frequently weakened, nay perhaps interrupted, by returns of doubt or fear) is the common privilege of Christians fearing God and working righteousness. Yet I do not affirm there are no exceptions to this rule. Possibly some may be in the favour of God, and yet go morning all the day long. But I believe this is usually owing either to disorder of body or ignorance of gospel promises. Therefore I have not for many years thought a consciousness of acceptance to be essential to justifying faith.[73]

In this quotation, we can see that Wesley delineated four possibilities regarding assurance. First, very few will have the assurance of hope, which is certainty of future salvation.[74] Second, more will have the assurance of

---

72. Wesley, *Letters*, 26:254–55.

73. Wesley, *The Letters of John Wesley*, 5:358–59.

74. Coppedge wrote: "Thus, assurance for Wesley, was primarily related to present pardon, whereas the hope of final perseverance continued to be grounded in a life of faith and obedience." Allan Coppedge, *John Wesley in Theological Debate* (Wilmore, KY: Wesley Heritage Press, 1987), 142.

faith, which is the current exclusion of all doubt and fear (as did Wesley at Aldersgate, but which he lost soon thereafter). Third, the common privilege of all Christians is the assurance of being in the favor of God. Fourth, some may deny being in the favor of God, and therefore may have no consciousness of assurance, yet still have justifying faith. Thus, a person can be a genuine convert and not have full assurance of faith. In other words, a genuine convert may lack faith and have fear of death, contra what Wesley argued earlier in his life. What we see is that, for Wesley, assurance of salvation is linked to the ongoing aspect of conversion rather than a confirmation of instantaneous conversion. In sum, Wesley's public and private theology came to a head in the years leading up to 1747 when Wesley proclaimed what would be his lasting and mature theology of assurance of salvation as it relates to conversion: assurance of salvation is available but not required for a genuine convert (synoptic statement 9).

3. CONVERSION AND THE VIA SALUTIS

We now turn our attention to Wesley's view of the relationship between conversion and his overarching soteriological schema, often called the *ordo salutis*, but more properly (as will be seen for Wesley), the *via salutis*. The motifs examined in chapter two presented the operant material from which the espoused theology of conversion of Wesley was articulated. While an analysis of the synoptic statements of conversion will be examined in detail in chapter six (alongside the conclusions regarding Whitefield's view of conversion), here we will see how conversion maps to Wesley's broader understanding of the *way* of salvation.

For Wesley, the *via salutis* includes that which is present *prior* to instantaneous conversion (prevenient grace, conviction of sin, and repentance), that which occurs in the *moment* of instantaneous conversion (genuine faith, regeneration, and justification—indicative of the inauguration of conversion), that which *follows* instantaneous conversion (obedience, the mind of Christ, and progress toward perfection [for some, reaching perfection]—indicative of the teleology of conversion), and the possibility of backsliding.

A proper espousal of Wesley's theology of conversion must take into account the broader scope of soteriology as found in Wesley's *via salutis* since no individual theological concept exists in isolation from the whole of theology. A study on conversion must attend to a broad range of theological loci: the nature of God, the nature of humanity, the atoning work of God, and the full redemption and restoration of all creation.[75] The *ordo salutis* is an attempt to describe the broader picture of redemption and salvation,[76] though its form in Wesley's theology is better described as a *via salutis*.[77] The critical advantage for describing salvation as a *via* rather than an *ordo* in Wesley's theology is that the concept of a *via* may allow for regression and reversal with more ease than the *ordo*, since the *ordo salutis* is a term which has been used typically among those who hold to irreversibility via the doctrine of the perseverance of the saints.[78]

3.1. THE THEOLOGICAL WAY PRIOR TO CONVERSION

Wesley addressed three critical soteriological dynamics which occur prior to conversion: prevenient grace, conviction of sin, and repentance.[79] Each of these dynamics is not relegated to the theological way prior to conversion;

---

75. There is an additional risk and temptation in the study of conversion to endlessly negotiate the details of salvation, which is to make salvation, and indeed conversion, an entirely individualistic topic.

76. Perhaps the most influential example of an *ordo salutis* is William Perkins, *A Golden Chain, or The Description of Theology*, ed. Greg Fox (Cambridge: Puritan Reprints, 2010). Rightmire draws attention to the comparison between Wesley and Aquinas's order of salvation. Aquinas's stages of grace are: (1) Preventing, (2) Convicting, (3) Justifying, and (4) Cooperating. R. David Rightmire, "Holiness and Wesley's 'Way of Salvation,' " *Word and Deed* 13, no. 1 (November 2010): 50–51n13.

77. Maddox suggested three reasons why the *via salutis* is preferred in Wesley's theology. First, it captures the gradual transitions in salvation compared to abrupt transitions. Second, it provides more flexibility for the reversibility of salvation. Third, it captures the pastoral context of Wesley's practical theology over the Scholastic approach embedded in the *ordo salutis*. Collins countered two of Maddox's arguments. The first point is countered on the basis of Maddox and Collins's overarching differences on the nature of salvation. The third point is countered by suggesting that Wesley often explained his reasoning in carefully organized ways not unlike Scholasticism. Collins leaves the second point, the reversibility advantage, untouched. At the end of the day, Maddox's footnote that Wesley likely would have seen little difference between the *via* and the *ordo* seems prudent. See Maddox, *Responsible Grace*, 157–58, 331n3; Collins, *The Theology of John Wesley*, 188, 307–10. For an earlier treatment by Collins, see Kenneth J. Collins, "A Hermeneutical Model for the Wesleyan Ordo Salutis," *Wesleyan Theological Journal* 19, no. 2 (Fall 1984): 23–37.

78. Wesley's 1765 sermon, *The Scripture Way of Salvation*, parallels the claims this section makes regarding Wesley's *via salutis*. Wesley, *Sermons*, 2:156.

79. Chapter two, section two, established Wesley's primary conversion motif of that which proceeds conversion: conviction, convincing, and awakening. In the current section, attention is given to an attendant theme in Wesley's theology, the relationship between the *via salutis* and conversion, which shows the broader, attendant influence of prevenient grace and repentance prior to conversion.

they continue on in the life of the converted person. In other words, for example, a person does not repent prior to conversion only; repentance is meant to continue throughout the Christian life. Similarly, prevenient grace exists before, during, and after the moment of instantaneous conversion. However, prevenient grace, conviction of sin, and repentance are a part of the theological way *before* conversion, or more specifically, instantaneous conversion, in a way that ensuing theological activity (for example, justification) is not. The motif of the *via salutis* prior to conversion highlights from a different angle the espoused synoptic statements of conversion found in chapter two. Wesley's *via salutis* shows that conversion is based upon the prevenient grace of God, which is a parallel observation to what was demonstrated in chapter two, section two: conversion is initiated and sustained by the grace of God (synoptic statement 1). Similarly, Wesley's belief that conviction comes before conversion is akin to what was also shown in chapter two, section two: conversion is foreshadowed by a deep sense of sinfulness (synoptic statement 4). In order to substantiate these claims regarding the theological way prior to conversion, attention will be given to Wesley's comments on prevenient grace, conviction of sin, and repentance as related to conversion.

Preventing grace should be given priority when discussing the *via salutis* prior to conversion because preventing grace exists before any human response, and thus, the human experience of conversion. Article X ("Of Free Will") of the *Thirty-Nine Articles* states that preventing grace enables people to have a good will despite the condition of mankind being fallen in Adam.[80] Wesley called preventing grace that which is "is common to all, is sufficient to bring us to Christ, though it is not sufficient to carry us any further till we are justified."[81] Wesley's discussion of preventing grace in the *Principles of a Methodist* are in the section entitled "Before justification." The inclusion of prevenient grace in the discussion of that which precedes justification confirms the place of preventing grace as being prior to conversion in the *via salutis* since justification comes upon instantaneous conversion (as will be shown in the next section). Similarly, preventing grace works to draw those people toward the gospel, even those whom do

---

80. Church of England, *Book of Common Prayer, 1662 Edition*, 615.

81. Wesley, *The Methodist Societies: History, Nature, and Design*, 9:64.

not respond in faith.[82] In a short letter to John Fletcher on March 22, 1771, Wesley argued:

> I always did for between these thirty and forty years clearly assert the total fall of man and his utter inability to do any good himself; the absolute necessity of the grace and Spirit of God to raise even a good thought or desire in our hearts; the Lord's rewarding no work and accepting of none but so far as they proceed from His preventing, convincing, and converting grace through the Beloved; the blood and righteousness of Christ being the sole meritorious cause of our salvation.[83]

Wesley's letter to Fletcher highlights Wesley's belief that preventing grace is present in fallen humanity as a part of Wesley's *via salutis* where preventing grace leads to convincing grace, which leads to converting grace.[84] Wesley's comment to Fletcher brings us to the next aspect of Wesley's *via salutis* prior to conversion: conviction of sin.[85]

The relationship between conviction of sin and conversion has already been established in chapter two, section two, where it was shown that Wesley taught that conviction (of sin), convincing, and awakening lead up to, but do not always end in, instantaneous conversion. What was not established in chapter two, since it is not primary in Wesley's writing on conversion, is the role of repentance prior to conversion. Repentance is not primary in Wesley's discussion of conversion due to his reluctance to return to the emphases of his pre-Aldersgate understanding of conversion, which included the extreme use of the means of grace (which included repentance) as a means to achieve perfection in order to be fully converted. Wesley does not deny, post-Aldersgate, that repentance comes before conversion;[86] the mature Wesley, instead, tends to emphasize that repentance

---

82. Wesley, *Journals and Diaries*, 21:66.

83. Wesley, *The Letters of John Wesley*, 5:231.

84. Wesley's theology of the presence of prevenient grace prior to conversion underscores the espoused synoptic statement of conversion which was identified in chapter two, section two: conversion is initiated and sustained by the grace of God (synoptic statement 1).

85. For more on Wesley's theology and prevenient grace, see Collins, *The Theology of John Wesley*, 73–82; Maddox, *Responsible Grace*, 83–90; Runyon, *The New Creation*, 27–41.

86. For example, in 1742, in *The Principles of a Methodist*, Wesley declared: "I believe every man is penitent before he is justified; he repents before he believes the gospel." Wesley,

occurs prior to and continuing from instantaneous conversion.[87] Having established that prevenient grace, conviction of sin, and repentance come prior to conversion in Wesley's *via salutis*, we now turn attention to the theological components nascent within the moment of conversion.

3.2. THE THEOLOGICAL WAY IN THE MOMENT
OF INSTANTANEOUS CONVERSION

The moment of conversion in Wesley's *via salutis* is the moment of instantaneous conversion; within this moment three discrete soteriological actions occur: genuine (lively) faith, regeneration, and the appropriation of justification.[88] Faith, regeneration, and justification all occur in the moment of instantaneous conversion but are not the same thing. In 1750, Wesley responded to George Lavington's attack when Wesley published *A Letter to the Author of "The Enthusiasm of Methodists and Papists Compared."* Wesley responded: "'Tis you who discover justification also to be 'the same as regeneration and having a lively faith'; I take them to be three different things—so different as not ever to come under one genus. And yet 'tis true that each of these, 'as far as I know', is at first experienced suddenly; although two of them (I leave it to you to find out which) gradually increase from that hour."[89] Wesley's words to Lavington establish that faith, regeneration, and justification are all different, so much so that they are of different genus; yet, faith, regeneration, and justification all happen in the same, sudden (instantaneous), moment.

The moment of conversion in Wesley's *via salutis* continues to develop a primary claim of the study, that for Wesley, conversion is accurately

---

The Methodist Societies: History, Nature, and Design, 9:62. Additionally, in a 1746 sermon, *The Witness of the Spirit I,* Wesley wrote: "Scripture describes repentance, or conviction of sin, as constantly going before this witness of pardon. So ... 'Repent ye therefore, and be converted that your sins may be blotted out.' In conformity whereto our Church also continually places repentance before pardon or the witness of it." Wesley, *Sermons,* 1:278.

87. In the sermon, *The Scripture Way of Salvation* (1765), Wesley proclaimed: "I allow there is a repentance consequent upon, as well as a repentance previous to justification." Wesley, *Sermons,* 2:164.

88. The moment of conversion, or in other words, the nature of instantaneous conversion is a primary motif of Wesley's operant teaching on conversion which was examined in chapter two, section three. The current section will examine the attendant themes that happen within this moment in the context of the *via salutis.*

89. Wesley, *The Appeals to Men of Reason and Religion and Certain Related Open Letters,* 11:369.

understood as inaugurated teleology.[90] The concept of conversion as inaugurated teleology deepens because genuine faith is inaugurated in the moment of instantaneous conversion,[91] but the *telos* of faith is not complete in instantaneous conversion; in other words, initial saving faith can form into mature faith. Similarly, regeneration and justification are inaugurated but their *telos* is not reached in instantaneous conversion. The *telos* of regeneration is not just birth but maturity.[92] Additionally, the *telos* of justification is not just "right standing" but full sanctification.[93] Wesley's theology of the *via salutis* as it relates to conversion requires progress toward its *telos* that goes past the inauguration of conversion, this is the theological way following instantaneous conversion.

3.3. THE THEOLOGICAL WAY FOLLOWING INSTANTANEOUS CONVERSION

Wesley delineated actions following instantaneous conversion in texts in which he speaks directly about conversion. In the words of Collins: "at this point of the *ordo salutis* that there is no standing still, so to speak, in the Christian life, that the way is ever forward. ... Each actualisation of grace, then, opens up the possibility of more. And though the new birth (or conversion for that matter) does indeed mark an important point along the

---

90. See chapter six, section three.

91. Genuine faith as the catalyst for instantaneous conversion has already been established in chapter two, section 3.2. where it yielded the espoused synoptic statement: conversion arrives by faith in an instant (synoptic statement 5).

92. In 1759 in A Letter to the Rev. Mr. Downes, Wesley wrote: "They talk of regeneration in every Christian as if it were suddenly and miraculously a conversion as that of St. Paul and the first converts to Christianity." Wesley continued: "We do believe in regeneration, or in plain English, the new birth. ... We likewise believe that the spiritual life which commences when we are born again must, in the nature of the living thing, have a first moment, as well as the natural." Wesley believed that conversion includes the act of regeneration; Wesley argued that regeneration, the new birth, and "being born again" are all synonymous. Wesley, *The Methodist Societies: History, Nature, and Design*, 9:360. See also Wesley, *Explanatory Notes Upon the New Testament*, Matt 18:3.

93. In 1742, Wesley wrote *The Principles of a Methodist* as a response to Josiah Tucker. In Wesley's work, he quoted Tucker and showed where Tucker was correctly and incorrectly characterizing Wesley. In a section where Wesley approved of Tucker's characterisation, and therefore was affirming, Wesley wrote: "I believe that conversion (meaning thereby justification) is an instantaneous work, and that the moment a man has living faith in Christ he is converted or justified." In other words, Wesley is saying that conversion and justification happen in the same instant. Wesley, *The Methodist Societies: History, Nature, and Design*, 9:60.

journey, it is not a resting place."[94] Wesley would never have recognized a soteriology which rested in instantaneous conversion alone.[95]

Wesley expected conversion to change the lifestyle of the convert into a lifestyle of obedience to Christ as the outworking of sanctification. It is possible to observe this view in his notes on Deuteronomy 30:6, in which Wesley wrote: "God will first convert and sanctify them, the fruit whereof shall be, that they shall return and obey God's commandments."[96] Thus, after conversion, an individual returns to God and obedience to God's commandments.[97] Wesley asserted that after instantaneous conversion, the way forward is "Christ being formed in him." In *The Principles of a Methodist*, Wesley wrote: "it is never before, and generally long after, he is justified, that 'Christ is formed in him'."[98] Wesley explained what he meant by "Christ formed in him" in his *Explanatory Notes*: "Till there be in you all the mind that was in him."[99] The mind of Christ is formed in the person not before conversion, but generally long after conversion. The theological way following instantaneous conversion, therefore, manifests obedience and a change of mind toward Christ-likeness. These changes are indicative of a broader category that is notoriously prominent in Wesley's theology: Christian perfection.

Christian perfection is the most notable theological marker in Wesley's *via salutis* following instantaneous conversion for at least two reasons. First, at the core of Wesley's personal journey for salvation was his aim

---

94. Collins, *The Theology of John Wesley*, 204.

95. The new birth captures a limited scope of Wesley's soteriological vision. See Sean McGever, "The Vector of Salvation: The New Birth as (Only) the Beginning of Conversion for Wesley and Whitefield," in *Wesley and Whitefield? Wesley versus Whitefield?*, ed. Ian J. Maddock (Eugene, OR: Pickwick Publications, 2018), 27–32, 40–41.

96. Wesley, *Explanatory Notes upon the Old Testament*, Deut 30:6.

97. Obedience after instantaneous conversion supports what emerged in chapter two, section four: Conversion is marked by ongoing good works (synoptic statement 7).

98. Wesley, *The Methodist Societies: History, Nature, and Design*, 9:62. In the 1772 revision of *The Principles of a Methodist*, Wesley omitted the phrase "and generally long after." Thus, this deletion does not change the meaning significantly for the purpose in this section, but it may be that Wesley believed that the mind of Christ could be formed in the new convert sooner than some may have understood from this passage. It is likely that by 1772 Wesley had a broader ministerial sampling to adjust his comments; see 9:62n96.

99. Wesley, *Explanatory Notes upon the New Testament*, Gal 4:19.

for Christian perfection.[100] In 1750, Wesley wrote against Lavington in *A Letter to the Author of "The Enthusiasm of Methodists and Papists Compared."* Wesley wrote: "A man is usually converted long before he is a perfect man."[101] Wesley went on to say that the recipients of the Letter to the Ephesians were most certainly converted and that Paul still urged them toward perfection.[102] Thus, Wesley argued that perfection was not to be expected at the moment of conversion. The disconnection of perfection and conversion dovetails with the previous point: neither the mind of Christ, nor Christ formed in him, nor perfection were to be expected at conversion, but they are possible following conversion. Second, Christian perfection is central to Wesley's *via salutis* following instantaneous conversion because Christian perfection captures the *telos* of conversion, as stated before; for Wesley conversion is accurately understood as inaugurated teleology.

3.4. THE POSSIBILITY OF BACKSLIDING

A primary reason that the ordering of Wesley's view of salvation is described as a *via* rather than an *ordo* is that, in Wesley's theology, a person can regress in their spiritual state. A twist of order, or reversal, is possible according to Wesley's discussion of conversion. This reversal is the practical and theological issue of backsliding. An introduction to Wesley's basic arguments concerning backsliding follows since the previous three subsections (before conversion, at conversion, and following conversion) could be assumed to be unidirectional when they are not. A discussion, therefore, of Wesley's theology of backsliding is required to understand his *via salutis*. Wesley's theology of backsliding, in relation to conversion, means that conversion can be lost, and that effectively, one could, foreseeably, need to re-convert.

Wesley's view of backsliding is exemplified in the 1745 *Minutes:*

Q. 12. Can faith be lost, but through disobedience?

A. It cannot. A believer first inwardly disobeys, inclines to sin with his heart. Then his intercourse with God is lost, i.e. his faith is lost,

---

100. See chapter two, section 3.1. for an account of Wesley's journey to understand salvation and conversion in light of seeking perfection.

101. Wesley, *The Appeals to Men of Reason and Religion and Certain Related Open Letters*, 11:369.

102. Wesley cites Eph 4:13.

and after this, he may fall into outward sin, being now weak and like another man.

Q. 13. How can such an one recover faith?

A. By repenting and doing the first works.[103]

Wesley's questions and answers show that disobedience is not the impetus for the loss of faith; the loss of faith leads to disobedience. Wesley shows that faith can be regained, but we should not move on so soon. The loss of faith, in Wesley's theology, comes with significant implications. One implication is that the Spirit will be removed from the believer and leave a person in darkness; this implication is exemplified in his sermon *The Great Privilege of Those that are Born of God* (1748). Wesley wrote: "But if we do not love him who first loved us; if we will not hearken to his voice; if we turn our eye away from him, and will not attend to the light which he pours upon us: his Spirit will not always strive; he will gradually withdraw, and leave us to the darkness of our own hearts."[104] The withdrawal of the Spirit is the loss of our guarantee of salvation.[105]

If Wesley was not clear regarding the significance and consequences of backsliding in 1748, Wesley was crystal clear in his 1751 work, *Serious Thoughts on Perseverance*. Wesley wrote: "If a believer make shipwreck of the faith, he is no longer a child of God. And then he may go to hell, yea, and certainly will, if he continue in disbelief ... he who is a child of God today, may be a child of the devil tomorrow."[106] Wesley explained that a future in hell could become one's destiny when the prior day the same person had been destined for heaven. Wesley's clarity on the topic of backsliding is blunt and bold: every converted Christian can regress in the *via salutis*.

Where other theological systems may have an irreversible order, there is a dynamic nature to the way of salvation in Wesley's theology. This dynamic is highlighted by his attention to backsliders and the reality of shipwrecked faith which has been lost and can be regained.[107] Wesley

---

103. Wesley, *The Methodist Societies: The Minutes of Conference*, 10:151.

104. Wesley, *Sermons*, 1:442.

105. See Collins, *The Theology of John Wesley*, 217–22; Maddox, *Responsible Grace*, 151, 163–65.

106. Wesley, *Doctrinal and Controversial Treatises II*, 13:257.

107. See Coppedge, *John Wesley in Theological Debate*, 139–40.

crystallized his view on backsliding in his mature (1778) sermon *A Call to Backsliders*. Wesley asked:

> Do any that "have made shipwreck of faith and a good conscience," recover what they have lost? ... In every place where the arm of the Lord has been revealed, and many sinners converted to God, there are several found who, "turn back from the holy commandment delivered to them." ... Innumerable are the instances of this kind, of those who had fallen but now stand upright. Indeed it is so far from being an uncommon thing for a believer to fall and be restored, than it is rather uncommon to find any believers who are not conscious of having been backsliders from God, in an higher or lower degree, and perhaps more than once, before they were established in faith.[108]

In effect, Wesley believed that there are those who have fallen from faith, those who shipwrecked their faith. Wesley said it was more common to find backsliders than those who have not backslidden. Wesley did not directly discuss conversion and backsliding together. However, Wesley was clear that inward disobedience can lead to a loss of faith which can lead to the withdrawal of the Spirit, leaving a person in darkness, no longer a child of God, with a potential destiny of hell—and the swiftness of backsliding could come as quickly as one day. Wesley's theology of backsliding provides the strongest argument to favor observing Wesley's *salutis* as a *via* over an *ordo*. Conversion, therefore, in Wesley's theology includes the logical possibility of "un-converting" and the need to convert again.

Wesley proclaims his theology of conversion as a *via* rather than an *ordo*, because a way is more fluid and flexible than an order. Fluidity and flexibility do not assume interchangeability, but rather, reversibility, with the possibility of backsliding being the primary driver for the conception of Wesley's soteriology as a *via* rather than an *ordo*. An insight can now be gleaned with the entirety of Wesley's *via salutis* stated: the possibility of backsliding implies that a person can lose his or her justification and regeneration. Wesley never states explicitly that a person could renounce his or her own justification or regeneration in relation to conversion, but Wesley believed that the benefits of baptism could be lost due to intentional sin

---

108. Wesley, *Sermons*, 3:224.

(thus providing the need for conversion). The presentation of Wesley's *via salutis* in this section has revealed not only the markers of each step along the way of salvation but the theological implications of the reversibility of the way of salvation. Wesley's conception of conversion, therefore, is one that can reverse and thus necessitate re-conversion.

4. CONCLUSION

This chapter has examined Wesley's writing on conversion in relation to three attendant themes in order to develop the account of Wesley's theology of conversion which is espoused in this study. More specifically, in the first section, Wesley's teaching on baptism as it relates to conversion yields synoptic statement 8: baptism marks one's entrance to the church but is not chronologically tied to conversion. The second section articulated Wesley's position on assurance of salvation as it relates to conversion, yielding the final espoused statement of conversion theology for Wesley: assurance of salvation is available but not required for a genuine convert (synoptic statement 9). In the third and final section, Wesley's *via salutis* was examined to show how the critical components of Wesley's soteriology come together to support a primary claim of this study, which is that Wesley's conception of conversion should be understood as inaugurated teleology.

When the totality of this chapter is taken with the previous chapter, it is possible to espouse a theology of conversion for Wesley from the operant material Wesley provided on conversion but did not synthesize himself in a systematic form. Seven of the nine synoptic statements of Wesley's conversion theology have been articulated in the previous chapter (the primary motifs), while the remaining two have been articulated in this chapter (the attendant themes). All of the synoptic statements, as well as the concept of conversion as inaugurated teleology, will be returned to in chapter six. But, first, another key contributor to the theology of conversion in early evangelicalism will be considered, John Wesley's ally, and sometimes adversary: George Whitefield.

4

GEORGE WHITEFIELD'S CONVERSION THEOLOGY MOTIFS

This chapter marks a turning point as the focus is now directed to George Whitefield's theology of conversion. While the focus has shifted from Wesley to Whitefield, the argument of the study is maintained: Wesley and Whitefield's theologies of conversion are best understood in terms of inaugurated teleology. This chapter articulates this claim through an exegesis of Whitefield's writings in order to describe systematically the four primary theological motifs of Whitefield's theology of conversion. These motifs (mirroring Wesley's) are presented in the four sections of this chapter: (1) conversion as an experience turning *from* and *to*; (2) preceding conversion: convicted, convinced, and awakened; (3) instantaneous conversion; and (4) continued evidence of conversion. In the course of these sections, several espoused synoptic statements regarding Whitefield's theology of conversion (to be presented below) emerge. To begin, we now turn to Whitefield's fundamental understanding of conversion.

1. CONVERSION AS AN EXPERIENCE TURNING "FROM" AND "TO"

George Whitefield's fundamental operant understanding of conversion is an experience turning *from* and *to* something or someone. More specifically, Whitefield understood conversion as a life-changing experience in which one turns *from* self-righteousness *to* the righteousness of Jesus Christ. Conversion, in Whitefield's articulation, is not a turn to a new denomination or theological emphasis; it is the radical experience of salvation that thrusts one into a life of holiness and Christian growth. This section will, first, show how Whitefield explained conversion as a turn *from* self and *to* Christ (synoptic statement 3). Second, it will be argued that conversion is initiated and sustained by the grace of God (synoptic statement 1) which is marked by ongoing good works (synoptic statement 7). Third, this section will show that Whitefield understood conversion as an experience, even in the midst of a society that shunned claims of enthusiastic religious experience and among some Calvinistic approaches which eliminated human participation in the experience of salvation. Fourth, the section will conclude by claiming that conversion is the experiential correlate of salvation (synoptic statement 2).

1.1. CONVERSION "FROM" AND "TO"

Conversion, in its most basic sense for Whitefield, is a turn *from* and *to* something or someone. Before attending to Whitefield's clearest articulation of conversion in his sermon *Repentance and Conversion*, a wider sampling of his usage of the terms "convert" and "conversion" provides the foundation for his general usage.

In some instances, Whitefield wrote of converting "from" something without mentioning the corresponding object "to" which one would turn. For example, Whitefield spoke of converting heathen from dumb idols,[1] converting from a wicked life,[2] and being converted from the error of one's ways.[3] Each of these instances of conversion describe a deficient prior orientation in Whitefield's thought. There is, in these instances, a lack of focus in Whitefield's usage of conversion; Whitefield does not make the alternative clear. In other words, in these instances, Whitefield does not state to where a person should turn. At one point, Whitefield spoke of people being "savingly converted" from the error of their ways.[4] It is this hint of being converted "savingly" that illuminates the ultimate object of conversion in Whitefield's understanding of conversion.

The object of conversion for Whitefield was the "to" toward which one would turn. The object of conversion was, essentially, the antithesis of what was described in the "from" orientation. For instance, Whitefield spoke of

---

1. George Whitefield, *Fourth Journal: During the Time He Was Detained in England by the Embargo* (London: James Hutton, 1739), 31.
2. Whitefield, *The Works of the Reverend George Whitefield*, 4:392.
3. Whitefield, *The Works of the Reverend George Whitefield*, 5:372.
4. Whitefield, *The Works of the Reverend George Whitefield*, 4:224.

conversion as a turning from darkness to light,[5] converting sinners from the "error of their ways, and turning them to the wisdom of the just,"[6] and converting from the power of Satan to God.[7] Conversion as a movement from one orientation to its antithesis is the essence of a "turning," and this is the general usage that Whitefield employs in his operant use of the idea of conversion.

While it has been established that Whitefield's general understanding of conversion is a turn *from* and *to* something or someone, this study is concerned with Whitefield's understanding of conversion in a soteriological context. Whitefield is keen to utilize conversion as a soteriological category to describe the work of God in salvation. Whitefield highlights how he understood conversion in the soteriological context in his sermon *On Repentance*. He preached:

> ... nothing short of a thorough sound conversion will sit thee for the kingdom of heaven. It is not enough to turn from profaneness to civility; but thou must turn from civility to godliness. Not only some, but "all things must become new" in thy soul. It will profit thee but little to do many things, if yet some one thing thou lackest. In short, thou must not only be an almost, but altogether a new creature, or in vain thou boasteth that thou art a christian.[8]

Whitefield's linguistic morphology of conversion was simply to turn from one thing to another; however, at the heart of Whitefield's true concern, conversion was not simply a turn from profaneness to civility, but from civility to godliness. Whitefield was fixated, ultimately, on the work of God on the soul in which one becomes a new creature; in short, conversion is a turning of a person to become a Christian.[9]

---

5. Whitefield, *The Works of the Reverend George Whitefield*, 3:160.

6. George Whitefield, *Fifth Journal: From His Embarking after the Embargo, to His Arrival at Savannah in Georgia* (London: James Hutton, 1740), 51.

7. Whitefield, *The Works of the Reverend George Whitefield*, 4:337.

8. Whitefield, *The Works of the Reverend George Whitefield*, 6:268.

9. Lambert observed the "turning" motif as well. Lambert wrote: "In preaching the necessity of the new birth, Whitefield's goal was that of 'turning People from Darkness to Light,' and making them new Creatures." Frank Lambert, "Whitefield and the Enlightenment," in *George Whitefield: Life, Context, and Legacy*, ed. David Ceri Jones and Geordan Hammond (Oxford: Oxford University Press, 2016), 70.

The clearest articulation of Whitefield's basic understanding of conversion is found in his sermon *Repentance and Conversion*. This sermon
argues that conversion is, first, different from repentance; second, is not,
ultimately, a turn to a different church or organization; third, is a turn
to the righteousness of Christ; and fourth, is a turn that occurs over and
over (continuously).

Conversion is different from repentance for Whitefield because repentance is, essentially, the efficient cause (together with faith) that initiates
conversion.[10] Whitefield described the relationship between repentance
and conversion as "nearly the same"[11] and "complex."[12] While similar and
complex, conversion, for Whitefield, is the reorientation that comes as a
result of repentance.[13] Conversion is the actual turning to a different direction which defines the experience and orientation of one's life. Whitefield
clarifies in this sermon the type of turning he has and does not have in
mind.

The type of conversion that Whitefield has in mind is not a turning
to a different church or particular group. While the general usage of the
term "conversion," even Whitefield's general usage as shown above, can
mean any type of turn from and to, Whitefield's focused concern is not a
conversion from one church to another or one group to another. Whitefield
wrote that the type of conversion he had in mind was not a conversion
"from the church of Rome to the Church of England."[14] Similarly, Whitefield
was not primarily concerned with a conversion to become a Methodist,
or obtaining a "Tabernacle-ticket."[15] Whitefield argued that these types
of conversions were just "a conversion only from party to party, not real,
and that which will bring a soul to heaven."[16] In other words, the type of
conversion Whitefield concerned himself with was conversion that would

---

10. See chapter five, section three.

11. George Whitefield, *Eighteen Sermons Preached by the Late Rev. George Whitefield*, ed.
Joseph Gurney (London: Joseph Gurney, 1771), 110.

12. Whitefield, *Eighteen Sermons*, 110.

13. See also Whitefield's sermon *A Penitent Heart, the Best New Year's Gift* where Whitefield
discusses how repentance leads to conversion. Whitefield, *The Works of the Reverend George
Whitefield*, 6:14.

14. Whitefield, *Eighteen Sermons*, 111.

15. Whitefield, *Eighteen Sermons*, 112.

16. Whitefield, *Eighteen Sermons*, 112.

"bring a soul to heaven." Whitefield made all other types of conversion (civility, denominationally, sub-groups within denominations) secondary, or perhaps, negligible in comparison to conversion which brought a soul to heaven: salvific conversion.

In his sermon *Repentance and Conversion*, Whitefield presented his positive and direct statement of what conversion is: a turn from one's own righteousness to the righteousness of Jesus Christ.[17] In other words, conversion is a turning *from* self and *to* Christ (synoptic statement of conversion 3). To turn to the righteousness of Christ means "to be washed in his blood; be clothed in his glorious imputed righteousness."[18] Whitefield argued that faith and repentance initiate conversion as a turn toward Christ, which brings with it the benefits of being a new creation, being saved, being washed in Christ's blood, and having the righteousness of Christ imputed. While the initial experience of conversion brings with it these benefits, other experiences follow a genuine conversion.

The imputation of Christ's righteousness brings with it what Whitefield calls a "consequence," which is a resultant ongoing holiness. Whitefield taught that conversion is not only the initial turn from and to, but the ongoing continuance of the orientation of the turn. Whitefield expected a genuine change to occur as a part of the experience of conversion. Whitefield wrote that conversion "will be a conversion from sin to holiness."[19] Section four of this chapter will detail Whitefield's teaching on the continued evidence required for a genuine convert, but, here, while articulating Whitefield's general approach to conversion, it must be noted that Whitefield called for converts to "take care to evidence their conversion, not only by the [sic] having grace implanted in their hearts, but by the [sic] grace diffusing itself through every faculty of the soul, and making a universal change in the whole man."[20] Whitefield's articulation of conversion brought with it the delicate tension of grace and works: the responsibility of the convert to give evidence of their conversion while understanding

---

17. Whitefield wrote: "What is conversion then? I will not keep you longer in suspense, my brethren: man must be a new creature, and converted from his own righteousness to the righteousness of the Lord Jesus Christ." Whitefield, *Eighteen Sermons*, 115.

18. Whitefield, *Eighteen Sermons*, 116.

19. Whitefield, *Eighteen Sermons*, 116.

20. Whitefield, *Eighteen Sermons*, 117.

that all evidence is a work of grace coming from God. Here we see that conversion is initiated and sustained by the grace of God (synoptic statement of conversion 1). Whitefield urged not only the unconverted but also the converted—including himself—to submit to the conception of conversion as ongoing and continuing. Whitefield stated:

> God convert you and me every hour in the day; for there is not a believer in the world, but has got something in him that he should be converted from; the pulling down of the old house, and building a new one, will be a work till death. Do not think I am speaking to the unconverted only, but to you that are converted.[21]

In this quotation one could replace the first instances of the words "convert" and "conversion" with "sanctify" and "sanctification" and arrive at a similar understanding. The use of the term conversion in this form may be a new way of understanding it for those who see conversion as a one-time occurrence. Whitefield's conception of conversion included ongoing repentance and Christian growth. As will be seen further in this chapter, conversion is marked by ongoing good works (synoptic statement of conversion 7). More comprehensively, for Whitefield, conversion is the initial and ongoing turning *from* and *to*; turning *from* self and *to* God, turning *from* my righteousness *to* Christ's righteousness. Whitefield attributed the initial and ongoing aspect of conversion solely to be a work of the Holy Spirit. His sermon argued: "The author of this conversion is the Holy Spirit; it is not their own free will … nothing short of the Spirit of the living God can effect this change in our hearts."[22] An emphasis on the work of the Spirit is at the center of Whitefield's articulation of conversion. The direct experience of the work of the Spirit in conversion (initially and ongoing) prompted questions about the nature of conversion as an enthusiastic experience.

1.2. CONVERSION AS EXPERIENCE

The previous section used the concept of experience without pausing to locate experience within Whitefield's theology (this move was necessary to establish the primary essence of conversion as a turn *to* and *from*).

---

21. Whitefield, *Eighteen Sermons*, 131.
22. Whitefield, *Eighteen Sermons*, 118.

Now, attention is turned to Whitefield's belief that conversion is an experience. Specifically, Whitefield did not hesitate to locate conversion as an experiential doctrine even in the face of two significant challenges: first, Whitefield's context which shunned enthusiastic religious experience; and second, some Calvinistic approaches which attempt to, effectively, mute participation in the experience of salvation.

Together with all Methodists in his era, Whitefield suffered the charge of being an enthusiast.[23] Enthusiasm is the claim to be able to directly perceive God's work in one's life. Conversion was identifiable, personal, and perceptible for him. His fiercest critics levied the charge of enthusiasm as the leading edge of their blade.[24] Yet, Whitefield did not relent; he insisted that conversion was a genuine "enthusiastic" experience whereby a person could actively *perceive* God's saving work in one's life.[25] Whitefield's publications provide the primary evidence of his belief in the experiential, enthusiastic, work of God. Much of Whitefield's accounts and journals were self-assessments of the work of God in his life and ministry, with Whitefield's conversion experience at its foundational center. These accounts have been characterized as the product of, in generous terms, a naive zealous young man, and in critical terms, the epitome of religion

---

23. Downey commented: "In an age when reasonable men had agreed to condemn outright all manifestations of enthusiasm, Whitefield was bound to engender criticism. His highly personal and emotional style of preaching indicted him as the apotheosis of enthusiasm." James Downey, *The Eighteenth Century Pulpit. A Study of the Sermons of Butler, Berkeley, Secker, Sterne, Whitefield and Wesley* (Oxford: Clarendon Press, 1969), 180.

24. Peter Toon captured the general critical spirit toward enthusiasm. Toon wrote: " 'Enthusiasm' was the word commonly used to describe the doctrinaire fanaticism of unbalanced minds." Toon continued and quoted John Locke: " 'It arises' wrote John Locke, 'from the conceits of a warmed and over-weening brain' and 'it takes away both reason and revelation, and substitutes ... the ungrounded fancies of a man's own brain, and assumes them for a foundation both of opinion and conduct.' " Peter Toon, *The Emergence of Hyper-Calvinism in English Nonconformity, 1689-1765* (Eugene, OR: Wipf & Stock, 2011), 31-32. Wallace commented on the view of enthusiasm a generation before Whitefield. Wallace wrote: "Enthusiasm was associated with religiously motivated disorder of the kind that Royalists blamed for the civil war and the execution of the king. Generally the term came to bear a meaning much like that later assigned to 'fanaticism.' " Dewey D. Wallace, *Shapers of English Calvinism, 1660-1714: Variety, Persistence, and Transformation* (New York: Oxford University Press, 2011), 39.

25. Downey commented: "[Whitefield] placed all store by a religion of the heart, a religion that could be felt. His emergence as a popular preacher signified the end of an era of reasoned restraint in religious experience. His impassioned oratory, and the paroxysms it engendered, seemed to many to mark a revival of that bugbear of Augustan England—enthusiasm." Downey, *The Eighteenth Century Pulpit. A Study of the Sermons of Butler, Berkeley, Secker, Sterne, Whitefield and Wesley*, 156.

manipulated for self-promotion.[26] It was not long until Whitefield apologized and edited these accounts to minimize the quasi-messianic and apostolic undertones of his own ministry. Nonetheless, these accounts were packed full of conversion experiences which fit the form of enthusiasm.

Whitefield did not avoid connecting conversion with enthusiastic experience, and thus the appropriation of salvation in the life of the believer; instead, he did the opposite and overtly connected conversion with enthusiastic experience. In the sermon *Walking with God* Whitefield said: "It is no doubt in this sense, that we are to be converted, and become like little children. And though it is the quintessence of enthusiasm, to pretend to be guided by the Spirit without the written word; yet it is every christian's bounden duty to be guided by the Spirit in conjunction with the written word of GOD."[27] Whitefield boldly identified with the pejorative label of enthusiasm but did so in a qualified sense. For Whitefield, enthusiasm was the guidance of God's Spirit within the prescriptions of the Bible. Whitefield was well-aware that he would be accused of enthusiasm, yet his emphasis on the vital connection and awareness of God's people with God's Spirit overruled his reservations provided by those who would attempt to censure him. In a letter written on February 16, 1741, Whitefield characterized conversion as an experience. Whitefield wrote: "I say complete salvation, for my dear friend knows that reformation is not conversion. O that you may experience a life hid with CHRIST in GOD!"[28] In Whitefield's accounts, journals, sermons, and letters, he characterized conversion as an experience, even in an era which rejected enthusiastic reasoning.[29]

---

26. For a generous assessment of Whitefield, see Arnold Dallimore, *George Whitefield: The Life and Times of the Great Evangelist of the Eighteenth-Century Revival*, vol. 1 (London: Banner of Truth Trust, 1970); Arnold Dallimore, *George Whitefield: The Life and Times of the Great Evangelist of the Eighteenth-Century Revival*, vol. 2 (Edinburgh: Banner of Truth Trust, 1980). For a more suspicious assessment of Whitefield, see Harry S. Stout, *The Divine Dramatist: George Whitefield and the Rise of Modern Evangelicalism* (Grand Rapids: Eerdmans, 1991); Frank Lambert, *Pedlar in Divinity: George Whitefield and the Transatlantic Revivals, 1737–1770* (Princeton, NJ: Princeton University Press, 1994). For a more balanced of Whitefield assessment, see Thomas S. Kidd, *George Whitefield: America's Spiritual Founding Father* (New Haven, CT: Yale University Press, 2014).

27. Whitefield, *The Works of the Reverend George Whitefield*, 5:30. See also Whitefield's sermon *Indwelling of the Spirit*, in *The Works of the Reverend George Whitefield*, 6:93.

28. Whitefield, *The Works of the Reverend George Whitefield*, 1:241.

29. Whitefield also taught that one reason people remained "unconverted" is that they had not yet experienced or felt the "power" of God. See Whitefield's sermons *Direction on How*

Whitefield taught that conversion is truly an experience, even though some Calvinistic schemes taught that sin so marred the image of God in humans that they were completely unable to perceive the regenerative work of God. While Whitefield was a Calvinist,[30] he was a moderate Calvinist. Moderate Calvinists of Whitefield's era were characterized by three aspects which parallel Whitefield's teaching on conversion.

First, moderate Calvinists often granted a hypothetical universal atonement, while holding to particular election.[31] Second, moderate Calvinists taught that human condemnation was due to disobedience and not an eternal decree (reprobation). Third, moderate Calvinists pressed for good works *after* justification as evidence of salvation.[32] Whitefield's moderate Calvinism was distinguished from hyper-Calvinism of his era in three ways. First, hyper-Calvinism taught that conversion was virtually empty of experience. Toon writes: "[Hyper-Calvinism] exalt[ed] the honour and glory of God and did so at the expense of minimizing the moral and spiritual responsibility of sinners to God."[33] Second, hyper-Calvinists taught that regeneration and conversion were entirely passive in order to uphold the doctrine of irresistible grace.[34] Third, and naturally following from

---

to Hear Sermons and The Conversion of Zaccheus, in The Works of the Reverend George Whitefield, 5:422, 6:56.

    30. More precisely, Whitefield started transitioning into Calvinistic doctrine shortly after his conversion in 1735, with clear moderate Calvinistic adherence emerging in his writing around 1737/8. For the best recent summary, and one that includes ground-breaking primary source research on Whitefield's codified diaries, see Hindmarsh, The Spirit of Early Evangelicalism: True Religion in a Modern World, 27–32.

    31. To those who may find the concept of hypothetical universalism surprising as a viable concept for Whitefield and others in his era, see the work of Oliver Crisp. Crisp writes: "Rather than being an aberration, hypothetical universalism is a notion that united many early Reformed thinkers." He goes on to conclude, "The scope of the atonement need not be conceived as 'limited.' There is a venerable tradition in Reformed theology (now largely forgotten, or treated as the eccentricity of a small minority) that thinks of the atonement as universal in its ordained, conditional sufficiency, though it is efficacious only for the elect. ... There is a scope within Reformed confessionalism, including the Canons of Dort and the Westminster Confession, for a doctrine of hypothetical universalism. ... Too often in recent theology, Reformed divines have presented their own tradition as something much narrower than it actually is." Oliver D. Crisp, Deviant Calvinism: Broadening Reformed Theology (Minneapolis: Fortress Press, 2014), 210, 238, 240.

    32. See Coppedge, John Wesley in Theological Debate, 39–40.

    33. Toon, The Emergence of Hyper-Calvinism, 144.

    34. Toon, The Emergence of Hyper-Calvinism, 145.

the first two statements, evangelism simply was not needed.[35] In contrast, Whitefield taught and validated the experiential work of the Spirit of God, primarily in the convicting of sinners. Whitefield taught that people must respond to the call of the gospel. Response to the gospel was enabled by the electing grace of God, but it still required experiential engagement.[36] Whitefield's moderate Calvinism, thus, allowed for a genuine experiential interaction between God and humans.

The experience of conversion in Whitefield's theology was, therefore, the human experience of the appropriation of salvation (initial conversion and ongoing conversion) in the life of the Christian. Salvation is accomplished solely by God in Christ and the experience of the appropriation of this salvation is called, by Whitefield, conversion. In other words, conversion is the experiential correlate of salvation (synoptic statement of conversion 2). The next section will show what Whitefield believed to always come before the initial turn of conversion: convincing, convicting, and awakening.

2. PRECEDING CONVERSION: CONVICTED, CONVINCED, AWAKENED

For Whitefield, to be convinced, convicted, and awakened describes a part of the spiritual journey which preceded and was set apart from conversion. All three terms described an inner work which was felt experientially. Each of these terms included a reference to one's sense of their sin and the possibility of espousing Whitefield's theology of conversion: conversion is foreshadowed by a deep sense of sinfulness (synoptic statement 4). These three terms also highlighted different aspects of the stage which collectively preceded conversion. To be *convicted* emphasized that one must move beyond rational agreement with the historical tenets of faith. To be *convinced* had a particular emphasis on one's understanding of Christ's righteousness, especially in contrast to ourselves, allowing a proper judgment

---

35. When William Carey suggested the formation of a missionary society, the hyper-Calvinist John C. Ryland shouted: "Sit down, young man; when God pleases to convert the heathen He will do it without your aid or mine." Toon, *The Emergence of Hyper-Calvinism*, 150.

36. In a letter to "Mr. B----" on July 24, 1741, Whitefield wrote: "O free grace! sovereign and electing love! how sweet to the soul, who really feels the power of it!" Whitefield, *The Works of the Reverend George Whitefield*, 1:281.

of the state of our soul. *Awakening* was used uniquely when highlighting a gap of time which existed before one was converted. Whitefield's theology of conversion taught that to be convinced, convicted, or awakened collectively describes the God-initiated experiential aspect of those in whom God was leading toward conversion. The God-initiated experiential aspect of being convinced, convicted, and awakened is not conversion and does not always end in conversion, but it always brings a strong inner experience of one's sin and a profound felt understanding of Jesus Christ's righteousness contrasted with the sinner's fallenness.[37]

2.1. CONVICTED

Whitefield taught that the experience of the conviction of sin preceded conversion. He contrasted being convicted *rationally* of the truths of the gospel (such as truths related to personal sinfulness and the righteousness of Christ) with being convicted *experientially* of these same truths; at times this experiential conviction would result in visible manifestations such as weeping. Whitefield was careful to distinguish between conviction and conversion, because one could be convicted, even experientially convicted, of his or her sin, and still not proceed to be converted.

Whitefield believed that it was good and proper to be convicted of the truths of the gospel, such as being convicted of sin, righteousness, judgement, and (more broadly) the "damnable state."[38] However, the journey toward conversion needed to go beyond simple rational or propositional conviction of these truths. In his sermon, *The Conversion of Zaccheus,*

---

37. Over time, Whitefield's view of election solidified and played a role in his understanding of how convincing, convicting, and awakening lead to conversion. Schwenk observes: "Whitefield was convinced that God, in his sovereignty, had chosen certain individuals for salvation, who would be awakened to their need through the preaching of the gospel, and would be gifted with the faith necessary to respond to God's call to forgiveness. Theology was important to Whitefield inasmuch as it fit into this framework, and resulted in the pragmatic awakening of the elect to their promised reward." See James L. Schwenk, *Catholic Spirit: Wesley, Whitefield, and the Quest for Evangelical Unity in Eighteenth-Century British Methodism* (Lanham, MD: Scarecrow Press; Center for the Study of World Christian Revitalization Movements, 2008), 99.

38. Whitefield most often discusses "conviction" without describing the object of conviction. For examples where Whitefield describes the object of conviction, see George Whitefield, *First Journal: A Voyage from London to Savannah in Georgia* (London: James Hutton, 1738), 59; Whitefield, *Fifth Journal: From His Embarking after the Embargo, to His Arrival at Savannah in Georgia*, 35; Whitefield, *The Works of the Reverend George Whitefield*, 6:137, 147.

Whitefield contrasted mere rational conviction with Zaccheus' experiential response when he ran to climb the tree to see Jesus.[39] Many of Whitefield's listeners would have been rationally convicted of gospel truths, since he often assumed that his listeners had been baptized and churched,[40] but Whitefield believed that the true gospel pushed for more than being rationally convicted. In the sermon, *The Holy Spirit Convincing the World of Sin, Righteousness, and Judgment*, Whitefield showed what was needed in addition to rational conviction of gospel truths: experiential conviction of the truth. Whitefield wrote: "Many, I believe, have a rational conviction of, and agree with me in this: but rational convictions, if rested in, avail but little; it must be a spiritual, experimental conviction of the truth, which is saving."[41] Rational convictions availed little; what was needed was a convicting experience. It was the convicting experience of truth which Whitefield believed "was saving."[42]

The *experience* of conviction could be manifested internally and externally. External conviction could come, for example, in the form of weeping. In Whitefield's *First Journal* he recorded: "God was pleased to set His seal to my sermon. Many officers and soldiers wept sorely, and a visible alteration was observed in the garrison for some days after. Oh that their convictions may end in their conversion, and that they may bring forth the fruits of the Spirit!"[43] In this passage, Whitefield hoped that their convictions would end in their conversion and that their conviction correlated with their weeping and "visible alteration."[44] The work of conviction in the officers and soldiers caused very expressive and visibly noticeable reactions which lasted not for just a moment or during the sermon but

---

39. Whitefield preached: "I am fully persuaded, numbers are rationally convicted of gospel-truths; but, not being able to brook contempt, they will not prosecute their convictions, nor reduce them to practice. Happy those, who in this respect, like Zaccheus, are resolved to overcome all impediments that lie in their way to a sight of CHRIST." Whitefield, *The Works of the Reverend George Whitefield*, 6:52.

40. See chapter five, section one.

41. Whitefield, *The Works of the Reverend George Whitefield*, 6:136.

42. See also the sermon *The True Way of Beholding the Lamb of God*, in Whitefield, *The Works of the Reverend George Whitefield*, 6:417.

43. Whitefield, *First Journal: A Voyage from London to Savannah in Georgia*, 40. See also the letter on October 27, 1753, in Whitefield, *The Works of the Reverend George Whitefield*, 3:34.

44. Whitefield, *First Journal: A Voyage from London to Savannah in Georgia*, 40.

for "some days."[45] While there were external expressions of conviction which Whitefield observed, conviction was also a strong internal feeling of damnation.[46] In Whitefield's sermon, *Saul's Conversion,* he preached: "As many of you that were never so far made sensible of your damnable state, as to be made feelingly to seek after JESUS CHRIST, were never yet truly convicted by, much less converted to, GOD."[47] Here, Whitefield made an argument from the negative. The people did not have a sense of their damnation, nor a feeling to seek Jesus. Thus, they were not yet convicted. Stated positively, therefore, conviction can be understood experientially as an internal sense and feeling of damnation. One way Whitefield liked to word this experience was through the phrase "arrows of conviction."[48] These arrows struck the heart of a person, and this metaphorical wound demanded attention toward one's spiritual state in order to lead them to convert.[49] The strong internal and external feelings (weeping, visible alteration, lack of sleep, sense of damnation, anguish, and more), which

45. Beebe described conviction as the experience of the miseries of one's lost and perishing condition, of the deep sense of the evil of sin as dishonoring to God, or even the very terror of hell. At times this experience brought about crying, fainting, swooning, and visions. Furthermore, Beebe described the responses to Whitefield's sermons at Cambuslang to include weeping, sighing, groaning, sobbing, screeching, and crying out; and all this in one sermon alone. See Keith Edward Beebe, "The McCulloch Manuscripts of the Cambuslang Revival, 1742: A Critical Edition" (PhD diss., Kings College, University of Aberdeen, 2003), 90, 136.

46. As noted in the introduction to this section: conversion is foreshadowed by a deep sense of sinfulness (synoptic statement of conversion 4).

47. Whitefield, *The Works of the Reverend George Whitefield,* 6:147.

48. For examples, see George Whitefield, *A Further Account of God's Dealings with the Reverend Mr. George Whitefield* (London: W. Strahan, 1747), 13; George Whitefield, *Sixth Journal: After His Arriving at Georgia, to a Few Days after His Second Return Hither from Philadelphia* (London: James Hutton, 1741), 25; Whitefield, *The Works of the Reverend George Whitefield,* 2:45, 118, 340, 3:29, 114, 205, 209, 212, 6:61.

49. One might wonder how Whitefield could know other people's strong internal feelings. Whitefield's observations were possible because people came and told him about their internal feelings. In his *Seventh Journal,* Whitefield wrote: "Many who before were only convicted, now plainly proved that they were converted [and had a clear evidence of it within themselves]. My chief business was now to build up and to exhort them to continue in the grace of God. Notwithstanding, many were convicted, almost every day, and came to me under the greatest distress and anguish of soul." Almost every day, during this period but perhaps later too, people came to Whitefield and told him of their great distress and anguish due to their conviction. George Whitefield, *Seventh Journal: From a Few Days after His Return to Georgia to His Arrival at Falmouth* (London: W. Strahan, 1741), 68.

could continue for days at a time, had a distinct purpose.[50] Whitefield taught that the end purpose of conviction and its associated experiences lead one to find one's need for a Savior and conversion.[51]

Conviction, usually of personal sinfulness, was an experience that preceded conversion. Whitefield often distinguished conviction from conversion.[52] Most clearly, he wrote "conviction is not conversion."[53] The purpose of conviction was to "end in sound conversions."[54] The instances of conversion in Whitefield's corpus show a strong and consistent pattern that reveals how he believed God to work in the process, namely the experience, leading up to instantaneous conversion.

2.2. CONVINCED

Whitefield taught that convincing was an experience that preceded instantaneous conversion in which a person came to feel the infinite gulf between his or her own righteousness and the righteousness of Jesus Christ; this experience persuaded the person of their impending eternal judgment. When compared to the two other experiences that Whitefield said occurred before conversion (conviction and awakening), Whitefield's concept of convincing is distinguished through its emphasis on the contrast between personal sinfulness and the righteousness of Christ; in other words, a person becomes convinced of their own sinfulness in light of Christ's righteousness in order to lead them to conversion.

---

50. See the letter on July 27, 1741, in Whitefield, *The Works of the Reverend George Whitefield*, 1:301.

51. Experiences of conviction varied in their degree from one person to the next. Whitefield taught that conviction varied from person to person since God cannot be confined to one way of acting. The "holy variety" God used to convert was an important concept since Whitefield had as broad a swathe of evangelistic experiences as perhaps any evangelist in recorded history. Whitefield repeated his methods and sermons time after time, but he did not dare to compare the work of God to a rigid rubric of response. Whitefield, *The Works of the Reverend George Whitefield*, 6:128.

52. See Whitefield, *First Journal: A Voyage from London to Savannah in Georgia*, 40; George Whitefield, *Third Journal: His Arrival at London to His Departure from Thence on His Way to Georgia* (London: James Hutton, 1739), 66; Whitefield, *Sixth Journal: After His Arriving at Georgia, to a Few Days after His Second Return Hither from Philadelphia*, 19; Whitefield, *Seventh Journal: From a Few Days after His Return to Georgia to His Arrival at Falmouth*, 8, 68; Whitefield, *The Works of the Reverend George Whitefield*, 1:233, 283, 320, 384, 2:302, 3:55, 194, 219, 448, 5:207, 6:130, 147.

53. Whitefield, *The Works of the Reverend George Whitefield*, 1:301.

54. Whitefield, *Fifth Journal: From His Embarking after the Embargo, to His Arrival at Savannah in Georgia*, 24.

Whitefield's clearest teaching on the relationship between conversion and convincing came in his sermon *The Holy Spirit Convincing the World of Sin, Righteousness, and Judgment.* This sermon explains "the manner in which the Holy Ghost generally works upon the heart of those, who, through grace, are made vessels of mercy, and translated from the kingdom of darkness into the kingdom of God's dear son."[55] Notice that, in this quotation, Whitefield utilizes the *from* and *to* conversion motif established earlier in this chapter. It is no surprise, then, that Whitefield wrote that this sermon would "explain the general way whereby the Holy Spirit works upon every converted sinner's heart."[56] Having established that this sermon addresses Whitefield's teaching on the relationship between convincing and conversion, we now turn to what Whitefield meant by convincing.

Convincing, in Whitefield's theology, is closely related to convicting. Whitefield defines convincing in terms of conviction, writing: "[Convincing] implies a conviction by way of argumentation, and coming with a power upon the mind equal to a demonstration [of the Spirit]."[57] The emphasis of convincing is the work of God upon the mind of humans to lead them to an experience of the Holy Spirit. Following the sermon's text (John 16:8), Whitefield explained how the Holy Spirit leads people to convert through a three-fold convincing: convincing a person of their sin,[58] convincing a person of Jesus' righteousness, and convincing a person of the coming judgement.[59] Whitefield's intent was to explain how God leads a person to convert, in other words, the pre-converting activity that is being examined in this section. Convincing is, thus, closely related to convicting, but is distinguished as a method the Holy Spirit uses to work upon a person cognitively to convince a person of their sinfulness in contrast to Christ's righteousness as a prelude to conversion.[60]

---

55. Whitefield, *The Works of the Reverend George Whitefield*, 6:128.

56. Whitefield, *The Works of the Reverend George Whitefield*, 6:129.

57. Whitefield, *The Works of the Reverend George Whitefield*, 6:129.

58. As noted in the introduction to this section: conversion is foreshadowed by a deep sense of sinfulness (synoptic statement of conversion 4).

59. Whitefield, *The Works of the Reverend George Whitefield*, 6:129–39.

60. Whitefield explained that the Holy Spirit first brings an obvious, heinous, or "worst" sin to mind in order to illuminate other sins such as the sin of self-righteousness, original sin, and most importantly, the sin of unbelief. Whitefield, *The Works of the Reverend George Whitefield*, 6:129–34.

2.3. AWAKENED

The third way Whitefield described the experiential stage before conversion was to be awakened. Whitefield used the word "awaken" to explain how the soul is pulled out of spiritual lethargy and given a sense of the weight of one's sins. To be awakened described the initial step of those who were impacted through Whitefield's ministry and who then converted upon Whitefield's return visit; sometimes this could be as much as a decade later.

Whitefield described awakening as a work in the soul, meaning it was a work in the inner person.[61] This awakening broke spiritual lethargy; in other words, one's spiritual life was otherwise asleep or dead until it was awakened.[62] When people were awakened, they were "awakened unto a sense of their sin."[63] Effectively, to be awakened was for the soul to be awakened from its slumber to recognize sin, which would, then, lead a person to be converted.[64]

Whitefield provided his fullest description of awakening in his *Short Account*:

> If thou art awakened to a sense of the Divine life, and art hungering and thirsting after that righteousness which is by faith only in Jesus Christ, and the indwelling of His blessed Spirit in thy heart, think it not absolutely necessary to pass through all the temptations that have beset me round about on every side. It is in the spiritual as in the natural life—some feel more, others less, but all experience some pangs and travails of soul, ere the Man Christ Jesus is formed

---

61. See Whitefield, *The Works of the Reverend George Whitefield*, 1:259, 382, 386, 410, 2:63, 92, 230, 476, 3:10, 155, 5:410, 6:410. Hindmarsh observed awakening as an internal experience in the era more broadly. Hindmarsh noted: "So often the convert used the metaphor of being woken from a deep sleep to describe his or her experience, so much so that to be 'awakened' became a cliché. This was the initial pricking of conscience, the very beginning of the process of disturbance that evangelicals hoped would lead to conversion." Hindmarsh, *The Evangelical Conversion Narrative*, 140.

62. See Whitefield, *The Works of the Reverend George Whitefield*, 1:29, 5:383. In the Cambuslang manuscripts, awakening was identified with physical feeling of "spiritual concern." Rather than presenting itself as a sharp, debilitating pain (as was the case with conviction), spiritual concern seemed to manifest itself more as a dull ache or low-grade fever that indicates to the body that something is wrong. See Beebe, "The McCulloch Manuscripts of the Cambuslang Revival, 1742: A Critical Edition," 87, 89.

63. Whitefield, *The Works of the Reverend George Whitefield*, 3:315, 5:134.

64. As noted in the introduction to this section, conversion is foreshadowed by a deep sense of sinfulness (synoptic statement of conversion 4).

within them, and brought forth and arrived unto the measure of His fulness Who filleth all in all. If God deals with thee in a more gentle way, yet so that a thorough work of conversion is effected in thy heart, thou oughtest to be exceeding thankful. Or, if He should lead thee through a longer wilderness than I have passed through, thou needest not complain. The more thou art humbled now, the more thou shalt be exalted hereafter. One taste of Christ's love in thy heart will make amends for all. And, if thou art one that hast felt the powers of the world to come, and art already converted and been made a partaker of the Holy Ghost, I know thou wilt rejoice, and give thanks for what God has done for my soul.[65]

Whitefield showed that to be awakened was to experience the divine life, which is exactly what brought Whitefield to his own conversion.[66] Being awakened was a process, for some quick, and for others slow, in which one sought righteousness and the indwelling of the Spirit.[67] In his *First Journal*, Whitefield wrote: "[Those awakened] cannot bear to read anything trifling, but throw away their useless books, as those did the books of divination and curious arts, whose conversion we read in the Acts, Chap. 5."[68] Thus, the effect of awakening began in the soul but also moved outward in the changing of habits.

Whitefield also used the term awakening when reflecting that there was a large gap in time between the initial onset of these experiences before conversion. Since the journals of Whitefield only recorded the first few years of Whitefield's ministry, they do not capture an important long-term aspect of his ministry. Whitefield would often preach and then return to the same location years later. Sometimes in doing so, he would observe the

65. George Whitefield, *A Brief and General Account of the First Part of the Life of the Reverend Mr. George Whitefield, From His Birth, to His Entering into Holy Orders* (Boston: Kneeland & Green; Edwards & Eliot, 1740).

66. See the discussion of the term "divine life" in section 3.3.4. in this chapter as it relates to Henry Scougal's *Life of God in the Soul of Man.*

67. A woman named Margaret Austin wrote a letter on May 19, 1740 which illustrates her understanding of conviction, awakening, and then finally conversion. Under her signature she wrote: "Awakened by the Reverend Mr Whitefield: Convicted by the Reverend Mr Jn Wesley: Converted by the Reverend Mr Charles"; see Hindmarsh, *The Evangelical Conversion Narrative*, 154.

68. Whitefield, *First Journal: A Voyage from London to Savannah in Georgia*, 50.

reaping of spiritual fruit that was sown but not reaped on his initial visit. Whitefield's letters beginning in the 1750s, roughly a decade after his initial journeys, capture these observations and give additional insight into his theology and understanding of awakening.[69] Thus, in Whitefield's teaching on conversion, "to be awakened" could indicate an initial step toward conversion, but a step that might take a good span of time—sometimes an entire decade—for conversion to manifest. For example, in a February 16, 1749, letter to Lady Huntington, Whitefield highlighted the gap of time between being awakened and converted: "I find a strange alteration in the people since I came first here, now above four years ago. Many were then awakened, and truly converted to the blessed JESUS."[70] Whitefield said that there was a four-year gap in this example between awakening and conversion.[71] Conversion was not always imminent upon awakening; conversion could take years after being awakened initially.

In Whitefield's use of the terms conviction, convincing, and awakening a consistent theme emerges: conversion is foreshadowed by a deep sense of sinfulness (synoptic statement 4). While all three terms relate to the experience of sinfulness, each one includes a particular emphasis in Whitefield's thought. Conviction emphasizes that a potential convert must experience more than a rational conviction of sinfulness; the potential convert must undergo an experiential conviction of sinfulness, and at times, the experiential conviction of sinfulness would manifest in visible ways such as weeping. When Whitefield spoke of people being convinced, he was stressing the potential convert's reckoning of the vast difference

---

69. Whitefield would have known the locations where people were previously awakened. During his sermons people would pass forward notes which would be collected. Whitefield wrote a letter on May 11, 1742, where he recalled that after he was done preaching, he had "pockets full of notes from people brought under concern, and read them ... rejoicing that so many sinners were snatched ... out of the very jaws of the devil. ... Three hundred and fifty awakened souls were received in one day, and I believe the number of notes exceeded a thousand." Whitefield, *The Works of the Reverend George Whitefield*, 1:386.

70. Whitefield, *The Works of the Reverend George Whitefield*, 2:231.

71. Dallimore noted: "Whitefield made no appeal for people to make a public profession of salvation at his services. ... He looked for the Spirit's work in arousing the sinner to a deep, and even overwhelming, sense of his need, but this work he called, not conversion, but awakening." Dallimore, *George Whitefield*, 1:137. For more examples of the "gap" between being awakened and conversion, see the letters on April 11, 1751, July 30, 1751, August 28, 1752, July 17, 1755, October 19, 1753, April 1, 1754, and October 27, 1756, in Whitefield, *The Works of the Reverend George Whitefield*, 2:409, 421, 441, 3:22, 34, 73, 190.

between personal sinfulness and Christ's righteousness. When there was a significant spiritual breakthrough or time gap between an initial work of the Holy Spirit when one came to understand one's own sin and potential conversion, Whitefield would often talk of these situations as awakening. These experiences are moot without Whitefield's belief in a conversion moment, and it is to the analysis of his theological understanding of this moment to which this chapter now turns its attention.

3. INSTANTANEOUS CONVERSION

Whitefield taught that conversion is instantaneous; more precisely, conversion arrives by faith in an instant (synoptic statement 5). He called his listeners and readers to respond instantly in order to find their salvation in Christ. He also understood his own conversion as one which happened suddenly and instantaneously. The *instant* and *sudden* nature of conversion is a repeated theme in Whitefield's operant theology; this chapter espouses instantaneous conversion as an essential element of his theology of conversion.

This section is organized in three parts to espouse what Whitefield taught regarding instantaneous conversion. First, it will be shown that Whitefield did not use the phraseology "instantaneous conversion" often; in fact, he only discussed it directly two times. From these two instances we learn that Whitefield affirmed his belief in the instantaneousness of conversion based upon the instantaneousness of regeneration. Despite Whitefield's very limited use of the precise terminology, this section will make clear that Whitefield spoke of the concept often, and, more so, never denied the instantaneousness of conversion. Second, three examples of the concept of instantaneous conversion will be examined from Whitefield's writing to show how he traded in the theological category even when it was not used as a term. Whitefield expounded upon biblical instances of instantaneous salvific response and invited his listeners (and readers) to convert without delay—effectively showing his firm belief in instantaneous conversion. Third, the chapter will undertake an in-depth analysis of Whitefield's own conversion as a foundational source of Whitefield's theology of instantaneous conversion arriving by faith. The analysis of Whitefield's conversion narrative will highlight the formative role of Henry Scougal's *The Life of God in the Soul of Man* as a key influence of Whitefield's conception of conversion as inaugurated teleology. Collectively, the three parts will show that Whitefield understood instantaneous conversion to be the inauguration of salvation in the life of the believer.

3.1. INSTANTANEOUS CONVERSION AS A TERM FOR WHITEFIELD

Whitefield did not use the phrase "instantaneous conversion" often. In fact, only two instances exist that connect the words "conversion" and "instantaneous" directly in Whitefield's corpus. First, in Whitefield's *Seventh Journal,* he asked: "Whether conversion was not instantaneous?"[72] The *Journal* went on to discuss the role of regeneration and baptism, but this quotation was the first instance in Whitefield's writing of "instantaneous" and "conversion" brought together directly. The second instance is found in Whitefield's *Remarks on a Pamphlet, Entitled, "The Enthusiasm of Methodists and Papists Compared."* In this publication, Whitefield responded line by line to the pamphlet, including its comments on instantaneous conversion. The author of the pamphlet described sudden and instantaneous conversion as an instance of "fanatical peculiarities." Whitefield replied: "Instantaneous conversion, a fanatical peculiarity! I presume instantaneous regeneration must be a *fanatical peculiarity* also."[73] Whitefield, once again, went on to connect instantaneous conversion with baptismal regeneration.[74] The sarcastic tone in this comment showed that Whitefield spoke approvingly of instantaneous conversion and based this approval on equating it with the moment of regeneration in baptism. Further, Whitefield never rejected the concept, or term, of instantaneous conversion. The lack of ample instances of term does not mean that the concept is not present throughout his corpus.

While instantaneous conversion was explicitly linked in Whitefield's thought as being related to regeneration and baptism, the idea of a sudden conversion or sudden change was one which Whitefield described more often in practice, anecdotally, and in exposition. At least 33 of the 59

---

72. Whitefield, *Seventh Journal: From a Few Days after His Return to Georgia to His Arrival at Falmouth,* 25.

73. Whitefield, *The Works of the Reverend George Whitefield,* 4:240. Italics are from the original text.

74. See chapter five, section one, for more concerning Whitefield's understanding of the relationship between instantaneous conversion and baptism.

standard sermons by Whitefield published by Gillies call for an immediate response to turn to Christ to be saved.[75] Whitefield's insistence that
people convert suddenly and instantaneously is strengthened by anecdotal
accounts from his audiences.[76] Whitefield did not use the term "instantaneous conversion" often, but, as seen above, the concept was readily present in his ministry. A closer look at several examples in the next section
will make this point clear.

3.2. EXAMPLES OF INSTANTANEOUS CONVERSION

Three examples of instantaneous conversion from Whitefield's teaching
will be examined to cement Whitefield's belief that conversion is brought
about instantaneously: first, his exposition of the thief on the cross; second,
his commentary on the conversion of three thousand at Pentecost; and
third, his anecdotal experiences with deathbed conversion. In Whitefield's
Observations on Select Passage of Scripture, Luke 23:40 and the thief on the
cross is discussed in catechetical form:

> Q: May wicked men draw any reasons from hence, to defer their
> repentance till a death-bed?
>
> A: No, by no means.
>
> Q: Why?
>
> A: Because probably this thief had never heard of Christ before ...
> God converted him, to honour his Son's death, that he might in the
> very agonies thereof triumph over the devil.[77]

---

75. See Whitefield, *The Works of the Reverend George Whitefield*, 5:35–36, 76–77, 139, 194–95,
213, 232, 248, 296–97, 317–18, 333–34, 351, 371–72, 390–91, 416–17, 438–39, 454–55, 472, 6:18, 33–34,
62–63, 77, 101–2, 125, 141, 159–60, 201–2, 225, 270–71, 299–300, 328, 386, 429.

76. One such account of instantaneous conversion is from David Hume, who said that he
heard Whitefield preach the following at the close of a sermon: " 'The attendant angel is just
about to leave the threshold, and ascend to heaven. And shall he ascend and not bear with
him the news of one sinner, among all this multitude reclaimed from the error of his ways.'
To give the greater effect to this exclamation he stamped with his foot, lifted up his hands and
eyes to heaven, and with gushing tears, cried aloud, 'Stop, Gabriel! Stop, Gabriel! Stop, ere you
enter the sacred portals, and yet carry with you the news of one sinner converted to God.' "
Hume's anecdote of Whitefield's call for one more person to convert, instantly, is an example
of Whitefield's belief in instantaneous conversion. John Gillies and Aaron C. Seymore, *Memoirs
of the Life of the Reverend George Whitefield, A.M.* (Philadelphia: Simon Probasco, 1820), 162.

77. Whitefield, *The Works of the Reverend George Whitefield*, 4:346.

While the scenario of the thief is certainly unique, it showed that Whitefield recognized the thief's quick recognition of Christ and understood the thief's response as conversion. The thief's conversion was sudden and did not require any salvific prerequisites such as the use of the means of grace or baptism. In this way, though the phrase "instantaneous conversion" was not used, an instance is displayed which showed Whitefield's approval of the instantaneous nature of conversion.

The second practical example of instantaneous conversion comes from Whitefield's comments on the conversion of three thousand people in Acts 2:14–41. In his sermon *The Wise and Foolish Virgins*, Whitefield wrote:

> If then you have crucified the Son of GOD afresh, and put him to an open shame, yet do not despair, only believe, and even this shall be forgiven. You have read, at least you have heard, no doubt, how three thousand were converted at St. Peter's preaching one single sermon, after our LORD's ascension into heaven; and many of the crucifiers of the LORD of glory undoubtedly were amongst them; and why should you despair? For "JESUS CHRIST is the same yesterday, to-day, and for ever." The Holy Ghost shall be sent down on you, as well as on them, if you do but believe; for CHRIST ascended up on high to receive this gift even for the vilest of men.[78]

Whitefield made the Pentecost sermon a model for response and conversion. Those who heard Whitefield's words could be like those who heard St. Peter's words. Whitefield's listeners could respond immediately, receiving the Holy Ghost and be converted, within the time it took to hear one sermon if they believed. With similar reasoning Whitefield's sermon *Directions How to Hear Sermons* described the potential for those who apply to their hearts what they hear: "The Holy Ghost would then fall on all them that hear the word, as when St. Peter preached; the gospel of CHRIST would have free course, run very swiftly, and thousands again be converted by a sermon."[79] The conversion of thousands was possible in the midst of one sermon. Thus, instantaneous conversion was possible in Whitefield's understanding. Again, the phrase is not used but its theological logic was

---

78. Whitefield, *The Works of the Reverend George Whitefield*, 5:388.

79. Whitefield, *The Works of the Reverend George Whitefield*, 5:426.

in place: conversion did not require days, weeks, or months. Conversion could happen suddenly, effectively instantaneously.

The thief on the cross and the reference to the three thousand converted at Pentecost are two examples of Whitefield's biblical evidence for instantaneous conversion. In addition to these two biblical examples, a third example will make it clear that Whitefield approved of instantaneous conversion: his reference to deathbed conversion. Whitefield wrote approvingly of at least two deathbed conversions and twice of another specific deathbed conversion. The first instance was included in his *Short Account*: "[A woman] called effectually by God as at the eleventh hour: She was a woman above threescore years old, and I really believe, died in the true faith of Jesus Christ."[80] On October 13, 1751, Whitefield wrote: "One of high rank, I really believe, was converted lately on a dying bed, and her death I trust hath proved the life of one or two more."[81] On the same day, Whitefield wrote a different letter highlighting the same occurrence. Whitefield penned: "I am now at my good Lady's with three clergymen that love and preach JESUS CHRIST. Several souls have been awakened here. One of high birth was lately converted on her dying bed; and by that means I trust one or two more are put upon securing the one thing needful."[82] In these letters, Whitefield affirmed the reality of a conversion which happened in an instant, without reference to any continued evidence or to a prolonged conversion experience.

While Whitefield anecdotally approved of deathbed instantaneous conversion, he certainly did not recommend it. As shown above, in Whitefield's comments on Luke 24 and the thief on the cross, Whitefield said explicitly that repentance should not be deferred until the deathbed; Whitefield's response to being asked if deathbed repentance should be normative was: "by no means."[83] Whitefield urged a youthful conversion in his sermon *The Benefits of an Early Piety*, saying that time spent living in piety gives "a

---

80. George Whitefield, *A Short Account of God's Dealings with the Reverend Mr. George Whitefield* (London: James Hutton, 1740), 50.

81. Whitefield, *The Works of the Reverend George Whitefield*, 2:383.

82. Whitefield, *The Works of the Reverend George Whitefield*, 2:384.

83. Whitefield made the same point in a letter dated July 27, 1741, in Whitefield, *The Works of the Reverend George Whitefield*, 1:300.

well-grounded assurance of the sincerity of our profession."[84] Though, presumably, the conversion preceding early piety could also be instantaneous, Whitefield's urging for an early conversion is in stark contrast to his reservations regarding deathbed repentance. Whitefield clarified the reason for early conversion: "For supposing a man to be sincere in his profession of repentance on a death-bed (which, in most cases, is very much to be doubted) yet, he is often afraid lest his convictions and remorse proceed not from a true sorrow for sin, but a servile fear of punishment."[85] Deathbed conversion left little assurance that the conversion was genuine. Whitefield, however, did not deny the veracity of deathbed conversion, thus, confirming his belief in instantaneous conversion.

These examples show that Whitefield based his theology of instantaneous conversion on his scriptural teaching and his pastoral theology, especially concerning deathbed conversion.[86] The examination of these operant instances of instantaneous conversion in Whitefield's corpus articulates the second half of one of the espoused statements of conversion for Whitefield: conversion arrives by faith in an instant (synoptic statement 5). The first half of this statement is that instantaneous conversion comes through *faith*.[87] Faith inaugurates conversion, initially through instantaneous conversion. As will be seen, Whitefield's own conversion narrative

---

84. Whitefield, *The Works of the Reverend George Whitefield*, 5:164.

85. Whitefield, *The Works of the Reverend George Whitefield*, 5:164.

86. Lambert shows that Whitefield was moving beyond the conversion pattern set by Puritans: "Whitefield also emphasized the immediacy of the new birth. Seventeenth-century New England Puritans had presented salvation as a process unfolding over a period of months in which sinners moved through successive stages from initial contrition to final conversion. Whitefield compressed the experience, raising the expectation that men and women could undergo conversion in a finite moment." Frank Lambert, "The Great Awakening as Artifact: George Whitefield and the Construction of Intercolonial Revival, 1739-1745," *Church History* 60, no. 2 (June 1991): 226–27. Furthermore, Whitefield's view of instantaneous conversion distinguished Methodism from Anglican belief. Chamberlain explained: "The nature of regeneration and conversion, then, was more of an issue between the Anglicans and Methodists than whether salvation is by grace or by works. Neither side actually espoused works for salvation, but the Methodists often considered the Anglicans to be moralists because they did not call for an experiential moment of faith in conversion." Jeffrey S. Chamberlain, "Moralism, Justification, and the Controversy over Methodism," *Journal of Ecclesiastical History* 44, no. 6 (1993): 678.

87. The relationship between faith and instantaneous conversion will be further examined later in this study in the section on Whitefield's *ordo salutis* (chapter five, section three).

provides a deep articulation of Whitefield's belief that conversion arrives by faith in an instant.

Whitefield's confidence in instantaneous conversion was rooted in his own conversion. While John Wesley's Aldersgate experience has drawn detailed study and reflection, few have mined Whitefield's conversion experience, three years prior to Wesley's, to understand how it shaped the early Methodist understanding of conversion, and more properly Whitefield's own theology of conversion.[88] What follows below is a thorough theological description of Whitefield's conversion. This description will conclude that his was an experience of instantaneous conversion, but one which also had much that preceded and followed after it (aligning with the four motifs of this chapter). In order to understand Whitefield's theology of conversion, we must understand his own conversion comprehensively.

3.3. WHITEFIELD'S CONVERSION

In 1740, at the height of Whitefield's meteoric rise to international fame, he published his life story from his birth in December 1714 up until his ordination in June 1736. This publication was entitled, *A Short Account of God's Dealings with the Reverend Mr. George Whitefield*, better known as his *Short Account*.[89] Upon enrolling at Oxford in 1732, Whitefield believed his soul was in peril despite his best efforts to find peace with God through piety. The catalyst for Whitefield's conversion came when he learned of the necessity of the new birth through reading Henry Scougal's *The Life of God in the Soul of Man*, a book given to him by Charles Wesley.[90] Whitefield believed himself to be damned without the experience of the new birth, and he went on to pursue the new birth through the excruciating use of the means of grace. The climax of this publication was the account of his

---

88. Engagement with the other scholarly accounts of Whitefield's conversion will be shown below.

89. Whitefield, *A Short Account of God's Dealings with the Reverend Mr. George Whitefield*.

90. Chapter five, section 3.2. will show that in Whitefield's theology, instantaneous conversion and the new birth occur in the same moment. While instantaneous conversion denotes more than the new birth for Whitefield, when he speaks of the new birth, he also means the moment of instantaneous conversion.

conversion. This account included a singular moment which is understood as his instantaneous conversion brought about by faith.[91]

3.3.1. *Whitefield's Early Life*

Since the *Short Account* climaxes carefully with Whitefield's conversion, it is important to see the details which led up to his conversion. For instance, Whitefield observed from his infancy that he had "early stirrings of corruption in my heart, as abundantly convinces me that I was conceived and born in sin."[92] Then, as a youth, Whitefield wrote that he could detect the "very early movings of the blessed Spirit upon my heart, sufficient to satisfy me that God loved me with an everlasting love."[93] Whitefield's youth also included "early convictions of sin."[94] During his youth, Whitefield desired to be a clergyman.[95] Late at night in his bedroom, Whitefield privately imitated ministers in their reading of prayers.[96] Whitefield wrote of his ethical dichotomy as he described stealing money and then giving it to the poor.[97] Similarly, Whitefield stole books, but the books he stole were of a devotional nature and he read them privately.[98] Around the age of fifteen, Whitefield composed two or three sermons and read the Bible while staying up at night.[99] While visiting his brother in Bristol, Whitefield recorded: "God was pleased to give me great foretastes of His love, and fill me with such unspeakable raptures, particularly once in St. John's Church, that I was carried out beyond myself."[100] Shortly after his experience in the church, Whitefield recorded a particular tempting season of his life. Whitefield wrote: "God even here stopped me, when running on in a full

91. Lambert wrote: "[Whitefield] linked his message to the personal experience of the messenger, filtering the message of the new birth through his own intense conversion." Lambert, "The Great Awakening as Artifact," 227.

92. Whitefield, *A Short Account*, 8.

93. Whitefield, *A Short Account*, 11.

94. Whitefield, *A Short Account*, 11.

95. Whitefield, *A Short Account*, 11.

96. Whitefield, *A Short Account*, 11.

97. Whitefield, *A Short Account*, 11.

98. Whitefield, *A Short Account*, 11.

99. Whitefield, *A Short Account*, 14.

100. Whitefield, *A Short Account*, 16.

career to hell."[101] Further, Whitefield described that "God so deeply convinced of hypocrisy."[102] Whitefield's early life was a dynamic period where he sought God in many ways and was convicted of his sinful nature (echoing the claim of the previous motif in this chapter). While Whitefield's conversion had not come, his journey and personal experience with God had been quite active from a young age.

3.3.2. Entering Oxford

In 1732 and at the age of seventeen, Whitefield found entrance as a student to Pembroke College, Oxford, by being a servitor—a low-level servant and academic aid to wealthy students.[103] Shortly before entrance to Pembroke, Whitefield turned to intense piety through fasting, attending worship twice a day, monthly sacrament, prayer more than twice a day in private, as well as a striking experience where he felt called to preach.[104] Upon beginning at Oxford, Whitefield's fellow students bid him to "join in their excess," but Whitefield said he was "given the grace to withstand them" and that "when they perceived they could not prevail, they let me alone as a singular odd fellow."[105] In turn, Whitefield was often alone and cold in his room. He still desired to play cards and read plays but stopped these activities too.[106] It was at this time that Whitefield purchased William Law's *A Serious Call to a Devout Life* and *Christian Perfection*.[107] Whitefield reflected on the impact these texts made on him, saying: "God worked powerfully

---

101. Whitefield, *A Short Account*, 20.

102. Whitefield, *A Short Account*, 21.

103. Dallimore states that Whitefield began at Pembroke on November 7, 1732. See Dallimore, *George Whitefield*, 1:61.

104. Whitefield, *A Short Account*, 22.

105. Whitefield, *A Short Account*, 25.

106. Whitefield, *A Short Account*, 25.

107. Both John Wesley and George Whitefield thought highly of and recommended *A Serious Call*. But as early as May 14, 1738, John Wesley issued a rebuke to Law in a letter where he described *A Serious Call* as a work which recommended works in order to be justified. In turn, Wesley produced his own abridgement of the work. Similarly, Whitefield "endeavoured to gospelize" the work and created his own version as well for publication. Thus, both Wesley and Whitefield produced edited versions for publication to remove any sense of righteousness won by works, thereby reforming *A Serious Call* in a more evangelical tone. See Whitefield, *The Works of the Reverend George Whitefield*, 2:144, 4:375–437; Law, *A Serious Call to a Devout and Holy Life*; Wesley, *Letters*, 25:540–41; William Law, *A Serious Call to a Holy Life [Abridgement by John Wesley]*, ed. John Wesley (Newcastle upon Tyne: John Gooding, 1744); Law, *A Practical Treatise Upon Christian Perfection*.

upon my soul."[108] Whitefield continued to pray, sing Psalms three times a day, fast on Fridays, and take the sacrament once a month.[109]

3.3.3. Meeting the Methodists

Whitefield had esteemed the Methodists and their Holy Club before his entry to Oxford, and longed to be acquainted with them.[110] Charles Wesley heard about Whitefield's piety through a situation at the University and invited him to breakfast.[111] At this breakfast, Charles Wesley gave Whitefield two books: Francke's *Treatise Against the Fear of Man* and *The Country Parson's Advice to His Parishioners*.[112] Later Charles Wesley gave Whitefield a copy of Henry Scougal's *The Life of God in the Soul of Man*, a text which had an enormous impact on Whitefield's theology of conversion.[113]

3.3.4. Reading Scougal

After reading Scougal, Whitefield recorded in his *Account*: "Though I fasted, watched and prayed, and received the sacrament so long, yet I never knew what true religion was, till God sent me that excellent treatise by the hands of my never-to-be-forgotten friend."[114] Whitefield went on to explain further how his thinking changed by reading Scougal's book:[115]

---

108. Whitefield noted that he had previously read Law's *Serious Account* but did not own it personally before coming to Oxford. See Whitefield, *A Short Account*, 25.

109. Whitefield, *A Short Account*, 26.

110. Whitefield, *A Short Account*, 26.

111. Whitefield, *A Short Account*, 27.

112. August Hermann Francke, *Nicodemus: Or, a Treatise Against the Fear of Man* (London: Joseph Downing, 1706); Anonymous, *Country Parson's Advice to His Parishioners* (London: Benjamin Tooke, 1680).

113. Henry Scougal, *The Life of God in the Soul of Man with Nine Other Discourses on Important Subjects* (London: J. Downing and G. Strahan, 1726). Kidd writes, "Aside from the Bible, Scougal was the most important book in introducing Whitefield to God-initiated conversion as the beginning of the Christian life." Kidd, *George Whitefield*, 29. For a fascinating account of the historical reception and adaptation of this book, see Isabel Rivers, "Scougal's *The Life of God in the Soul of Man*," in *Philosophy and Religion in Enlightenment Britain*, ed. Ruth Savage (Oxford: Oxford University Press, 2012), 29–55.

114. Whitefield, *A Short Account*, 27–28.

115. Hindmarsh notes that Whitefield told the *General Evening Post* in 1739 that Scougal's book alerted him to the necessity of the new birth; this was before Whitefield published his *Short Account*. Hindmarsh, *The Spirit of Early Evangelicalism: True Religion in a Modern World*, 33.

At my first reading it, I wondered what the author meant by saying, "That some falsely placed religion in going to church, doing hurt to no one, being constant in the duties of the closet, and now and then reaching out their hands to give alms to their poor neighbours," "Alas!" thought I, "if this be not true religion, what is?" God soon showed me; for in reading a few lines further, that "true religion was union of the soul with God, and Christ formed within us," a ray of Divine light was instantaneously darted in upon my soul, and from that moment, but not till then, did I know that I must be a new creature.[116]

Reflecting on Scougal's writing was a turning point for Whitefield. Previously, Whitefield sought his faith through externals: through the strict adherence to church attendance, private prayer, and the giving of alms. Now, he understood his religion to be, primarily, an inner experience of the soul. Whitefield went on to reveal further how this book changed his thinking. Whitefield wrote: "I had no rest in my soul till I wrote letters to my relations, telling them there was such a thing as the new birth."[117] For the first time, Whitefield understood the need for the new birth, an inner change in the soul of a person whereby they were a new creation. A careful reading shows that Whitefield discovered the new birth as an idea, not as something he had yet experienced himself. The instantaneous dart which hit him was that until then Whitefield did not know that there "was such a thing as the new birth."[118] This new knowledge of the new birth would change nearly every aspect of Whitefield's life and pave the path to his conversion.

Whitefield was well aware of his corruptions and that he was born in sin. He had "movings of the blessed Spirit upon my heart"; he experienced "early convictions of sin," as well as "great foretastes of His love";

---

116. Whitefield, *A Short Account*, 28. Whitefield recalled that he was "made instrumental in converting one who is lately come into the church." Nothing more is said regarding this convert. It is unclear if this example of conversion is an example of a rich theological understanding of the word or if it is simply a plain description of someone changing, such as joining the Holy Club. The latter is more likely, in my opinion, since the *Short Account* at this point is not using a rich theological language of conversion.

117. Whitefield, *A Short Account*, 28.

118. Whitefield, *A Short Account*, 28.

also, he was "deeply convinced of hypocrisy." Yet, with all of this Whitefield did not know of the new birth until reading Scougal and did not claim to have the new birth at this point. Whitefield's experiences taught him that instantaneous conversion was possible, but it did not preclude the significant working and experience of God in one's life before being born again. Much to the contrary, for whatever breakthrough instantaneous conversion may be, it was not the absolute *beginning* of God's work in one's life. For Whitefield conversion was better thought of as a significant turn in one's life surrounded by a larger narrative, including that which preceded instantaneous conversion.

In a sermon entitled *All Men's Place*, given shortly before Whitefield's death in 1771, Whitefield recalled: "I must bear testimony to my old friend, Mr. Charles Wesley; he put a book into my hands, called, The Life of God in the Soul of Man, whereby God shewed me that I must be born again or be damned."[119] Thirty-six years of reflection allowed Whitefield to summarize his primary revelation from Scougal: God used Scougal to show him he must be born again, or be damned; Whitefield was convinced and convicted. This epiphany was no small revelation. Whitefield read Scougal three years before the conversions of Charles and, then, John Wesley, and the importance of the new birth for the transatlantic revivals and the emergence of evangelicalism via the Wesleys and Whitefield cannot be overstated. A brief look at Scougal's work is in order.

Scougal saw at least two significant errors in the common religious practice of his day as people sought an assurance of their salvation: first, mechanical performance of duty; second, emotionally-enhanced performance of duty.[120] These two errors are the two extreme ends of an emotional spectrum of religious duty. Scougal changed the grounds for assurance and true religion. Counter to religion defined by duty, Scougal argued: "True religion is an union of the soul with God, a real participation of the divine nature, the very image of God drawn upon the soul, or, in the apostle's phrase, *it is Christ formed within us*."[121] The phrase that

---

119. Whitefield, *Eighteen Sermons*, 18.

120. Scougal, *The Life of God in the Soul of Man*, 2–3.

121. Scougal, *The Life of God in the Soul of Man*, 4. Italics in the original.

Scougal used to describe "Christ being formed within us" is what Scougal called the "divine life."[122]

Returning to Whitefield's retrospective sermon, Whitefield painted a vivid picture as he wrestled with *The Life of God*. Whitefield wrote: "Yet shall I burn that book, shall I throw it down, shall I put it by, or shall I search into it? I did, and holding the book in my hand, thus addressed the God of Heaven and earth: Lord, if I am not a Christian, if I am not a real one, God, for Jesus Christ's sake, show me what Christianity is, that I may not be damned at last."[123] Whitefield's description takes us into the depths of his personal faith and thoughts. We know that Whitefield had been burdened by his sin his entire life and had sought to be freed from his anxiety. In his description, we see clearly that more than an afflicted soul was at stake—Whitefield was not assured at all that he was a Christian. But, then Whitefield wrote:

> I read a little further, and the cheat was discovered; O, says the author, they that know anything of religion, know it is a vital union with the Son of God, Christ formed in the heart; O what a ray of Divine life did then break in upon my poor soul; I fell a writing to all my brethren, to my sisters, talked to the students as they came in my room, put off all trifling conversation, put all trifling books away, and was determined to study to be a Saint, and then to be a scholar; and from that moment God has been carrying on His blessed work in my soul.[124]

Union with the Son of God in Whitefield's soul was the breakthrough that he had been seeking. Two things require elaboration: first, the important terminology from Scougal to which Whitefield returned to over and over in his ministry; second, an analysis of the moment which is best understood as Whitefield's conversion.

After Scougal had introduced his basic thesis that religion was neither mechanical performance nor emotional performance of Christian duties, Scougal used several important phrases. True religion was, in Scougal's

122. Scougal, *The Life of God in the Soul of Man*, 4.
123. Whitefield, *Eighteen Sermons*, 360.
124. Whitefield, *Eighteen Sermons*, 360–61.

terms, "union of the soul with God, a real participation of the divine nature, the very image of God drawn upon the soul, or in the Apostle's phrase, it is Christ formed in us ... the divine life."[125] When true religion was defined this way, the duties of a Christian which were subsequently performed mechanically and emotionally were performed differently. Scougal wrote: "The love which a Pious man carries to God and goodness [is] ... by a new nature instructing and prompting him to do it ... the proper emanations of the divine life, the natural employments of the new-born soul."[126] The rest of *The Life of God* was organized around the pivotal term "divine life," of which Scougal explained: "The root of the divine life is faith; the chief branches are: love to God, charity to man, purity, and humility."[127] Of these four roots Scougal wrote: "He who hath attained [love to God, charity to man, purity, and humility] needs not desire to pry into the hidden rolls of God's decrees or search the volumes of heaven to know what is determined about his everlasting condition, but he may find a copy of God's thought concerning him written in his own breast."[128] The rest of *The Life of God* was organized around these four roots which feed into the *proof* of the divine life. In other words, for Scougal the divine life was the aim of true religion. The divine life was proof of a new nature, proof of the new-born soul, proof of conversion. A primary claim of this study is that Whitefield's view of conversion can be described as inaugurated teleology. Whitefield is indebted to Scougal's concept of the divine life as the aim (*telos*) of true religion. Scougal introduced to Whitefield the concept of the necessity of the new birth (which captures the essence of inauguration) as well as the divine life brought upon by the new birth (which captures the essence of teleology).

Scougal expounded upon the divine life, but Scougal's teaching could be accused of theologically circular reasoning. What was to be avoided was the mechanical or emotional performance of duties, but this could not be done without a new nature, being a new born soul. Scougal then set out a way to perform these functions in different ways in order to attain the new

---

125. Scougal, *The Life of God in the Soul of Man*, 4–5.

126. Scougal, *The Life of God in the Soul of Man*, 5–6.

127. Scougal, *The Life of God in the Soul of Man*, 15.

128. Scougal, *The Life of God in the Soul of Man*, 17. Notice that Scougal, like Whitefield, was not concerned with the precise articulation of the hidden decrees.

born soul. But, this could not be done properly without being a new born soul. Scougal's logic created the practical problem that Christian duties must continue to be done, but they were hoped to be done with the empowerment that comes from a new born soul.[129] This confusion led Whitefield into further extreme efforts to experience the divine life Scougal described.

3.3.5. Seeking the New Birth through Increased Fervor

Upon reading Scougal, Whitefield was drawn toward what he now understood as the divine life. Whitefield continued with the Holy Club and the Wesleys to be built in the knowledge and fear of God: enduring hardships like a good soldier, living by a rule, wasting no time, taking of the weekly sacrament, fasting on Wednesdays and Fridays, visiting prisoners in jail, giving charity to the poor, visiting the sick, and reading only books related to heart religion.[130] Effectively, Whitefield desired the new birth and sought it through continued religious practices. The only real change was his awareness and desire for the new birth, not a change in his approach to religious practices. If there was any change it was in the intensity of his effort. He would encounter additional challenges, however. Whitefield wrote: "When religion began to take root in my heart, and I was fully convinced my soul must be totally renewed ere it could see God, I was visited with outward and inward trials."[131] These trials began and the first challenge was that he gave up his own care for his reputation among those at Oxford.[132] Upon Whitefield's new intensity and approach to religion,

---

129. The "divine life" is a phrase Whitefield returned to many times throughout his entire ministry. I have identified over fifty uses of this phrase where it is synonymous with the idea of conversion and the new birth. A full example is given here in Whitefield's sermon, *The Potter and Clay*: "This moral change is what some call, repentance, some, conversion, some, regeneration; choose what name you please, I only pray GOD, that we all may have the thing. The scriptures call it holiness, sanctification, the new creature, and our LORD calls it a 'New birth, or being born again, or born from above.' These are not barely figurative expressions, or the slights of eastern language, nor do they barely denote a relative change of state conferred on all those who are admitted into CHRIST's church by baptism; but they denote a real, moral change of heart and life, a real participation of the divine life in the soul of man." Whitefield, *The Works of the Reverend George Whitefield*, 5:210.

130. Whitefield, *A Short Account*, 29–30.

131. Whitefield, *A Short Account*, 33.

132. Relinquishing your own reputation was also a major theme of Francke. See Francke, *Nicodemus: Or, a Treatise Against the Fear of Man.*

students at Oxford mocked him.[133] Whitefield at this point called himself
awakened to the desire for humility.[134] He then entered a period which
included an incredible weight, inward darkness, dry soul, weight and
sweat in his body when he kneeled, lack of sleep, and days spent pros-
trate on the ground.[135] He gave up eating fruit, gave his fruit money to the
poor, and chose the worst food for himself on purpose.[136] He fasted twice
a week; he did not attend to his unkempt hair; he wore woollen gloves, a
patched gown, and dirty shoes. In all this Whitefield "found [self-denial]
great promoters of the spiritual life."[137] He did this for many months but
then, after reading Castaniza's *Spiritual Combat*, shut himself in his study
and changed his tactics: he began praying silently and stopped speaking
to other people.[138] Lacking enough energy to do his schoolwork, he even
went to Christ Church meadow to be among the animals in an attempt to
have his own experience of Christ's temptation in the wilderness among
the animals.[139]

---

133. Whitefield, *A Short Account*, 34. Whitefield called those who mocked him "almost
Christians." This description would be a common theme in Whitefield's works, including the
title of a sermon he first delivered in 1737 and was published the following year. John Wesley
also delivered a sermon of the same title and in the critical notes provided by Outler, Outler
wrote: "The distinction between 'almost' and 'altogether' Christians was by now commonplace." Outler then listed a handful of examples of the usage of the phrase beginning in 1657.
See Wesley, *Sermons*, 131n1. What was less clear is the way that Whitefield used this phrase in
his *Short Account* at this point. The *Short Account* described Whitefield in 1734 when he would
have understood himself to be an 'almost Christian,' yet it was written in 1739 and published
in 1740 as part of his evangelistic publishing. Thus, in 1734 it is unlikely that Whitefield would
have criticized others for being "almost Christians," but by 1739/40 he was able to label them
this way for the purposes of his writing.

134. Whitefield, *A Short Account*, 36.

135. Whitefield, *A Short Account*, 37–38.

136. Whitefield, *A Short Account*, 39.

137. Whitefield, *A Short Account*, 39.

138. Whitefield, *A Short Account*, 40.

139. John Castaniza, *Spiritual Combat: Or, the Christian Pilgrim in His Spiritual Conflict and
Conquest*, 2nd ed. (London: Sam Keble, 1710). The work Whitefield cites as Castaniza was likely
authored by the ascetic Fr. Lawrence Scupoli, first published in Venice in 1589. An introduction
to this work states: "The purpose of this work is to lead the soul to the summit of spiritual
perfection, by the means of a constant, courageous struggle against our evil nature, which
tends to keep us away from that goal." The text itself states that to attain Christian perfection, "you must resolve on a perpetual warfare with yourself ... providing yourself with four
weapons ... in this spiritual combat: distrust of one's self, confidence in God, proper use of the
faculties of the body and mind, and the duty of prayer." Lorenzo Scupoli, *The Spiritual Combat*,
trans. James William Lester and Robert Paul Mohan (London: Catholic Way Publishing, 2013),
1, 6. Whitefield went further than the already-extreme Castaniza: "When Castaniza advised

Upon learning of Whitefield's asceticism, Charles Wesley directed him toward John Wesley's closer care. John instructed Whitefield to resume his "externals"—that is his public interaction, church activities, and a more sustainable lifestyle. But Wesley noted that Whitefield should not "depend on them."[140] During this time, Whitefield kept close attention to reading à Kempis, Castaniza, and his Greek New Testament.

Whitefield took up externals again just prior to the 1735 season of Lent, which began on February 23 and ended on Easter Sunday, April 10.[141] During this time Whitefield ate no meat, except on Saturdays, and ate nothing else on the other days except coarse bread and sage-tea without sugar. He walked in the frigid mornings until one hand turned black due to the harsh weather. He described his body as emaciated. He was so weak that he could not go upstairs.[142] He recalled that "sickness continued ... a glorious visitation it was ... purifying the soul."[143] After seven weeks of these self-induced trials, in the midst of nearly a year of other trials, Whitefield had a breakthrough.

Before outlining this breakthrough, however, some theological reflection on the preceding account is required. Whitefield had grown up in the Anglican context, which included infant baptism and regular partaking of the Eucharist. He had strong experiences with God throughout his life in regard not only to his sin, but also exciting revelations from God. Implicit in Whitefield's story was a push for something more, and most of the time the push came from his burdened soul. He did what any studious and pious Anglican steeped in the Holy Living tradition would do: he pushed further into the means of grace that he knew. Whitefield's most significant revelation was learned from Scougal: Whitefield's soul needed to be in union with Christ formed within him. Effectively, Whitefield recognized that

---

to talk but little, Satan said I must not talk at all. So that I, who used to be the most forward in exhorting my companions, have sat whole nights almost without speaking at all. Again, when Castaniza advised to endeavour after a silent recollection and waiting upon God, Satan told me I must leave off all forms, and not use my voice in prayer at all." Whitefield, *A Short Account*, 40, see also 40–43.

140. Whitefield, *A Short Account*, 44.

141. Whitefield, *A Short Account*, 46.

142. Whitefield, *A Short Account*, 47. On a personal note, the stairs at Pembroke are very few. That Whitefield was unable to go up these stairs showed his weak state.

143. Whitefield, *A Short Account*, 48.

his soul was not in union with God, and Christ was not formed in him. Whitefield had taken steps to push further using the only tool he knew: the means of grace. But, during this phase of Whitefield's life, the means of grace were pushed to their extreme through Whitefield's reading of the Catholic mystic Castaniza (Whitefield applied the means of grace even further than Castaniza recommended). Whitefield hoped that the extreme use of the means of grace would bring a breakthrough in which he would be converted.

3.3.6. Whitefield's Breakthrough: Conversion

About seven weeks after the Lenten season Whitefield had the breakthrough he had been hoping for in his life. The primary source which describes this event is Whitefield's *Short Account*. Whitefield went back later and edited many of his earliest publications, including the *Short Account*. Relevant extracts from both are presented below for comparison.

1740 1ST EDITION	1756 REVISION
About the end of the seven weeks and after I had been groaning under an unspeakable pressure both of body and mind for above a twelvemonth, God was pleased to set me free in the following manner. One day, perceiving an uncommon drought and a disagreeable clamminess in my mouth and using things to allay my thirst, but in vain, it was suggested to me, that when Jesus Christ cried out, "I thirst," His sufferings were near at an end. Upon which I cast myself down on the bed, crying out, "I thirst! I thirst!" Soon after this, I found and felt in myself that I was delivered from the burden that had so heavily oppressed me. The spirit of mourning was taken from me, and I knew what it was truly to rejoice in God my Saviour: and, for some time, could not avoid singing psalms wherever I was; but my joy	About the end of the seven weeks, after having undergone innumerable, buffetings of Satan, and many months inexpressible trials by night and day under the spirit of bondage, God was pleased at length to remove the heavy load, to enable me to lay hold on His dear Son by a living faith, and, by giving me the spirit of adoption, to seal me, as I humbly hope, even to the day of everlasting redemption. But oh! with what joy—joy unspeakable— even joy that was full of, and big with glory, was my soul filled, when the weight of sin went off, and an abiding sense of the pardoning love of God, and a full assurance of faith broke in upon my disconsolate soul! Surely it was the day of my espousals—a day to be had in everlasting remembrance. At first my joys were like a spring tide, and, as it were, overflowed the banks.

gradually became more settled, and, blessed be God, has abode and increased in my soul, saving a few casual intermissions, ever since. Thus were the days of my mourning ended. After a long night of desertion and temptation, the Star, which I had seen at a distance before, began to appear again, and the Day Star arose in my heart. Now did the Spirit of God take possession of my soul, and, as I humbly hope, seal me unto the day of redemption.[144]

Go where I would, I could not avoid singing of psalms aloud; afterwards it became more settled—and, blessed be God, saving a few casual intervals, has abode and increased in my soul ever since. But to proceed.[145]

The difference between the two accounts is striking. The original account spoke of Whitefield being "set free" via his imitation of Christ's cry from the cross, "I thirst!" At this moment Whitefield said he was delivered from his burden, oppression, and mourning. He knew that God was his Savior and from that time God took possession of his soul. The hope that Whitefield found in Scougal's writing had now come to fruition. Whitefield's soul had been united with God in a sudden moment; Whitefield had experienced the breakthrough conversion he sought. The 1756 revision omitted Whitefield's allusions to Christ's words on the cross. Instead, Whitefield inserted more theologically specific language such as adoption, sealing, redemption, pardoning, and assurance; but, the end was the same and Whitefield's soul was filled, though in a more muted tone.[146] Luke Tyerman gives a coherent explanation of the two accounts. Tyerman

144. Whitefield, A Short Account, 48–49.

145. George Whitefield, The Two First Parts of His Life, with His Journals, Revised, Corrected, and Abridged, by George Whitefield (London: W. Strahan, 1756), 17.

146. Whitefield did speak of adoption in the 1740 original edition just a few pages after his conversion, saying that he received "the Spirit of Adoption in my heart," though, strangely, this comment was removed in the 1756 edition. One explanation might be that it was removed as it may have seemed to be redundant since the idea was added to his conversion narrative. See Whitefield, A Short Account, 50. Amazingly, John Gillies, Whitefield's friend and executor of his writings, in his biography Memoirs of the Life of the Reverend George Whitefield, published a year after Whitefield's death, does not speak at all about Whitefield's conversion. While chronicling this time Gillies recorded, "His tutor therefore thought proper to call a physician, and it appeared by the event, he had rightly judged in doing so: for it pleased God to make the physician's care and medicines successful to his recovery. His bodily health being restored, his soul was likewise filled with peace and joy in believing on the Son of God." Gillies made this experience more of a medical story than a religious one. See John Gillies, Memoirs of the Life of the Reverend George Whitefield (London: Charles Dilly, 1772), 8.

explains: "It cannot be denied that Whitefield's first account of the way in which he obtained this gift of God is tinged with fanaticism. The second and revised account, published sixteen years afterward, is unobjectionable."[147] Nonetheless, both accounts described the time when Whitefield had the change in his soul he had been longing for: the moment of his instantaneous conversion.

One critical aspect of Whitefield's conversion is articulated clearer in his 1756 account than in his earlier one: the role of faith in instantaneous conversion. Whitefield described faith as the instrumental cause of his instantaneous conversion. Whitefield wrote: "God was pleased at length to remove the heavy load, to enable me to lay hold of His dear Son by a living faith … it was the day of my espousals."[148] Whitefield is careful to note that God, and not Whitefield, was the source of his converting faith; God's enabling allowed Whitefield to respond in faith.[149] Whitefield's instantaneous conversion was indeed in an instant, but it also was the culmination of a long process of intentional spiritual devotion for Whitefield. We can now espouse from Whitefield's conversion narrative a primary claim of this study: conversion arrives by faith in an instant (synoptic statement 5).

Whitefield understood instantaneous conversion as the life-changing moment that brought one from eternal death into eternal life through faith in Jesus Christ. Throughout his entire ministry, Whitefield called for people to convert, but he also knew that the journey toward conversion would be different for each person.[150] In some people, instantaneous conversion happened in their last moments, whether for a thief on a cross or an elderly person on their deathbed. In other words, a discrete instant was

---

147. Luke Tyerman, *The Life of the Rev. George Whitefield* (London: Hodder and Stoughton, 1876), 1:25–26.

148. Whitefield, *The Two First Parts of His Life*, 17.

149. Reliance on Whitefield's 1756 account is not required to show that Whitefield understood instantaneous conversion to arrive by faith. In the 1740 account, a few pages after his conversion narrative, Whitefield described that some experience a difficult path (such as Whitefield) and others a gentler path on their way toward conversion; but, that both become right with God by faith. Whitefield, *A Short Account*, 72–73.

150. Whitefield said: "It is in the spiritual as in the natural life—some feel more, others less, but all experience some pangs and travails of soul, ere the Man Christ Jesus is formed within them, and brought forth and arrived unto the measure of His fulness Who filleth all in all." Whitefield, *A Short Account*, 73.

clear for them when they converted.[151] For others, instantaneous conversion happened in the instant of hearing a powerful sermon, such as that given by St. Peter at Pentecost. Still others experienced instantaneous conversion in the midst of a long process, with Whitefield's preeminent example being his own conversion narrative.[152] While the specific timeframe of each person may vary leading up to their instantaneous conversion, Whitefield's operant teaching on conversion has, in this chapter, been espoused to show that conversion, for Whitefield, arrives by faith in an instant. Furthermore, this chapter has shown that Whitefield's understanding of conversion in terms of inaugurated teleology is indebted to Scougal's influence in his book *The Life of God in the Soul of Man.*

4. CONTINUED EVIDENCE OF CONVERSION

Having argued that the primary motifs of Whitefield's theology of conversion are defined as an experience *from* and *to* (section 1), with convicting, convincing, and awakening experiences which precede conversion (section 2), and a defined moment of instantaneous conversion (section 3), it is now important to show that Whitefield taught the necessity of continued evidence of conversion after instantaneous conversion. This section will proceed, first, to show that Whitefield taught that a conversion date is normative, but not required. Whitefield believed that some individuals may not have a recollection or a specific date of any instantaneous moment when they converted. In the course of this discussion, synoptic statement 6 will emerge: conversion is instantaneous but is not always recognizable on behalf of the true convert. This section will continue, second, to argue that

---

151. Kidd said of Whitefield's view of the conversion moment, "He or she could often (though not always) know the time and circumstances under which that union occurred. ... Most true believers, he contended, could remember the moment of their conversion, just as they would remember their own wedding." Kidd, *George Whitefield*, 164. Many accounts of the conversion experience in this period name the season of the year, the date, and frequently the hour of the conversion experience. Brauer adds, "This represents a movement beyond the classical Reformation concern for conversion as exemplified in Luther and Calvin." Jerald C. Brauer, "Conversion: From Puritanism to Revivalism," *The Journal of Religion* 58, no. 3 (1978): 241.

152. While the moment of conversion was seen as instantaneous, the events and experiences preceding this moment could still take place of several years, months, weeks, or days. While the Methodist scheme differed from Puritanism preparationism and conversion, this prolonged process could make the exterior appearance of the progress seem nearly identical. Brauer, "Conversion," 232–33; Dallimore, *George Whitefield*, 1:137.

Whitefield understood conversion as an ongoing and repeated turning to God throughout the Christian life; at times Whitefield called the repeated turning to God a second conversion. The section will continue, third, to reveal that ongoing marks of holiness were evidential of a genuine conversion in Whitefield's thought. In other words, and denoted in the synoptic statement of conversion 7: conversion is marked by ongoing good works. This section comes to a close, fourth, by showing that Whitefield's view of election did not lead to antinomianism, as it could for some hyper-Calvinists. Instead, the ongoing nature of conversion showed the proper fruits of a rightly understood doctrine of election in Whitefield's moderate Calvinism.

4.1. CONVERSION DATE NORMATIVE BUT NOT REQUIRED

Whitefield did not require a person to be able to recall the exact moment of his or her instantaneous conversion. A cursory reading of Whitefield's corpus, however, could give the impression that he gave a mixed message whether or not one must be able to recount his or her conversion moment. For instance, Whitefield asked in his sermon *The Holy Spirit Convicting the World of Sin, Righteousness, and Judgment* (1742): "How long have you believed? Would not most of you say, as long as we can remember; we never did disbelieve? Then this is a certain sign that you have no true faith at all."[153] The context of the sermon related to the role of the Holy Spirit to convict one of righteousness.[154] Whitefield taught that since the Holy Spirit's role is to convict one of unbelief in order to convert, one must be able to identify a time when he or she did not believe. Therefore, for Whitefield it was simple: if you could not recall when you did not believe, then you could not possibly believe at all, and your faith was false. Whitefield gave one caveat: "Unless you were sanctified from your infancy, which is the case of some."[155] Being sanctified from infancy suggested the fate of infants who were baptized and protected through their baptism until such a time came when they sinned it away. A hurried reading of this sermon could lead one to believe that Whitefield held that a conversion date was required in order for the conversion to be genuine. Other evidence leads one to think

---

153. Whitefield, *The Works of the Reverend George Whitefield*, 6:133.
154. Whitefield, *The Works of the Reverend George Whitefield*, 6:129.
155. Whitefield, *The Works of the Reverend George Whitefield*, 6:133.

that Whitefield did not hold that a conversion date was required in order for the conversion to be genuine. For instance, in his sermon *Christ the Believer's Husband* (1747), Whitefield declared:

> Not that all who can say, their Maker is their husband, can give the same clear and distinct account of the time, manner and means of their being spiritually united and married by faith, to the blessed bridegroom of the church. Some there may be now, as well as formerly, sanctified from the womb. And others in their infancy and non-age, as it were silently converted. Such perhaps may say, with a little Scotch maiden, now with GOD, when I asked her, whether JESUS CHRIST had taken away her old heart, and given her a new one? "Sir, it may be, (said she,) I cannot directly tell you the time and place, but this I know, it is done." And indeed it is not so very material, though no doubt it is very satisfactory, if we cannot relate all the minute and particular circumstances, that attended our conversion; if so be we are truly converted now, and can say, the work is done, and that, "our Maker is our husband." And I question, whether there is one single adult believer, now on earth, who lived before conversion, either in a course of secret or open sin, but can, in a good degree, give an account of the beginning and progress of the work of grace in his heart.[156]

In this sermon, Whitefield did not require one to be able to give an account of their conversion in order to prove the legitimacy of their conversion. All that was needed was certainty that one was converted; the specific recollection of the moment, or date, was not required. It is possible that Whitefield was giving a mixed message on the necessity of a genuine convert to be able to recall the moment of their instantaneous conversion.[157] It is also possible that Whitefield had matured and was relaxing his insistence on a precise recollection of one's instantaneous conversion. Another

---

156. Whitefield, *The Works of the Reverend George Whitefield*, 5:180.

157. Whitefield was not shy to point out changes in his views and to make amendments to his previous publications. As seen above, Whitefield edited his *Accounts* in order to present them in a more mature tone. Similarly, Whitefield went back and edited his early sermons which came before his Calvinistic turn. See Whitefield, *The Works of the Reverend George Whitefield*, 4:46–47.

possibility arises from a careful reading of the second part of the quoted portion above in *Christ the Believer's Husband*. Whitefield could be talking about the beginning of the conversion process, "an account of the beginning," and not the pivotal conversion, or instantaneous conversion moment itself. Extending the marriage analogy Whitefield provided, spouses may not know when they fell in love, but they do know when they were married. While it is possible to read these accounts as contradictory, such a reading would be unlikely because the beginning of the quotation appears to indicate that not requiring a conversion date is exactly Whitefield's point. It is more likely that in the 1742 sermon Whitefield was addressing conviction, sin, and belief primarily, while the 1747 sermon has in mind the need for a very specific conversion narrative.[158]

Therefore, Whitefield did not require people to be able to state their conversion *instant*, though he expected that adults would recall times when they were convicted of their sin and lack of belief. While it was normative in Whitefield's theology of conversion that an individual did experience an instantaneous conversion, Whitefield allowed for a "holy variety" of conversion explanations which included the possibility that some simply would have an ongoing conversion from their infancy. It is, therefore, possible to espouse from Whitefield's operant teaching that conversion is instantaneous but is not always recognizable on behalf of the true convert (synoptic statement 6).

4.2. CONTINUED CONVERSION AS TURNING TO
GOD THROUGHOUT THE CHRISTIAN LIFE

Another variety of ongoing conversion in Whitefield's theology was his mention of a second conversion and a present tense conversion, best understood as the ongoing turning back to Jesus through Christian humility and spiritual growth, or in other words, the process of sanctification.[159]

---

158. It is also possible that Whitefield was retaining the variety of conversion experiences he would have encountered in his broad Puritan reading. As Hambrick-Stowe states, for Puritans, "Conversion could be gradual, sudden, violent, mild, or scarcely perceptible." Charles E. Hambrick-Stowe, *The Practice of Piety: Puritan Devotional Disciplines in Seventeenth-Century New England* (Chapel Hill, NC: University of North Carolina Press, 1982), 85.

159. The idea of an "ongoing" conversion is not without precedent. The Puritan Thomas Shepard spoke of his own progress in grace as "renewed conversions." The stages of these deeper experiences followed the original conversion pattern. The freshness of each successive

In the sermon, *Peter's Denial of His Lord*, Whitefield discussed Jesus' prediction of Peter's denial of Jesus. In his sermon, Whitefield spoke of a second conversion: "[Peter's] recovery out of [Peter's denial of Christ] would be, as it were, a second conversion."[160] But this second conversion was not a second conversion at all. A second conversion would imply, in Whitefield's theology, that a converted person would need to be regenerated and justified more than once.[161] What Whitefield meant by a second conversion is clarified by a closer look at the sermon's text, Luke 22:32 in the King James Version, in which Jesus stated: "But I have prayed for thee, that thy faith fail not: and when thou art converted, strengthen thy brethren." A question needs to be answered: Was Peter converted before his denials of Jesus? Whitefield anticipated and answered this question earlier in this sermon: "Peter, before his fall, was certainly a converted man."[162] Clarification on Peter's conversion (whether he needed to convert once or twice) is found in the translation of the word *epistrepho* in Luke 22:32, which can be translated as either "convert," "repent," or "to turn" (physically). Modern translations consistently translate *epistrephō* in Luke 22:32 as "to turn," with a representative example being the New Revised Standard Version: "But I have prayed for you that your own faith may not fail; and you, when once you have turned back, strengthen your brothers." As one who read and prayed over every word of his Greek New Testament while on his knees in the morning, Whitefield was well aware of the word *epistrephō* and its meaning.[163] Accordingly, Whitefield stated "that [Peter's] fall would be so

---

infusion of grace came in spite of, or because of, Shepard's long and well-assured first conversion. Others spoke of "renewed conversions" as "deeper experiences of the stages of redemption." Increase Mather recorded in a sermon, "There are Second Conversions of the same Christians, though not as to their State, but in respect of Growth in Grace." See Hambrick-Stowe, *The Practice of Piety*, 199–200; Increase Mather, *Ichabod or, A Discourse, Shewing What Cause There Is to Fear That the Glory of the Lord Is Departing from New-England* (Boston, 1702), 31.

160. Whitefield, *The Works of the Reverend George Whitefield*, 6:392.

161. See chapter five, section three for more on Whitefield's understanding of conversion, regeneration, and justification.

162. Whitefield, *The Works of the Reverend George Whitefield*, 6:391.

163. Dallimore, *George Whitefield*, 1:81–93. Additionally, Whitefield relied heavily on Matthew Henry's commentary. Henry understood Luke 22:32 as a turn from sin and not a regenerative, salvific conversion. See Matthew Henry, *Matthew Henry's Commentary on the Whole Bible: Complete and Unabridged in One Volume* (Peabody, MA: Hendrickson, 1994), 1904.

exceeding great, that his recovery out of it would be, as it were, a second conversion."[164] The fall would be significant but not complete. Therefore, the second conversion was not a conversion at all in a salvific sense. One way to understand the second conversion is the theme of an ongoing conversion in the sense of ongoing Christian growth through sin and repentance, or in other words the process of sanctification. Put another way, conversion is *not only* instantaneous; for Whitefield conversion is also ongoing Christian growth through turning back to Christ for one who was already firmly converted.

An ongoing conversion for one who was already firmly converted is a good way to understand some passing comments Whitefield made about himself throughout several letters. For example, on December 20, 1752, Whitefield wrote: "And O that I may be converted myself more and more every day and hour! I am ashamed of my being such a dwarf in religion, and of my having so little of the mind of CHRIST."[165] In this instance, Whitefield's wandering mind led him to want to draw closer to God as an ongoing conversion; he was not expressing that he was no longer converted. Similarly, on March 26, 1754, he recorded: "O that I may begin to begin to be converted myself.—I am a dwarf.—Less than the least of all, shall be my motto still."[166] This is an instance of Whitefield's recognition of his sinfulness, the ongoing struggle of sanctification; it is not a statement that Whitefield was no longer converted and needed to convert again. Likewise, on December 1, 1763, he wrote: "LORD JESUS, spare root and branch, for thy own glory, and thy people's good! LORD JESUS, convert us all more and more, and make us all like little children!"[167] In each of these instances, Whitefield was desiring more and more turning for himself and his recipients. There is no sense that Whitefield thought that he had lost his initial conversion to Christ; instead, ongoing conversion was indicative of ongoing Christian growth after experiencing instantaneous conversion.

---

164. Whitefield, *The Works of the Reverend George Whitefield*, 6:392.
165. Whitefield, *The Works of the Reverend George Whitefield*, 2:463.
166. Whitefield, *The Works of the Reverend George Whitefield*, 3:69.
167. Whitefield, *The Works of the Reverend George Whitefield*, 3:303.

4.3. THE MARKS OF A SOUND CONVERSION: ONGOING REPENTANCE, OBEDIENCE, AND LOVE

We have seen that to be a genuine convert one was not required, according to Whitefield, to recall an exact conversion moment, though many did; and that Whitefield at times spoke of a second conversion, which can be understood as the process of sanctification. There is a third, and closely linked, aspect to Whitefield's theology of conversion whereby a true convert was expected to show the marks of a sound conversion.

The analysis of Whitefield's view on the marks of conversion require care. For Whitefield, the difference between the exterior and the interior, the outward and the inward, the head and the heart, made a world of difference in his theology of conversion. The marks of conversion were an outside-in view, seeing exteriors. In contrast, the inside-out view was the personal experience where so much of Whitefield's pastoral emphasis rested. This discussion of the marks of a sound conversion is an evaluation based on exteriors. In chapter five, a discussion of how Whitefield's theology of conversion impacted one's personal experience of assurance will be examined.[168] The two aspects (exterior and the interior) cannot be completely separated, since fruit indicates the type of tree; still, some distance between exterior actions and interior reality is required in the evaluation of Whitefield's theology. In other words, Whitefield believed that conversion was an interior orientation when one responded in faith through understanding oneself as a benefactor of Christ's righteousness; this orientation would then manifest in the outward marks of conversion. Care is required because the outward marks are simply indicators, or signs, not conversion itself. Now that Whitefield's priority on interior change has been established, it is now possible to proceed in the analysis of the marks of conversion in its proper context.

The marks of a sound conversion for Whitefield were the general trend of growth in the Christian life. These marks were indicated by the forsaking of sin through repentance, bringing forth fruit in godly living, and

---

168. Chapter five, section two.

going beyond general civility toward actual godliness. Instances abound in Whitefield's writing regarding the marks of a sound conversion.[169]

For those who were genuinely converted, one mark of conversion was that a convert would repent and forsake their sin. In his sermon, *Marks of Having Received the Holy Ghost*, Whitefield taught:

> And so is every one that is born again: to commit sin, is as contrary to the habitual frame and tendency of his mind, as generosity is to the inclinations of a miser; but if at any time, he is drawn into sin, he immediately, with double zeal, returns to his duty, and brings forth fruits meet for repentance. Whereas, the unconverted sinner is quite dead in trespasses and sins: or if he does abstain from gross acts of it, through worldly selfish motives, yet, there is some right eye he will not pluck out.[170]

Whitefield taught that a clear contrast would exist between a genuine convert (one who had been born again) and the unconverted (one who had not been born again). When true converts sinned, Whitefield expected them to repent with "double zeal." The false convert will not repent or will respond more out of personal gain than true piety.[171]

Whitefield's belief that instantaneous conversion required continued evidence of conversion through the marks of conversion is indicated through the organizational structures that he developed in order to nurture new converts. While the legacy of Methodism came through the line of the Wesleys, it is not well known that Whitefield was the one who originally set out to organize people, prior to the Wesleys, into bands and societies to tend to the spiritual needs of converts and others.[172] Within a few years

---

169. See Whitefield, *First Journal: A Voyage from London to Savannah in Georgia*, 50, 51, 53; Whitefield, *The Works of the Reverend George Whitefield*, 4:90, 363.

170. Whitefield, *The Works of the Reverend George Whitefield*, 6:166.

171. Dallimore wrote: "[Whitefield] refused to count converts. He chose to wait until conversion had been manifested by months of a transformed life, and his attitude is well expressed in his words, 'Only the judgement morning will reveal who the converts really are.'" Dallimore, *George Whitefield*, 1:137.

172. Some scholars overlook Whitefield's organizational efforts for discipleship; see Maddock who published an otherwise exceptional monograph on the relationship between Whitefield and Wesley. Maddock wrote: "Whitefield deliberately eschewed any effort to organize those converted under his preaching ministry." Ian J. Maddock, *Men of One Book: A*

of Whitefield's return from America in 1741, there were thirty-six Whitefieldian Methodist societies with the Tabernacle location in London as its center.[173] The public was invited to the services but members needed to pass an examination of their spiritual state for a ticket of admission which required renewal every three months upon evaluation of a satisfactory manner of life. The organization of Societies showed the high commitment Whitefield and his associates had for the ongoing growth of converts, so as not to fall into an antinomian or nominal Christianity. On April 7, 1743, the Calvinistic Methodist Association (CMA) was formed out of the Whitefieldian Methodist societies. The CMA spanned England and Wales. Whitefield was appointed the "Life Moderator" of the CMA. The CMA began eighteen months before the Wesleys organized their first Methodist Conference in June 1744.[174] Later, the CMA came more and more under the leadership of Daniel Rowland and Howell Harris. Subsequently, the group underwent a split and developed its own history apart from Whitefield.[175] In a letter to John Wesley on September 1, 1748, Whitefield wrote that he would stop forming his own Whitefieldian Methodist societies and any attempts to lead a similar movement. Whitefield wanted to focus his effort, instead, on being an evangelist at-large. He made this decision because he did not have men capable of leading the groups without him and he also wanted to avoid strife with the growing societies of Wesley.[176] The formation of these groups is important for understanding Whitefield's theology of conversion because, due to his prodigious and lasting reputation as an orator and not an organizer, one may be tempted to think that Whitefield's theology of conversion was wholly concerned with instantaneous conversion and scant attention was given to people after experiencing instantaneous conversion. The truth of the matter is that Whitefield was *the* pioneer of the Methodist bands, societies, and classes,

---

Comparison of Two Methodist Preachers, John Wesley and George Whitefield (Eugene, OR: Pickwick Publications, 2011), 31.

173. Dallimore, *George Whitefield*, 2:151–53.

174. Dallimore, *George Whitefield*, 2:158.

175. See Jones, White, and Schlenther, *The Elect Methodists*; David Ceri Jones, "George Whitefield and the Revival of Calvinism in Eighteenth-Century Britain," *International Congregational Journal* 14, no. 1 (Summer 2015): 97–115.

176. See Whitefield, *The Works of the Reverend George Whitefield*, 2:169.

and their organization was a testament to Whitefield's theological and pastoral sensibilities regarding the ongoing nature of conversion.

A contemporary of Whitefield, Josiah Smith, published his own assessment of Whitefield's evangelistic soteriology in 1740 in which he concluded, along with the analysis above, that Whitefield taught that ongoing marks, evidenced through good works, were required to evidence genuine saving faith. Smith wrote:

> [Whitefield] vindicated himself from all suspicions of antinomian error ... on the one hand, he earnestly contended for our justification as the free gift of God, by faith alone, in the blood of Christ ... on the other hand he took special care to guard against the licentious abuse of it, and would not make void the Law, when he asserted that good works are necessary fruit and evidences of true faith; telling us plainly, and with the clearest distinction, that a man was justified these three ways; meritoriously by Christ, instrumentally by faith alone, declaratively by good works.[177]

All three aspects were needed for those who were truly justified, and thus converted: first, the merit of Christ; second, faith in Christ; and third, good works.[178] Smith's evaluation aligns with the preceding analysis of Whitefield's teaching on the need for the ongoing marks, or good works, as a sign of conversion.

As seen from the preceding, Whitefield expected those who experienced instantaneous conversion to manifest an external change in their behaviors. As further evidence of his theology for the need of ongoing conversion, Whitefield formed societies and organizational structures to nurture new converts in their faith. Outsiders, such as Josiah Smith, recognized in Whitefield's teaching and ministry the expectation of the outward marks of conversion. Therefore, it is concluded that, in the operant instances of Whitefield's teaching on conversion, the espoused theology of conversion for Whitefield includes the fact that conversion is marked by ongoing good works (synoptic statement 7). This section now turns its

---

177. Josiah Smith, *The Character, Preaching, &c, of the Reverend Mr. George Whitefield, Impartially Represented and Supported, in a Sermon* (Boston: G. Rogers, 1740), 5.

178. Schwenk concluded that Whitefield believed "holy living was not optional; God expected it." Schwenk, *Catholic Spirit*, 41.

attention to the relationship between Whitefield's commitment to election and the necessity of the marks of conversion.

4.4. ELECTION AND THE ONGOING MARKS OF CONVERSION

A genuine mark of conversion was simply that a true convert would bring forth fruit. Whitefield's Calvinism (and more specific reflections on election) will be shown in the discussion of assurance in chapter five as well as chapter six (where John Wesley and George Whitefield will be compared). Whitefield's view of election did not lead to antinomianism. This is established from Whitefield's theology of ongoing conversion. Soon after Whitefield began to emphasize election in his teaching, he responded to those who thought election would negate the seeking of these marks (that is, antinomianism). For example, the sermon *The Conversion of Zaccheus* (1739) spoke directly to these accusations. Whitefield wrote: "Say not within yourselves, this is a licentious Antinomian doctrine; for this faith, if true, will work by love, and be productive of the fruits of holiness. See an instance in this convert Zaccheus: no sooner had he received JESUS CHRIST by faith into his heart, but he evidences it by his works."[179] Whitefield presented Zaccheus as a foundational example of a genuine convert whose natural response was to evidence his conversion through good works. True faith and true conversion resulted, for Whitefield, in true fruits of holiness in the life of the believer.

Whitefield maintained that a genuine change must occur after a person converted; in other words, Whitefield's view of election did not lead to antinomianism after God's work to bring instantaneous conversion. Four examples from Whitefield's corpus can be given to support this claim. First, St. Paul was deemed truly converted by Whitefield because of his actions following his encounter with Jesus.[180] Second, those who had undergone the revival in Cambridge were deemed truly converted because, as Whitefield wrote, "the voice of prayer and praise fills their chambers; and sincerity, fervency, and joy, with seriousness of heart, sit visibly on their faces."[181] These evidences were the proof that convinced Whitefield of the

---

179. Whitefield, *The Works of the Reverend George Whitefield*, 6:56.

180. Whitefield, *The Works of the Reverend George Whitefield*, 6:156.

181. Whitefield, *The Works of the Reverend George Whitefield*, 4:85.

genuineness of their conversion (and thus, election). Third, in a letter to the Bishop of London, Whitefield wrote: "How can it be proved that they reckon them real converts, till they see them bring forth the fruits of the Spirit, in doing justly, loving mercy, and walking humbly with their GOD?"[182] In other words, Whitefield taught that conversion could only be deemed genuine later, after genuine evidence of good works had emerged. Fourth, Whitefield's clearest teaching on the marks was in his sermon, *Marks of a True Conversion*, where he stated plainly that true converts must be obedient to God and love one another.[183] Whitefield was clear that genuine converts, whom he believed to be elect, must show a change in their life.

The continued evidence of conversion was, for Whitefield, a distinct mark of his view of election. Whitefield taught that the "seeming convert" (the person who was not genuinely converted) would experience initial progress in holiness but would later return to their folly.[184] Conversely, those who were genuinely converted would maintain their holiness as they made "all diligence to make your calling and election sure."[185] Similarly, in Whitefield's famous letter to Wesley on the topic of election, Whitefield was careful to remind Wesley of "many dear children of GOD, who are predestinarians, and yet are meek, lowly, pitiful, courteous, tender-hearted, kind, of a catholic spirit, and hope to see the most vile and profligate of men converted."[186] Whitefield confronted Wesley's accusations of the doctrine of election leading to antinomianism by reminding Wesley of people that Wesley knew who believed in election and evidenced their election through godliness. Whitefield, thus, believed that his affirmation of the doctrine of election was a natural correlate to his belief in the ongoing nature of conversion which was evidenced by ongoing good works, holiness, or in other words, sanctification.

Whitefield's belief that conversion required continued evidence in order to be genuine has been demonstrated through four main points. First, for Whitefield, a conversion date is normative but not required (synoptic statement 6). Whitefield did not require a conversion date because he was

---

182. Whitefield, *The Works of the Reverend George Whitefield*, 4:162.

183. Whitefield, *The Works of the Reverend George Whitefield*, 5:348, 351.

184. Whitefield, *The Works of the Reverend George Whitefield*, 2:402.

185. Whitefield, *The Works of the Reverend George Whitefield*, 2:402.

186. Whitefield, *The Works of the Reverend George Whitefield*, 4:61.

more concerned with the substance of conversion more so than a one-time experience. Second, Whitefield's emphasis on the substance of conversion (a changed life) has been shown in Whitefield's language of an ongoing and second conversion, which describe the process of growth in holiness and godliness, or, in other words, sanctification. Third, Whitefield's emphasis on continued evidence of conversion has been supported by his teaching on the marks of a sound conversion, of which Whitefield also initiated societies and organizations in order to nurture. From Whitefield's insistence on the necessity of continued good works emerged the synoptic statement of conversion: conversion is marked by ongoing good works (7). Fourth, and finally, Whitefield's doctrine of election was shown to align with his expectation of ongoing good works.

5. CONCLUSION

This chapter has examined George Whitefield's theology of conversion in relation to four primary motifs and has enabled the identification of seven espoused synoptic theological statements of conversion in order to support the primary claim of this study that Wesley and Whitefield's theology of conversion can be articulated as inaugurated teleology.[187] The first section of this chapter showed that, for Whitefield, conversion is a life-changing experience in which one turns from self-righteousness to the righteousness of Christ. The second section revealed that Whitefield observed conviction, convincing, and awakening, each of which related to an experience with personal sinfulness, to occur prior to instantaneous conversion. The third section articulated Whitefield's conversion motif of instantaneous conversion as a moment in which conversion arrives by faith in an instant. In this section, Whitefield's conversion narrative was analyzed to show his own instantaneous conversion and the pivotal influence of Scougal's concept of the new birth in Whitefield's conversion theology. The fourth section articulated Whitefield's belief that genuine conversion will be evidenced by good works and holiness throughout the convert's life, and that this evidence is indicative of Whitefield's doctrine of election, which was opposed to antinomianism. With the primary motifs

---

187. The other two espoused statements of conversion theology of Whitefield (regarding baptism and assurance) emerge in the analysis located in chapter five.

of Whitefield's theology of conversion in place, this study now moves to the attendant themes which are needed to develop the establishment of a theology of conversion for Whitefield.

5

—

GEORGE WHITEFIELD'S CONVERSION THEOLOGY ATTENDANT THEMES

This chapter exegetes theologically the three attendant themes relating to Whitefield's conversion theology. These themes attend to practical matters which Whitefield faced in his ministry. The first theme considers Whitefield's view of baptismal regeneration and conversion since baptism brought about regeneration per the Church of England's baptismal rites. Whitefield had to substantiate his claim that people who were baptized still needed to experience the new birth (by which he meant regeneration that happens in the moment of instantaneous conversion). The second attendant theme to be addressed in relation to conversion is assurance of salvation. For Whitefield, the experience of assurance was the trust and knowledge that one's faith was genuine and salvific. The discussion in the first and second sections highlights the need for a careful understanding of Whitefield's use of several critical soteriological terms related to conversion (such as regeneration and new birth). The third and final section thus espouses Whitefield's *ordo salutis* as it pertains to conversion.

This chapter strengthens the claim of this study that the espousal of Whitefield's theology of conversion can be described as inaugurated teleology in two ways. First, conversion requires an inauguration, which, in Whitefield's theology, comes properly upon the advent of personal faith and repentance in the moment of instantaneous conversion. Second, conversion requires a teleological aspect since a person is regenerated and justified for a purpose, which is to grow in their sanctification toward glorification. Whitefield's hypothetical universal election used the doctrine of election as a source for Christian well-being in the face of discouragement because of ongoing sin while maintaining that genuine converts needed to continue in their good works. Thus, Whitefield's use of the doctrine of election was a theological source for the teleological aspect of conversion since it supplied the foundation for Christian fortitude in the face of the ongoing struggle against sin.

1. CONVERSION AND BAPTISMAL REGENERATION

Whitefield's theology of conversion is deepened by an examination of the relationship between conversion and baptism. Attention to this attendant theme is necessary to develop Whitefield's theology of conversion because, as will be shown, the Anglican rite of baptism plainly declared the baptized person as regenerated, born again, and saved. Whitefield, therefore, had to substantiate the need for conversion since many people in Whitefield's era would have not sensed the need to be converted because of their participation in baptism.[1]

1.1. WHITEFIELD'S COMMITMENT TO BAPTISMAL REGENERATION IN THE CHURCH OF ENGLAND

The crux of Whitefield's view of conversion and baptismal regeneration hinges upon his commitment to the documents of the Church of England, specifically Article XXVII and the rite for infant baptism. We have seen earlier that Wesley's 1784 *Sunday Service* amended the language in the baptismal rites to align with his view of regeneration. Whitefield, instead, worked within the documents of the Church of England to arrive at a similar endpoint, though, as this section will show, his approach requires much more nuance.

Critics accuse Whitefield of eschewing his commitment to the Church of England because of issues such as his field preaching and extemporaneous prayer.[2] Whitefield, however, boasted in his confidence in the doc-

---

1. In 1740 Josiah Smith evaluated Whitefield's theology and commented on Whitefield's focus on regeneration. Smith wrote: "Hardly a single sermon, but he mentioned [regeneration], sometimes more than twice; and one, and perhaps the best, of his discourses, was ex professo, upon this subject." Smith, *The Character, Preaching, &c, of the Reverend Mr. George Whitefield, Impartially Represented and Supported, in a Sermon*, 6.

2. Loane highlights some of these critics: Edward Loane, "Wesley, Whitefield, and the Church of England," in *Wesley and Whitefield? Wesley versus Whitefield?*, ed. Ian J. Maddock

uments of his church. Whitefield wrote: "God is my judge, I should rejoice to see all the world adhere to her articles. ... I am a friend to her articles, I am a friend to her homilies, I am a friend to her liturgy."[3] Loane observes that, despite Whitefield's critics inside and outside of his church, he was never defrocked or officially sanctioned by his church.[4]

An incident in 1737 in Whitefield's *First Journal* highlights his commitment to the baptismal standards of his church. During his ocean journey from Gibraltar to Georgia, the captain of Whitefield's ship desired to have one of the boys on the boat baptized. Unfortunately, the boy fell ill and died quickly while aboard the boat. Though it seems that the boy was approaching his baptism amid his death, Whitefield comments that while the dead boy was "thrown into the sea. I could not read the Office over him being unbaptized."[5] Whitefield could not perform a burial service, nor the confidences of hope proclaimed in the service, since the rite states "the Office ensuing is not to be used for any that die unbaptized."[6] Similarly, in Whitefield's catechetical comments on John 3, Whitefield writes: "How God will deal with persons unbaptized we cannot tell. What have we to do to judge those that are without?"[7] Whitefield, thus, held a high view, even in difficult circumstances, of the baptismal standards of his church. He did, however, look to an even higher standard than the documents of his church.

Whitefield relied upon Scripture to respond to ministerial questions which were unclear from the documents of his church. Whitefield discussed baptismal regeneration with Dr. Cutler but turned the topic to being born again. Whitefield captured the conversation:

> [Whitefield said] "That if every child was really born again in baptism, then every baptised infant would be saved." "And so they are," said Dr. Cutler. "How do you prove that?" "Because the Rubric says, 'that all infants dying after baptism before they have committed actual sin, are undoubtedly saved.'" I asked, "What text of Scripture

(Eugene, OR: Pickwick Publications, 2018), 66–67.

3. Whitefield, *The Works of the Reverend George Whitefield*, 5:131.

4. Loane, "Wesley, Whitefield, and the Church of England," 70.

5. Whitefield, *First Journal: A Voyage from London to Savannah in Georgia*, 50.

6. Church of England, *Book of Common Prayer, 1662 Edition*, 326.

7. Whitefield, *The Works of the Reverend George Whitefield*, 4:356.

there was to prove it?" "Here" said he, (holding a Prayer Book in his hand) "the Church says so." We then just hinted at predestination.[8]

In this instance, Whitefield had every opportunity to reject baptismal regeneration outright—but he doesn't. Whitefield's discussion, and the context surrounding it, exudes caution and doubt but not rejection of the claims of Dr. Cutler regarding the salvific promise of baptismal regeneration. Rather than rejecting the rubric, Whitefield anchors the discussion in Scripture.

Whitefield, again, neither rejected nor verbatim affirmed regeneration in baptism in the painful experience of the death of his four-month-old son. Instead, Whitefield looked to Scripture. Though Whitefield baptized his son a week after his birth, Whitefield's journal entry shows that his consolation was not in the confidence of his son's baptism but in a passage from 2 Kings 4. Whitefield wrote: "I was comforted from that passage in the book of Kings, where is recorded the death of the Shunamite's child, which the Prophet said, 'The LORD had hid from him;' and the woman's answer likewise to the Prophet when he asked, 'Is it well with thee? Is it well with thy husband? Is it well with thy child?' And she answered, 'It is well.' This gave me no small satisfaction."[9] Again, when given a gut-wrenching, yet clear, opportunity to put his confidence in the salvific promise of baptismal regeneration, he does not; instead he looked to Scripture. At the same time, it is critical to observe that Whitefield did not use this opportunity to deny baptismal regeneration.

Whitefield's approach to neither explicitly affirm nor deny baptismal regeneration leaves his interpreters with a difficult task. On one hand, one can see why scholars such as Haykin might claim Whitefield was "ardent and plain" in his rejection of baptismal regeneration.[10] On the other hand, Whitefield never plainly denied baptismal regeneration; in fact he relied

8. Whitefield, *Seventh Journal: From a Few Days after His Return to Georgia to His Arrival at Falmouth*, 25.

9. Whitefield, *The Works of the Reverend George Whitefield*, 2:52.

10. Michael A. G. Haykin, *The Revived Puritan: The Spirituality of George Whitefield* (Dundas, Ontario: Joshua Press, 2000), 45. See also McKnight, though McKnight shows an awareness of further nuance in Whitefield's baptismal theology; Tim McKnight, *No Better Gospel: George Whitefield's Theology and Methodology of Evangelism* (Timmonsville, SC: Seed Publishing Group, 2017), 104, 240–41, 241n328.

upon it (as shown above and will be continued below). It is not surprising that later paedobaptistic evangelicals debated this issue at length,[11] and that Bebbington highlights this exact issue in his discussion of conversionism among evangelicals.[12] In the case of Whitefield, his discussions of baptismal regeneration and regeneration are less clear than they could be because he does not explicitly delineate what others had done, but what he intonated in other ways: Whitefield believed in two types of regeneration.

1.2. ANGLICAN DELINEATION OF TWO TYPES OF REGENERATION

Some readers might be surprised or dismayed in the discussion of two types of regeneration. The Anglican delineation of two types of regeneration is unlikely to quell the quarrels of the credobaptistic-paedobaptistic debates. Theologians in the Anglican church, however, used this distinction as a way forward to remain aligned to their formative documents and practices.

In the wake of the eighteenth-century evangelical revivals and their insistence on the new birth, the nineteenth-century scholar William Goode determined that the leading theologians and voices in the Church of England prior to the revivals did not hold to fully-effectual baptismal regeneration for infants. The conclusion of his 181-page analysis (in the midst of his 571 page tome on the topic) of over 40 "leading Reformers and Divines" from 1553 to 1626 including (given in the order discussed by Goode) Cranmer (d. 1555), Ridley (d. 1555), Latimer (d. 1555), Hooper (d. 1554), Coverdale (d. 1553), Davenant (d. 1641), Lancelot Andrews (d. 1626), Ussher (d. 1656), and Richard Hooker (d. 1600),[13] concludes: "There is not one of them that holds that spiritual regeneration, is in all cases, conferred upon infants at baptism. And almost all of them take what is called the 'Calvinistic' view, and make the gift of such regeneration to depend altogether upon God's free mercy."[14] Thus, Whitefield entered a church which

---

11. For example, see the case of George Gorham concluded in 1848. Boultbee, *A Commentary on the Thirty-Nine Articles*, 235; Gatiss, "The Anglican Doctrine of Baptism," 83.

12. Bebbington, *Evangelicalism in Modern Britain*, 9–10.

13. Hooker wrote, "All receive not the grace of God which receive the sacraments of His grace"; Richard Hooker, *The Works of Mr. Richard Hooker in Eight Books of Ecclesiastical Polity* (London: Thomas Newcomb, 1666), 223.

14. William Goode, *The Doctrine of the Church of England as to the Effects of Baptism in the Case of Infants* (London: J. Hatchard and Son, 1850), 387.

held to infant baptism, and a declaration of regeneration in the infant baptismal service, but that also did not understand the minister's declaration of the child being "regenerated" to be universally and fully effectual. Put differently, whatever baptismal regeneration meant to the Church of England, it did not mean the same thing as, what Goode calls, "spiritual regeneration." Goode parses the Church of England's understanding of what actually happens in the infant baptismal service, what is described as baptismal regeneration, by distinguishing two kinds of regeneration.

Challenges arise in terminology since the terms baptismal regeneration and spiritual regeneration (per Goode) beg the question: Which instance is when regeneration actually happens? To navigate this challenge Goode notes that some confined the term "regeneration" as that which happens only at baptism and that a later "spiritual regeneration" should be labeled "renovation" or "conversion."[15] Others argued that Scripture describes regeneration (and the new birth) "as something which has a transforming effect upon the heart and conduct, and therefore [regeneration] must include renovation."[16] Goode even gives an instance where a theological companion book replaced the word "regeneration" with the word "renovation" without notice.[17] Goode closes his discussion of infant baptism and baptismal regeneration unhelpfully by concluding: "I leave the reader to determine the true doctrine of the Church of England on this important subject."[18] While Goode allowed the reader to make his or her own determinations, two extremes were ruled out by the Church of England.

---

15. Goode, *The Doctrine of the Church of England as to the Effects of Baptism in the Case of Infants*, 524–25; see also Boultbee, *A Commentary on the Thirty-Nine Articles*, 235–48.

16. Goode, *The Doctrine of the Church of England as to the Effects of Baptism in the Case of Infants*, 527. Thomas also comments on the twofold terminology of regeneration: "Baptismal Regeneration is twofold. Regeneration is birth into the visible Church; conversion is birth into the Church invisible ... so that Baptism is the introduction of the recipient, whether adult or child, into a new condition or relation. It must not be overlooked that since the Puritan age Regeneration has come to mean renovation or conversion. But this was not the meaning of the Reformers, nor has the idea been changed in the Prayer Book." Thomas then goes on to discuss the "visible" and "invisible" Israel and church viz. circumcision and baptism. W. H. Griffith Thomas, *The Principles of Theology: An Introduction to the Thirty-Nine Articles* (Eugene, OR: Wipf & Stock, 2005), 385.

17. Goode, *The Doctrine of the Church of England as to the Effects of Baptism in the Case of Infants*, 527.

18. Goode, *The Doctrine of the Church of England as to the Effects of Baptism in the Case of Infants*, 528.

The Church of England eliminated two extremes in regard to baptismal regeneration.[19] On one end, the church ruled out the Roman Catholic view of baptismal regeneration of *ex opere operato*.[20] On the other end the church rejected a Zwinglian view of baptism in which the baptism is a mere sign or badge with no promise attached to the baptism itself. Within these bounds several options exist, and all require careful terminology and descriptions of what happens in the infant baptismal service and what is required subsequent to the service. Whitefield ministered in an era which had in many cases eased toward a nearly Roman Catholic view of baptism. Whitefield navigated these challenges by distinguishing between baptism in the *name* of the Spirit with baptism in the *nature* of the Spirit.

1.3. BAPTISMAL REGENERATION: WATER
BAPTISM IN THE NAME OF THE SPIRIT

As mentioned above, there are some whose reading of Whitefield might conclude, as Sherriff does, that Whitefield "speaks as if the rite matters not at all, as if the sacrament was entirely inefficacious."[21] If this is the case, why would Whitefield bother with his continued practice of infant baptism, including the baptism of his own son? We can see from Whitefield's corpus that he believed baptismal service, while not imparting spiritual baptism as described in the next section, should be retained for two reasons: it is an office of Christ and it imparts preparatory grace.

Whitefield believed that infant baptism is an ordinance of Christ. Whitefield preached: "I think infant-baptism is an ordinance of Christ, because if our children are not to be baptized, they are left inferior in their privileges to the Jews, their children were circumcised to God, and they should not our children be as soon initiated into Christ as they?"[22]

---

19. Boultbee, *A Commentary on the Thirty-Nine Articles*, 227–29.

20. Gatiss writes that Anglican teaching "is certainly not saying that everyone who is baptised is a true believer or that they are going to heaven as a result of their baptism! The formularies are everywhere opposed to such *ex opere operato* theologising." Gatiss, "The Anglican Doctrine of Baptism," 75. J. C. Ryle wrote: "To maintain that every child who is baptized with water is at once regenerated and born again, appears to turn the sacrament of baptism into a mere form, and to contradict both Scripture and the Thirty-Nine Articles." J. C. Ryle, *The Upper Room* (Edinburgh: Banner of Truth Trust, 1990), 354.

21. Collin Bedford Sherriff, "The Theology of George Whitefield (1714–1770)" (PhD diss., University of Edinburgh, 1950), 170.

22. Whitefield, *Eighteen Sermons*, 300–301.

Similarly, Whitefield again affirmed that baptism is an ordinance of Christ and should be maintained, even if it does not impart complete confidence in salvation. Whitefield wrote:

> I remember when I began to speak against baptismal regeneration in my first sermon, printed when I was about twenty-two years old, or a little more; the first quarrel many had with me was, because I did not say that all people who were baptized were born again. ... I do believe baptism to be an ordinance of Christ, but at the same time, no candid person can be angry for my asserting, that there are numbers that have been baptized when grown up, or when very young, that are not regenerated by God's Spirit.[23]

This sermon, which he preached late in his life, showed that Whitefield indeed spoke against baptismal regeneration but only in order to mean that baptismal regeneration was not synonymous with being "born again" or "regenerated by God's Spirit." Baptismal regeneration, while an ordinance of Christ, did not make a person born again or regenerated by God's Spirit; instead, Whitefield taught that the concept of baptismal regeneration brought preparatory grace.

Whitefield described to the Bishop of Litchfield and Coventry the nature of the regeneration which took place at baptism: "What a miserable condition then are those in, who have only those [sic] baptismal regeneration to depend on? For who is there that has improved, nay who is there that has not sinned away this preparatory grace?"[24] Preparatory grace implied preparation for something. In Whitefield's theology, the benefits of infant baptism prepared the adult for the grace of the reception of the inward baptism of the Holy Spirit by being born again through conversion. These preparatory benefits include access to the Lord's Supper, the nurture of the church's teaching and community, and a visible sign of covenant membership in the church community (vis-à-vis circumcision).[25]

---

23. Whitefield, *Eighteen Sermons*, 350–51.

24. Whitefield, *The Works of the Reverend George Whitefield*, 4:190.

25. Gatiss writes "Most evangelical Anglicans have taken the hypothetical conditional view of baptismal efficacy. Others have held to the view that as well as signifying these conditional blessings, baptism truly does admit a child into the privileges of the church in a covenant relationship to God, and that this is such a great and distinctive blessing as to

While Whitefield believed that baptismal regeneration should be held because it is an ordinance of Christ and it brought preparatory grace, he also used the theological logic of baptismal regeneration within the baptismal right to support his understanding of instantaneous conversion. Whitefield believed that the instantaneous nature of regeneration in baptism logically supported the instantaneous nature of conversion.[26] Whitefield leveraged regeneration found in the baptismal rites as a part of his theology of conversion; he substantiated the instantaneousness of conversion based upon the instantaneousness of regeneration in the baptismal rite. The instantaneousness of regeneration in the baptismal rite is evident from the grammar used in the rite. Prior to the actual act of baptism with water in the rite, regeneration is spoken of in a future tense (that is, "that he ... may receive remission ... by spiritual regeneration");[27] while, after the act of baptism with water, regeneration is spoken of in a past tense (that is, "see now ... that this Child is regenerate"),[28] thus, meaning that regeneration happened suddenly and instantaneously in the baptism. The language of the *Book of Common Prayer* made it clear, therefore, that regeneration occurs instantaneously and in a sudden moment.[29] Whitefield leveraged the instantaneousness of regeneration to substantiate his claim that

---

deserve the name regeneration. Yet regeneration is not by them understood as conversion, or the spiritual transformation of the soul." Gatiss, "The Anglican Doctrine of Baptism," 84.

26. Jeffery Chamberlin summarized that "the dispute over the mode of regeneration and moment of conversion is pivotal. ... The nature of regeneration and conversion, then, was more of an issue between the Anglicans and Methodists than whether salvation is by grace or by works. Neither side actually espoused works for salvation, but the Methodists often considered the Anglicans to be moralists because they did not call for an experiential moment of faith in conversion." Chamberlain, "Moralism, Justification, and the Controversy over Methodism," 677–78.

27. Church of England, *Book of Common Prayer, 1662 Edition*, 264–65.

28. Church of England, *Book of Common Prayer, 1662 Edition*, 269–70.

29. The clear present tense used in the rite appears to trump Chamberlain's observation that for Anglicanism, "regeneration, for the Anglicans, was not necessarily sudden. It was a growing process, not like the instantaneous conversion preached by Wesley and Whitefield. A metaphor frequently used was the recovery of a sick person: the patient did not recuperate overnight; he needed a long period of convalescence during which he gradually grew strong again. In like manner the Christian, who languished with the disease of sin, grew gradually in the state of grace after he was regenerated in baptism. As long as progress is being made, he can be confident that regeneration has occurred (or is occurring) and that redemption will be complete at the end of his life." While Chamberlain's observation may be true regarding the theology of Anglicans in the era of Whitefield, Chamberlain does not engage with the plain reading of the *Book of Common Prayer* itself. Chamberlain, "Moralism, Justification, and the Controversy over Methodism," 677.

conversion can be instantaneous. In a *Letter to the Bishop of London* where Whitefield was replying to a previous letter from the Bishop concerning conversion, Whitefield argued:

> Does not the author himself [the Bishop of London], if he holds baptismal regeneration, found his comfort on the doctrine of a sudden and instantaneous change? And do not the greatest part of the poor souls now in England, go on secure that they shall be eternally happy, and yet have no better foundation of comfort, and assurance of a gospel new-birth, than that which is founded on the doctrine of a sudden and instantaneous change wrought upon them in baptism?[30]

Whitefield showed from Anglican baptismal theology that since regeneration is instantaneous, conversion can be also. Whitefield affirmed the import and benefit of instantaneous regeneration to support the veracity of instantaneous conversion, but, he also argued that mere reliance on the memory of regeneration from baptism falls short of the aims of instantaneous conversion. Whitefield asked: "How can it be proved that they reckon them real converts, till they see them bring forth the fruits of the Spirit, in doing justly, loving mercy, and walking humbly with their GOD?"[31] Whitefield's question is meant to show that while God works instantaneously to regenerate and convert, it is what these actions import that actually matters: a changed life (consistent with the trajectory of the *telos* of inaugurated teleology).

1.4. INWARD-ACTUAL REGENERATION: BAPTISM IN THE NATURE OF THE SPIRIT

A careful examination of the infant baptismal rite shows the responsibility of what the infant, when grown, must do: "This infant must also faithfully ... [when] he come of age to take it upon himself ... will renounce the devil ... constantly believe God's holy Word, and obediently keep his commandments."[32] The benefits of baptism are, thus, contingent in adulthood

---

30. *Letter to the Bishop of London*, August 25, 1744, in Whitefield, *The Works of the Reverend George Whitefield*, 4:162.

31. *Letter to the Bishop of London*, August 25, 1744, in Whitefield, *The Works of the Reverend George Whitefield*, 4:162.

32. Church of England, *Book of Common Prayer, 1662 Edition*, 267.

upon obedience, belief, and renunciation of the devil. For Whitefield, this meant that the benefits of baptism could be lost through sinful choices. Whitefield said that those who "wilfully and daringly live as without God" have "renounced [their] baptism."[33] In one of Whitefield's last sermons before his death, *All Men's Place*, he echoed this thought. Whitefield preached: "I believe that a person who gives no evidence of being a saint, from the time of his baptism to the time perhaps of his death, that never fights against the world, the flesh, and the devil, and never minds one word of what his god-fathers and god-mothers promised for him, can I believe that person is a real Christian? No."[34]

Whitefield's view of preparatory grace, as described in the preceding section, prepared a person to receive the inward baptism of the Holy Spirt which came through conversion and by which the person was saved. Whitefield spoke of baptism in the *name* of the Father, Son, and Holy Spirt which prepared one for baptism in the *nature* of the Father, Son, and the Holy Spirt through the inward baptism of the Holy Spirit.

To be baptized in the name of the Father, Son, and the Holy Spirit meant to be only baptized in an outward sense, a sense that was not necessarily salvific. To be baptized in the nature of the Father, Son, and the Holy Spirit meant to be baptized inwardly, in which a genuine change had occurred through conversion. In Whitefield's sermon, *Dying Saints Triumph*, he preached: "We are not only to be baptized in the name of the Father, Son, and Holy Ghost, but we are to be baptized into the nature of the Father, Son, and Holy Ghost, this is the baptism of the Spirit, and this is that salvation which God grant we may all partake of."[35] Whitefield detailed how the difference between name and nature can be confused. A name is a label, a sign, or thing it is related to; it is not the substance of the thing it describes. The nature, however, is the substance of the thing itself. In the sermon *The Indwelling of the Spirit*, Whitefield preached: "Though we translate the words, 'baptizing them in the *name*' yet, as the name of GOD, in the LORD's prayer, and several other places, signifies his nature, they might as well be translated thus, 'baptizing them into the *nature* of the

33. Whitefield, *The Works of the Reverend George Whitefield*, 6:285.

34. Whitefield, *Eighteen Sermons Preached by the Late Rev. George Whitefield*, 350–51.

35. Whitefield, *Eighteen Sermons Preached by the Late Rev. George Whitefield*, 99.

Father, into the *nature* of the Son, and into the *nature* of the Holy Ghost.' "[36]
What is at stake is more than a technicality in wording. What is at stake
is actually having the indwelling presence of God as opposed to the mere
claim of having God's indwelling presence. Whitefield called the difference between having the indwelling Spirit and not having the indwelling
Spirit the basis for salvation. Whitefield wrote: "Consequently, if we are
all to be baptized into the nature of the Holy Ghost, before our baptism
be effectual to salvation, it is evident, that we all must actually receive
the Holy Ghost, and ere we can say, we truly believe JESUS CHRIST. For no
one can say, that JESUS is my LORD, but he that has thus received the Holy
Ghost."[37] The preparatory grace given through baptismal regeneration, in
Whitefield's analysis, was realized through the filling of the Holy Spirit in
a believer through conversion.[38]

For Whitefield, if people had been baptized, young or old, and had none
of the fruit of the Spirit in their life, then they may not have the Spirit of
God in them and thus not be converted. In the sermon, *Repentance and
Conversion*, Whitefield preached: "For to be baptized when young, or as
some to come out of the water at age, and turn out as bad as ever, is a plain
proof of the necessity of being baptized by the Holy Ghost."[39] Effectively,
in Whitefield's theology, a second experience was needed for those who
had been baptized, which was a personal experience through conversion of being indwelt by the Holy Spirit. The need for a personal experience with the Holy Spirit was echoed in the sermon, *Spiritual Baptism*, in
which Whitefield argued: "So it may be said of outward baptism, he is not a
Christian who is baptized only outwardly, but he that is baptized inwardly
of the Spirit."[40] For Whitefield, the Holy Spirit must be *in* the Christian,

---

36. Whitefield, *The Works of the Reverend George Whitefield*, 6:93–94.

37. Whitefield, *The Works of the Reverend George Whitefield*, 6:94.

38. Kidd writes: "Whitefield strictly differentiated between infant baptism with water
and subsequent baptism with the Holy Spirit that accompanied salvation." Kidd, *George
Whitefield*, 64.

39. Whitefield, *Eighteen Sermons*, 120.

40. Whitefield, *Eighteen Sermons*, 301. See also Whitefield, *The Works of the Reverend George
Whitefield*, 6:162.

evidenced by personal experience and spiritual growth for one to know that he or she was converted and born again.[41]

Whitefield understood the preparatory grace of baptism to be realized when one performed the *act* of her baptismal covenant; a person performed her baptismal covenant when she converted and lived a godly life.[42] In other words, baptismal regeneration provided the grace which prepared the way for a person to turn again to God: to be converted.[43] Whitefield wrote in his sermon, *Persecution Every Christian's Lot*: "Unless we are thus converted, and transformed by the renewing of our minds, we cannot properly be said to be in CHRIST, much less to live godly in him. To be in CHRIST merely by baptism, and an outward profession is not to be in Him in the strict sense of the word."[44] Whitefield, thus, taught that conversion was the means (the act) by which people became Christians through the preparatory grace of

---

41. A related topic in this discussion is the rite of confirmation. While the *Book of Common Prayer* has clear instructions for the rite of confirmation, in the eighteenth century this rite received little attention and was virtually ignored. It is not clear that either of the Wesleys or Whitefield were ever confirmed, though being the sons of a minister we should assume the Wesleys were confirmed. Cornwall stated: "Evangelicals placed greater emphasis on the act of conversion rather than on rites of initiation." Critical to this discussion is the focus which the Holy Spirit receives in confirmation. With confirmation being overlooked it is not surprising that Whitefield, and others, emphasized the personal experience of the Holy Spirit in conversion and the new birth. See Church of England, *Book of Common Prayer, 1662 Edition*, 297–300; Robert Cornwall, "The Rite of Configuration in Anglican Thought during the Eighteenth Century," Church History 68, no. 2 (June 1999): 359, 368–69; John Douglas Close Fisher, *Christian Initiation: Confirmation Then and Now* (Chicago: Hillenbrand Books, 2005), 137–52; Maxwell E. Johnson, *The Rites of Christian Initiation: Their Evolution and Interpretation* (Collegeville, MN: Liturgical Press, 2007), 353–81.

42. For a similar discussion attempting to reconcile baptismal regeneration with conversion in Wesleyan spirituality, see Campbell, "Conversion and Baptism in Wesleyan Spirituality," 160–74.

43. Whitefield held to infant baptism throughout his ministry and never supported rebaptism. A minister named Rev. James Reed recalled that in 1764 Whitefield "condemned the rebaptizing of Adults & the doctrine of the irresistible influence of the spirit, for both of which, the late Methodists in these parts had strongly contended & likewise recommended infant Baptism, & declared himself a member & minister of the Church of England." Bill Hand, "The Return of George Whitefield," New Bern Sun Journal, April 28, 2013, accessed May 3, 2016, www.newbernsj.com/20130428/bill-hand-the-return-of-george-whitefield/304289940. Mr. Hand's contribution was located by Kidd who contacted and confirmed the historical details. See Kidd, *George Whitefield*, 238, 304n38.

44. Whitefield, *The Works of the Reverend George Whitefield*, 6:347. Whitefield made a similar comment in his sermon, *Worldly Business No Plea for the Neglect of Religion*: "We are all under the necessity of performing our baptismal covenant, and perfecting holiness in the fear of GOD: for the holy scriptures point out to us but one way of admission into the kingdom of CHRIST, through the narrow gate of a found conversion." It is noticeable that Whitefield said that "all" need to perform this covenant; this was a reminder that his audience must have

God given to them in their baptism. As an example of the need for conversion after baptism, Whitefield did not exclude himself from his requirement to perform his baptismal covenant through conversion and holiness. Whitefield recounted on Christmas day of 1738 in his *Third Journal*: "This day 24 years ago was I baptised. Lord! to what little purpose have I lived? However, I sealed my baptismal covenant with my dear Saviour's most blessed Body and Blood, and trust in His strength I shall keep and perform it. Amen, Amen."[45] Whitefield had sealed his baptismal covenant through his instantaneous conversion and continued conversion via manifesting good works through sanctification.[46] Baptismal regeneration brought the opportunity through preparatory grace to respond in faith, be converted, and move beyond being baptized merely in the name of the Father, Son, and the Holy Spirit to, instead, be baptized in the nature of the Father, Son, and the Holy Spirit.

While it has been necessary to analyze Whitefield's understanding of baptismal regeneration as an attendant theme to his theology of conversion, and it has been shown that he held to baptismal regeneration as an ordinance of Christ and as preparatory grace which was not necessarily salvific, we must remember that Whitefield was concerned with the *telos* of the Christian life over its *arché*. When confronted with debates over baptism, Whitefield redirected the focus from the imports of baptism to the outcome and fruit of baptism. Whitefield encouraged a reader to be "kept free, and not fall into disputing about Baptism or other non-essentials."[47] Instead, Whitefield urged: "When we come together, talk of the heart, and enquire whether, when we received the outward sign by sprinkling or dipping, we really received the thing signified in our hearts, and exemplify that thing signified in our lives."[48] Similarly, he wrote: "This is religion

---

been virtually unanimously baptized and many were still in need of conversion and holiness. Whitefield, *The Works of the Reverend George Whitefield*, 5:301.

45. Whitefield, *Third Journal: His Arrival at London to His Departure from Thence on His Way to Georgia*, 3.

46. Unfortunately, Whitefield's nuanced view of baptism, regeneration, and conversion is lost when historians and theologians use the terms regeneration and conversion synonymously. For two examples see Schwenk, *Catholic Spirit*, 35; Robert Elliot, "A Summary of Gospel Doctrine Taught by Mr. Whitefield," in *Select Sermons of George Whitefield*, ed. J. C. Ryle (Carlisle, PA: The Banner of Truth Trust, 1953), 53–54.

47. Whitefield, *The Works of the Reverend George Whitefield*, 1:394.

48. Whitefield, *Eighteen Sermons*, 299.

common to all, whether we are Baptist or Paedo-baptist; for we may call one another by this and that name, it is no matter what we are called, the grand matter is, what God looks upon us to be; whether we are become by baptism, and with the powerful operations of the Spirit of God accompanying that ordinance."[49] The best guide to Whitefield's attitude toward the intricacies of baptismal regeneration can be seen in his recommendation of the works of the credo-baptist John Bunyan. Whitefield wrote: "I must own, more particularly endears Mr. Bunyan to my heart; he was of a catholic spirit, the want of water adult baptism with this man of GOD, was no bar to outward christian communion. And I am persuaded, that if, like him, we were more deeply and experimentally baptized into the benign and gracious influences of the blessed Spirit, we should be less baptized into the waters of strife, about circumstantials and non-essentials."[50] Therefore, while we analyze Whitefield's theology of baptismal regeneration in our study of conversion, we must recognize that this analysis misses the aim and thrust of his ministry which pressed people to be "experimentally baptised" in the nature of the Holy Spirit through conversion.

This section contributes to synoptic statement of conversion (8). Baptism marks one's entrance to the church but it is not chronologically tied to conversion. A baptized person entered the church when they were baptized, but their conversion may come at a later date when they respond in faith, personally, to the vows made at their baptism. Having established Whitefield's understanding of conversion and baptism, a second theological and pastoral topic needs to be addressed and was frequently commented on by Whitefield: assurance of salvation.

2. CONVERSION AND ASSURANCE

Whitefield attended substantially to one soteriological trope which he directly related to ongoing conversion: assurance. At the outset of this discussion, it should be known that, for Whitefield, assurance was to have a "well-grounded hope,"[51] to know clearly "that his Maker is his husband,"[52]

49. Whitefield, *Eighteen Sermons*, 300.
50. Whitefield, *The Works of the Reverend George Whitefield*, 4:307.
51. Whitefield, *The Works of the Reverend George Whitefield*, 5:368.
52. Whitefield, *The Works of the Reverend George Whitefield*, 5:178.

and to know that "we are born again, that we are members of Christ, that we are united to him."[53] Conversely, Whitefield believed that assurance is the opposite of doubt; therefore assurance can be thought of as trust.[54] Whitefield spoke of having assurance of pardon,[55] finding rest,[56] hope,[57] the gospel new birth,[58] free salvation;[59] but, what Whitefield spoke most often of was assurance of faith.[60] Since the next section will show that Whitefield taught that faith was instrumental to instantaneous conversion, when Whitefield spoke of assurance he was, therefore, referencing the trust and knowledge that one's faith was genuine and salvific. Whitefield taught that it was possible to have assurance that one was truly and genuinely saved after his or her experience of instantaneous conversion—even when sinful choices after instantaneous conversion continued. Whitefield was equally insistent that a genuine convert would not be content with continued sinfulness but would instead work to make their calling and election sure.

In order to support the aforementioned claims, this section will first argue that Whitefield located assurance as a felt experience which he described as the witness of the Spirit. The divine origin of the experience of assurance aligned with Whitefield's doctrine of election since salvation has its origin in God's decrees and not in human merit; thus, assurance had to be a divinely given experience and not an experience based on human merit. Establishing the experiential nature of assurance enables this section to argue, second, that Whitefield taught that those who continue to sin after instantaneous conversion can still experience assurance since its origin is supernatural. Divinely given assurance of salvation was a comfort which Whitefield received immediately after his own instantaneous

53. Whitefield, *The Works of the Reverend George Whitefield*, 1:39.
54. Whitefield, *The Works of the Reverend George Whitefield*, 1:203.
55. Whitefield, *The Works of the Reverend George Whitefield*, 6:268.
56. Whitefield, *The Works of the Reverend George Whitefield*, 5:309.
57. Whitefield, *The Works of the Reverend George Whitefield*, 5:169.
58. Whitefield, *The Works of the Reverend George Whitefield*, 4:161, 162.
59. Whitefield, *The Works of the Reverend George Whitefield*, 4:117, 154.
60. Whitefield, *Sixth Journal: After His Arriving at Georgia, to a Few Days after His Second Return Hither from Philadelphia*, 20, 44; Whitefield, *Seventh Journal: From a Few Days after His Return to Georgia to His Arrival at Falmouth*, 78; Whitefield, *The Works of the Reverend George Whitefield*, 1:164, 203, 239, 243, 270, 277, 321, 360, 434, 2:246, 3:431, 4:64, 66, 179, 241, 5:178, 435, 6:148, 153, 214, 382.

conversion. However, and as a third claim of this section, Whitefield taught that assurance of salvation, while normative for genuine converts, was not experienced by all who had genuinely converted. This is a conclusion he reached based on his ongoing pastoral experience. In other words, assurance is not required to be a genuine convert (synoptic statement 9). Assurance, while not experienced by all true believers, was nonetheless available to all genuine believers because of the doctrine of election. He taught, as the fourth claim of this section, that assurance would not be possible without the doctrine of election because, without the doctrine of election, people would be required to base their assurance of salvation in their own evaluation of their own righteousness (and not in the righteousness of Christ). Whitefield's moderate Calvinism hypothetically assumed that all people were among the elect. In turn, the doctrine of election aided assurance of salvation rather than adding anxiety (whether one was among the elect, and thus saved). Whitefield rooted assurance doctrinally in election as a work of the Spirit while also maintaining that good works must follow instantaneous conversion in order to be deemed a genuine convert. Whitefield held these views in tension since his emphasis was on continued Christian growth. In order to support these four claims, this section turns to its first argument to establish the experiential nature of assurance.

2.1. ASSURANCE: A FELT EXPERIENCE

Assurance was an experiential feeling in Whitefield's understanding. It is important to understand that Whitefield understood assurance as a felt experience since feelings can come and go. For Whitefield, the variability that comes naturally through feelings and experiences needs to be articulated because, as a Calvinist who was convinced of God's eternal decree of election in which the economy of God's work of salvation does not vary, the experience, feeling, and confidence found in assurance often does vary. When people doubted their assurance (their assurance of salvation), this doubt brought the veracity of their conversion into question.

Whitefield taught that assurance was the feeling of the witness of the Spirit. Whitefield wrote that assurance "[comes] by receiving his blessed Spirit into our hearts, and feeling him witnessing with our spirits, that

we are the sons of GOD."[61] The witness of the Spirit was the absence of
doubt or fear that one was a child of God.[62] Thus, feelings of doubt and
fear were contrary to assurance, meaning that feelings of confidence and
trust in one's salvation were the witness of the Spirit and were indicative
of a person who had experienced instantaneous conversion and was continuing in their conversion.

The origin of the feeling of assurance, in Whitefield's theology, was
divine. Assurance came from the witness of the Spirit, not the witness of
humanity or physiology. While many feelings and emotions come naturally
through physiology, such as adrenaline and human impulse, Whitefield
taught that assurance was a feeling deposited by God in humans; this
feeling was supernatural, not natural. Whitefield wrote a letter to the
Reverend Bishop of Litchfield and Coventry on September 20, 1744, in
which Whitefield spoke of *supernatural assurance*:

> What signifies talking of his assistances, and at the same time
> declare, that they can neither be inwardly felt, or perceived, nor
> believers be *supernaturally* assured thereby of their salvation? Or
> if we are to expect no operations of the Spirit that are supernatu-
> ral, as his Lordship again and again intimates, what are the natu-
> ral operations that we are to look for? Or can there possibly be any
> operation of the Holy Spirit which is not supernatural?[63]

Whitefield made it clear that assurance was felt inwardly along with
salvation, as a supernatural occurrence, meaning that it was a work of
the Holy Spirit in the life of the believer. Later in this letter, Whitefield
grounded his argument in the *Book of Common Prayer's* Order for the
Visitation of the Sick, where the sick were assured of their comfort and
salvation.[64]

---

61. Whitefield, *The Works of the Reverend George Whitefield*, 5:368.

62. Whitefield, *The Works of the Reverend George Whitefield*, 4:63.

63. Whitefield, *The Works of the Reverend George Whitefield*, 4:187. Italics in the original.

64. See Whitefield, *The Works of the Reverend George Whitefield*, 190; Church of England, *Book of Common Prayer, 1662 Edition*, 312–25. Whitefield's *Fifth Journal* recorded a letter written to a young person regarding the young person's dying aunt. In this letter, Whitefield spoke of her "being filled with the full assurance of faith in Christ, and a joyful hope of eternal salvation through his merits and mediation." The letter went on to say that in the agonies of

The feeling of assurance was critical in Whitefield's arguments regarding election. In his debates with Wesley concerning election, Whitefield made the feeling of assurance an important consideration, as seen in his well-known August 9, 1740 letter to John Wesley in answer to Wesley's sermon *Free Grace*. Whitefield wrote:

> I believe your fighting so strenuously against the doctrine of election, and pleading so vehemently for a sinless perfection, are among the reasons or culpable causes, why you are kept out of the liberties of the gospel, and from that full assurance of faith which they enjoy, who have experimentally tasted, and daily feed upon GOD's electing, everlasting love.[65]

Simply stated, Whitefield believed in assurance for the present moment and grounded this belief in his affirmation of the doctrine of election, while Wesley believed in assurance for today and contingently upon continued faith for the future. While Whitefield and Wesley differed on the theological foundation for assurance, the reality was that Whitefield kept addressing the topic of assurance throughout his life because the feeling of assurance was difficult to maintain while experiencing continued sin after instantaneous conversion. It is now to this topic that we turn.

2.2. ASSURANCE AVAILABLE DESPITE CONTINUED SIN

The divine supernatural source of the feeling of assurance provided the basis for Whitefield's contention that assurance was available to genuine converts despite continued sin after instantaneous conversion. Following Whitefield's conversion a few weeks following Easter 1735, he began to describe for the first time his sense of assurance.[66] Whitefield recorded in his *Short Account*: "How assuredly have I felt that Christ dwelt in me, and I in Him! and how did I daily walk in the comforts of the Holy Ghost,

---

last hour, she cried out, "I see him! I see him! Now I see the light." Whitefield, *Fifth Journal: From His Embarking after the Embargo, to His Arrival at Savannah in Georgia*, 78–79.

65. Whitefield, *The Works of the Reverend George Whitefield*, 4:66–67.

66. Henry comments, that prior to Whitefield's conversion, "asceticism had not brought him the assurance that he sought." Henry views Whitefield's conversion as the beginning of his assurance. See Henry, *George Whitefield*, 23, 105.

and was edified and refreshed in the multitude of peace!"[67] Before his
conversion, Whitefield had little comfort, peace, or assurance. After his
conversion, even when Whitefield struggled at times with the guilt of his
past sins, he sensed assurance. In his *Fifth Journal* on September 22, 1739,
Whitefield wrote: "Underwent inexpressible agonies of soul for two or
three days, at the remembrance of my sins, and the bitter consequences
of them. All the while I was assured God had forgiven me; but I could not
forgive myself, for sinning against so much light and love."[68] Thus, even
when Whitefield had inner turmoil due to his sin, he maintained his sense
of assurance. He continued these sentiments a few months later in a letter
to a friend on November 10, 1739. Whitefield wrote: "As yet, blessed be God,
in my darkest hours my evidences have not been in the least clouded. I
have been assured my LORD hath forgiven all my iniquities, transgressions
and sins, but I cannot forgive myself."[69] The same theme continued in a
letter two years later, dated July 26, 1741. Whitefield recorded: "Dear Sir,
JESUS is a precious Master. He, as it were, dandles me upon his knees. He
carries me in his arms, he fights all my battles, and makes me more than
conqueror thro' his love. My work is great, but my supports are greater. He
assures me from day to day, that he will never leave me nor forsake me. My
infirmities often make me blush, and yet JESUS passes them all by."[70] The
assurance which Whitefield experienced was in the midst of his multiple
failures, sin, and guilt (past and present). Whitefield's theology of assurance was not based on successful Christian living. Following his conversion,
the assurance that Whitefield experienced was supernatural assurance.

In his sermons and letters, Whitefield was clear about *when* assurance
was made available to individuals; it came upon the moment of instantaneous conversion, not as a result of the absence of sin. As one experienced
instantaneous conversion, assurance of salvation became available. In his

67. Whitefield, *A Short Account*, 54–55.

68. Whitefield, *Fifth Journal: From His Embarking after the Embargo, to His Arrival at Savannah in Georgia*, 17.

69. Whitefield, *The Works of the Reverend George Whitefield*, 1:77.

70. Whitefield's quote brings to mind Wesley's last statement he made in his journal on May 24, 1738, his Aldersgate moment: "But then I was sometimes, if not often, conquered, now, I was always conqueror." Whitefield appears to share the same experience of assurance after his own conversion. See Wesley, *Journals and Diaries*, 18:250; Whitefield, *The Works of the Reverend George Whitefield*, 1:293.

1739 sermon, *What Think Ye of Christ*, Whitefield proclaimed: "All we have to do, is to lay hold on this righteousness by faith: and the very moment we do apprehend it by a lively faith, that very moment we may be assured, that the blood of JESUS CHRIST has cleansed us from all sin."[71] Conversely, Whitefield clarified that assurance was not available until one was born again.[72] Therefore, Whitefield taught that assurance was available for all those who truly believed and were converted, even when sin continued after instantaneous conversion.[73] While assurance was available for all who had experienced instantaneous conversion, Whitefield came to believe some genuine converts did not have the experience of assurance.

2.3. ASSURANCE NOT REQUIRED TO BE A GENUINE CONVERT

Although Whitefield taught that assurance was available to all Christians, he eventually observed that not everyone felt that they had assurance. Whitefield's mature belief was that assurance was not needed to be a Christian, but it was necessary for one's well-being. In other words, Whitefield taught that assurance of salvation is available but not required for a genuine convert (synoptic statement 9).

Whitefield believed early in his career that one must have a sense of assurance in order to be a true believer, but he made clear in a April 28, 1741 letter that he had changed his mind to believe that assurance was not required to be a genuine convert. Whitefield stated:

> As for assurance, I cannot but think, all who are truly converted must know that there was a time in which they closed with CHRIST: But then, as so many have died only with an humble hope, and have been even under doubts and fears, though they could not but be looked upon as christians; I am less positive than once I was, left haply I should condemn some of GOD's dear children.[74]

---

71. Whitefield, *The Works of the Reverend George Whitefield*, 5:361; see also 4:28.

72. Whitefield, *The Works of the Reverend George Whitefield*, 6:310.

73. Whitefield wrote explicitly about the nature of sin before and after (instantaneous) conversion being forgiven in relation to assurance: "I have seen him and Mr. J——, and hear that Mr. B—— died comfortably, being fully assured, 'That not only all his sins before, but after conversion were forgiven him.' " Whitefield, *The Works of the Reverend George Whitefield*, 2:354–55.

74. Whitefield, *The Works of the Reverend George Whitefield*, 1:260.

Whitefield's initial years as an ordained minister had given him enough experiences with people who were dying that his theology was tempered by his ministerial experiences. He encountered dying people who had doubts, fears, and only humble hope.[75] These pastoral experiences changed his theological assertion that people needed assurance in order to be considered genuinely saved.[76] In his *Fifth Journal*, Whitefield wrote: "It is a dreadful mistake to deny the doctrine of assurances ... though all are not to be condemned who have not an immediate assurance, yet all ought to labour after it."[77] Whitefield made it clear that assurance was available and should be sought, but assurance was not required in order to escape condemnation.

Assurance was an essential ingredient for Christian well-being according to Whitefield (even if it was not required for salvation). As shown above, Whitefield taught that the source of the feeling of assurance was divine and not human; but, he did not disregard the role of good works to compliment the feeling of assurance, and he taught that good works aided the well-being of a Christian. Whitefield wrote in his 1747 sermon, *Christ the Believer's Husband*: "I dare not affirm, that a full assurance of faith is absolutely necessary for the very being, yet I dare assert, that it is absolutely necessary, for the well being of a christian."[78] Assurance was available for the well-being of the Christian, but assurance was not a requirement *to be* a Christian.

Whitefield taught that assurance was not required upon conversion, but seeking assurance was sincerely urged by Whitefield for the well-being of a Christian, and was truly available—the believer simply needed to ask for assurance, press after it, and plead for it.[79] Whitefield urged his followers to seek assurance of salvation so much that he prayed for one person that

---

75. Whitefield, *The Works of the Reverend George Whitefield*, 1:260.

76. Whitefield, *The Works of the Reverend George Whitefield*, 1:260.

77. Whitefield, *Fifth Journal: From His Embarking after the Embargo, to His Arrival at Savannah in Georgia*, 68.

78. Whitefield, *The Works of the Reverend George Whitefield*, 5:179.

79. See Whitefield, *Fifth Journal: From His Embarking after the Embargo, to His Arrival at Savannah in Georgia*, 68; Whitefield, *Sixth Journal: After His Arriving at Georgia, to a Few Days after His Second Return Hither from Philadelphia*, 44; Whitefield, *The Works of the Reverend George Whitefield*, 2:246.

"God to give you no rest" until it came.[80] While assurance was not experienced by all those who were genuine converts, the experience of assurance was normative and to be sought by all those who had experienced conversion. Whitefield's doctrinal reason that assurance was available to all people was a consequence of his affirmation of the doctrine of election.

2.4. ASSURANCE WAS ROOTED IN ELECTION

Whitefield believed that the doctrine of election was required in order to maintain a defense of the experience of assurance for those who had converted. His doctrine of election taught that no one could know that he or she was not among the elect. In other words, everyone should assume that after instantaneous conversion they were among the elect; they did not need to speculate that they were among the reprobate (perhaps because of ongoing and continued sin). Whitefield did, however, maintain tension between the assurance of salvation that was rooted in the righteousness of Christ and the need for ongoing obedience in order to give evidence of the genuineness of their conversion. This tension was not resolved in Whitefield's theology. He maintained simultaneously that assurance was available to a Christian because of the merits of Christ while also maintaining that obedience was necessary to confirm one's faith. This tension contributes to the claim that conversion is best understood as inaugurated teleology, emphasizing initiation and continuance over the exact explanation of the hidden decrees of God.

Whitefield taught that without the doctrine of election, the experience of assurance was not possible. Since the experience of assurance was a divinely-given experience, the experience would be consistent with God's divine will, which included election in Whitefield's theology. The clearest example of assurance being rooted in election is in Whitefield's letter to Wesley regarding Wesley's sermon *Free Grace*. Whitefield wrote: "But, without the belief of the doctrine of election, and the immutability of the free love of GOD, I cannot see how it is possible that any should have a comfortable assurance of eternal salvation."[81] Whitefield asked repeatedly how people could truly have any peace of mind as Christians, knowing that

---

80. Whitefield, *The Works of the Reverend George Whitefield*, 1:321.
81. Whitefield, *The Works of the Reverend George Whitefield*, 4:64.

they would inevitably sin in the future, unless they based their salvation
on their election in God.[82] Whitefield argued that assurance needed to be
based in the doctrine of election. He supported his view by referencing
Article XVII, which states: "Election in Christ, is full of sweet, pleasant,
and unspeakable comfort to godly persons."[83] In a later letter to the Right
Reverend Bishop of London, Whitefield wrote against creating a foundation of comfort and assurance in any gradual improvement in grace and
goodness, but only in the "all sufficient righteousness of Jesus."[84] The doctrine of election, thus, based the experience of assurance of salvation on
the righteousness of Christ and not on the righteousness of a Christian.
Therefore, converts could be confident and assured of the genuineness
of their instantaneous conversion because of Christ's righteousness for
them personally due to their election by God. The topic of election, however, brought up another experiential issue: whether one could know if
he or she was among the elect.

   Whitefield's doctrine of election was couched in a pastoral theology
which hypothetically assumed that all people were among the elect, and,
thus, election did not threaten the possibility that assurance was available
to everyone who converted to Christ.[85] In other words, after the experience of instantaneous conversion, people did not need to ponder whether
they were among the reprobate. Anxiety over whether individuals were
among the elect caused people to question whether they could ever have
assurance of salvation.[86] Whitefield attempted to reverse this anxiety. In
Whitefield's response to Wesley's *Free Grace* sermon, Whitefield stated:
"None living, especially none who are desirous of salvation, can know that

---

82. Whitefield, *The Works of the Reverend George Whitefield*, 4:64–69.

83. See Whitefield, *The Works of the Reverend George Whitefield*, 4:62; Church of England, *Book of Common Prayer, 1662 Edition*, 618.

84. Whitefield, *The Works of the Reverend George Whitefield*, 4:162-63.

85. See chapter four, section 1.2. for more on Whitefield's moderate Calvinism and the place of hypothetical universal election in Anglican theology. See also Crisp, *Deviant Calvinism: Broadening Reformed Theology*, 175-212; Coppedge, *John Wesley in Theological Debate*, 39-40; Toon, *The Emergence of Hyper-Calvinism in English Nonconformity, 1689-1765*.

86. Wesley's *Free Grace* sermon raises this exact concern. Wesley wrote: "I appeal to any of you who hold [the doctrine of election], to say, between God and your own hearts, whether you have not often a return of doubts and fears concerning your election." Wesley, *Sermons*, 5:549-50.

they are not of the number of GOD's elect. None, but the unconverted, can have any just reason, so much as to fear it."[87]

In the course of all of Whitefield's personal reflection and public theology, there was no sense of him ever asking if he was one of the elect. Whitefield's starting place was that no one could *not* know they were not elect. In other words, everyone should assume that they were elect and then move on considering conversion from there. Whitefield taught that people should not even ponder if they were among the elect. If the *terrible decree* or reprobation was ever a deterrent of conversion (since people may become disillusioned thinking that they were not among the elect), Whitefield attempted to turn this worry on its head and, thus, neutralized potential anxiety from possible converts because assurance was available to all people who converted to Christ (because, in retrospect, those who experienced instantaneous conversion were proven to be among the elect).

Whitefield did not resolve an internal tension within his theology between assurance of salvation due to election and the need for ongoing obedience in order to give evidence of being a genuine convert. Election, available through the righteousness of Christ alone, was the true source of assurance for Whitefield; yet, this did not negate the need for continued evidence of conversion which was shown to be a primary motif of conversion for Whitefield in chapter four, section four. Whitefield explained that the natural outworking of election was that the elect person would work to make their election sure. A letter from March 1, 1751, exhorted a man: "The love of CHRIST therefore constrains me, dear Sir, to exhort you to make thorough work of it, and to give all diligence to make your calling and election sure. Now indeed is the accepted time!"[88] Whitefield simultaneously argued for the experience of full assurance of salvation based solely upon the righteousness of Christ applied to the elect while maintaining that true converts would produce evidence of their conversion. Whitefield's associate R. Elliot said that Whitefield believed "no one indeed can prove, or know his election, but by his conversion to God and obeying the gospel."[89] Therefore, only an obedient person who experienced

---

87. Whitefield, *The Works of the Reverend George Whitefield*, 4:62.

88. Whitefield, *The Works of the Reverend George Whitefield*, 2:402; see also 1:101.

89. Elliot, "A Summary of Gospel Doctrine Taught by Mr. Whitefield," 69.

conversion could know they were elect. Elliot commented further on his appraisal of Whitefield's theology: "They who do thus believe on the Son of God, turning to the Lord with their whole hearts, evidence thereby their election in Christ … they that willingly continue in sin and unbelief unto the last, do thereby prove themselves not to be of the number of God's elect, but of them whom he hath justly reprobated."[90] Ironically, Elliot's analysis sounded very Arminian in real-life application. Whether or not this was Whitefield's "Arminian accent" coming through is difficult to tell.[91] It is also possible that Elliot did not properly represent Whitefield on this matter. What is clearer is that, as shown earlier, Whitefield did not rest assurance of salvation on good works (past, present, or future), yet good works were expected of any true convert and one could ascertain their assurance and election based on their good works. It is a both-and conundrum to which Whitefield's theology lent itself. High Calvinists and hyper-Calvinists attempted to push the logic and consequences of this tension further, but Whitefield was not among their ilk.[92] Whitefield urged those who had experienced instantaneous conversion to put their assurance of salvation in Christ's righteousness (and not their own) while also telling them to work to give evidence of their conversion and election.

One of the reasons Whitefield could maintain tension between election and the necessity of ongoing good works after conversion was that Whitefield's theology of assurance placed less emphasis on the exact articulation of hidden decrees of God regarding salvation. Whitefield made predestination and election secondary to his call for conversion.[93] John Wesley and George Whitefield both taught that one must keep turning to Christ wholeheartedly since any true convert would respond to waywardness by an ongoing turning back to Christ. Whitefield's approach was similar to

---

90. Elliot, "A Summary of Gospel Doctrine Taught by Mr. Whitefield," 70.

91. Rack spoke of the "Arminian accent" as a phrase used to describe how Whitefield's stated Calvinism still had a strong free-will response appeal in nearly every sermon he preached. My thanks go to Joel Houston for highlighting this phrase for me. See Henry D. Rack, *Reasonable Enthusiast*, 3rd ed. (Peterborough, UK: Epworth Press, 2014), 201.

92. See the discussion of Whitefield's moderate Calvinism and other forms of Calvinism in chapter four, section 1.2.

93. Whitefield said: "Let a man go to the grammar school of faith and repentance, before he goes to the university of election and predestination." Whitefield, *Seventh Journal: From a Few Days after His Return to Georgia to His Arrival at Falmouth*, 66–67.

Calvin's suggestion to not push too far into things we simply cannot know.[94] Whitefield believed that conversion is best understood as inaugurated teleology, emphasizing initiation (instantaneous conversion) and continuance (ongoing conversion) over an explanation of the hidden decrees of God.

Whitefield's view of conversion and its relation to assurance of salvation is essential to the argument of the study that, for Whitefield, conversion is best understood in terms of inaugurated teleology in which not only the beginning of conversion receives attention (instantaneous conversion), but also the continuance of conversion in the life of the convert, because Whitefield recognized that assurance of salvation (and the vacillating sense of confidence of salvation many experience due to sin and doubt) is a common aspect of the experience of the ongoing nature of conversion. The topic of baptismal regeneration in the previous section brought to light a host of theological questions regarding soteriological loci related to conversion such as justification, the new birth, grace, faith, and repentance. The current section on assurance of salvation highlighted Whitefield's doctrine of election. Attention is given, therefore, in the next section to Whitefield's understanding of conversion and these topics in his *ordo salutis*.

3. CONVERSION AND THE ORDO SALUTIS

Whitefield's *ordo salutis* orients the place of conversion in his soteriology while cementing how he understood the arrangement of soteriological vocabulary such as grace, faith, repentance, justification, regeneration, and the new birth in relation to conversion. It should be noted that shortly after Whitefield's conversion, he adopted Calvinistic theology.[95] While some Calvinists hold all aspects of the *ordo salutis* very tightly, Whitefield's focus was on the experiential aspects which related to evangelism and Christian

---

94. Calvin warned: "For this debate about predestination is in some way obscure in itself and it is made dark and perplexing and even dangerous by human curiosity, because human understanding cannot rein itself in from great detours and elevating itself too high, desiring (if it were possible) to leave nothing secret to God which it does not seek out and examine minutely." John Calvin, *Institutes of the Christian Religion: 1541 French Edition*, trans. Elsie Anne McKee (Grand Rapids: Eerdmans, 2009), 414.

95. For one account of this transition see Mark K. Olson, "Whitefield's Early Theological Formation," in *George Whitefield: Life, Context, and Legacy*, ed. David Ceri Jones and Geordan Hammond (Oxford: Oxford University Press, 2016), 29–45.

growth. Whitefield held firmly to election, predestination, and final perseverance, but he did not attempt to speculate on the exact order of the hidden decrees of God.[96] In his *Free Grace* letter to Wesley, Whitefield wrote: "Though I would observe, that after all our reading on both sides the question, we shall never in this life be able to search out GOD's decrees to perfection. No, we must humbly adore what we cannot comprehend."[97] Thus, this section concentrates on the order of salvation which related directly to the experience of the believer since this was Whitefield's focus.[98] Specific attention will be given to that which preceded conversion: prevenient grace, faith, and repentance. Next, the section will explore Whitefield's understanding of regeneration, the new birth, and justification, each of which occur in the moment of instantaneous conversion and do not occur again. Last, it will be argued that Whitefield did not have a robust articulation of what happens after conversion in terms of an *ordo salutis*; instead, it will be shown that he simply expected Christian growth, or sanctification, to occur through the continued use of the means of grace such as ongoing repentance and faith which end in glorification as a reflection of the teleology of conversion. The analysis in this section will revisit four of the synoptic statements of conversion which were established in the previous chapter.

3.1. PRECEDING CONVERSION: PREVENIENT GRACE, FAITH, AND REPENTANCE

Prevenient grace, faith, and repentance precede instantaneous conversion in Whitefield's *ordo salutis*. To precede (for example, "preceding conversion") is being utilized in a particular way in this section; to precede, here, means initializing or being catalytic toward the experience of instantaneous conversion. In other words, Whitefield taught that when, by the

---

96. Late in his life Whitefield did note that he was not a supralapsarianist. Whitefield, *The Works of the Reverend George Whitefield*, 3:379.

97. Whitefield, *The Works of the Reverend George Whitefield*, 4:70.

98. Following the discussion in chapter four, section 1.2., Whitefield is best classified as a moderate Calvinist. Coppedge wrote: "[Moderate Calvinists] believed many Calvinists had gone beyond Scripture on positions like predestinated reprobation and supralapsarianism. ... Man's condemnation was due to his own disobedience and not to any eternal decree. ... This explains why many Moderate Calvinistic Evangelicals, whenever possible, avoided preaching on the doctrines of predestination, election, and final perseverance. They concentrated instead on justification by faith alone, holiness, and assurance." Coppedge, *John Wesley in Theological Debate*, 39–40.

prevenient grace of God, faith and repentance occurred, a person then experienced the moment of instantaneous conversion. Put another way: faith and repentance, by the prevenient grace of God, are the spark that comes immediately before the fire of instantaneous conversion.

3.1.1. Prevenient Grace (before conversion)

The moment of instantaneous conversion, in Whitefield's *ordo salutis*, was preceded by the work of God's prevenient (also called preventing) grace. Prevenient grace is the grace of God that goes before, or precedes, a work of grace. Prevenient grace is important to Whitefield's beliefs regarding instantaneous conversion because prevenient grace is the work of God that enables the sinful person to be able to respond to God and convert. Whitefield's theology of prevenient grace as the grace that enables sinful people to convert is supported by the teaching of the Church of England in Article X, *On Free Will*. This article states: "The condition of Man after the fall of Adam is such, that he cannot turn and prepare himself ... without the grace of God by Christ preventing us."[99] In other words, the preventing grace of God is the grace that enables a sinful person to "turn and prepare himself." It was shown in chapter four, section one that Whitefield defined conversion as a turn. Therefore, Whitefield's *ordo salutis* requires prevenient grace to precede and enable the instantaneous (turn of) conversion.

Whitefield spoke frequently in his journals, sermons, and letters of God's grace coming before (prevenient grace) and enabling people to convert.[100] Whitefield spoke specifically of "converting grace" and that St. Paul was "converted by the almighty power of efficacious grace."[101] Whitefield understood that all merit and all capacity to respond to God in any form was in response to God's grace.[102] For instance, in the sermon *The Pharisee and the Publican*, Whitefield wrote:

---

99. Church of England, *Book of Common Prayer, 1662 Edition*, 615.

100. Whitefield, *Sixth Journal: After His Arriving at Georgia, to a Few Days after His Second Return Hither from Philadelphia*, 18; Whitefield, *The Works of the Reverend George Whitefield*, 2:69, 3:229–30, 448, 4:221, 464–65, 5:180, 348, 6:107, 158, 338.

101. Whitefield, *The Works of the Reverend George Whitefield*, 3:229–30, 6:158.

102. J. I. Packer said that Whitefield presented his view of conversion in a "two-sided way, as Augustinians typically do." Packer stated that one side was the psychological and evangelistic way in which one realized his or her sin and need, followed by prayer and seeking God, which led to faith and repentance as a personal response. The other side was the

For whatever degrees of goodness there may be in us, more than in others, it is owing to GOD's restraining, preventing, and assisting grace. We are all equally conceived and born in sin; all are fallen short of the glory of GOD, and liable to all the curses and maledictions of the law; so that "he who glorieth, must glory only in the LORD." For none of us have any thing which we did not receive; and whatever we have received, we did not in the least merit it, nor could we lay the least claim to it on any account whatever: we are wholly indebted to free grace for all.[103]

Conversion is made possible only because of God's grace that comes before instantaneous conversion. For Whitefield, however, prevenient grace was not efficacious for every person to be converted; electing grace was available only for the elect.[104] Whitefield taught that the efficaciousness of prevenient grace to convert was only manifested for the elect. For example, Whitefield wrote in his sermon *The Conversion of Zaccheus*: "Praise, magnify, and adore sovereign, electing, free, preventing love; JESUS the everlasting GOD, the Prince of peace."[105] In Whitefield's Calvinism, the prevenient love by which Zaccheus was converted was available through God's election of Zaccheus.[106] Whitefield's moderate Calvinism, as discussed in chapter four, section 1.2., granted a hypothetical universal atonement, while holding to particular election. Therefore, Whitefield taught that prevenient grace was available to all people before instantaneous conversion but was only effective to bring instantaneous conversion to the elect

---

theological and doxological way he described as the "entire process as one which the Holy Spirit works from first to last, in which each of our steps Godward is taken only because the Holy Spirit is moving us forward by his secret ambition within us. God's irresistible prevenient grace (meaning, the Holy Spirit's work that dissolves resistance away) overcomes our natural inability, as slaves of sin, to turn ourselves to God: that is how we come to be born again and converted." J. I. Packer, "The Spirit with the Word: The Reformational Revivalism of George Whitefield," in *Honouring the People of God: The Collected Shorter Writings of J. I. Packer*, vol. 4 (Carlisle: Paternoster, 1999), 55.

103. Whitefield, *The Works of the Reverend George Whitefield*, 6:40–41. Whitefield published this sermon in 1740, which is after Whitefield embraced Calvinism. Whitefield did not shy away from the term "preventing" or "prevenient" grace as some Reformed people do today.

104. Coppedge, *John Wesley in Theological Debate*, 136.

105. Whitefield, *The Works of the Reverend George Whitefield*, 6:53.

106. When discussing Whitefield's sermon on "Zaccheus," the spelling of "Zaccheus" by Whitefield has been retained.

(synoptic statement 1: conversion is initiated and sustained by the grace of God). Now that it has been established that Whitefield taught that prevenient grace came before and enabled sinful people to convert to God, it will now be shown that faith also came prior to instantaneous conversion in Whitefield's *ordo salutis*.

3.1.2. Faith (before conversion)

Whitefield taught that faith preceded instantaneous conversion.[107] Faith, in Whitefield's teaching, went beyond (but also included) belief in rational or historical Christianity. Faith is a gift of God in which one puts one's trust in God that, by the merits of Christ, one's sins are forgiven. Whitefield argued that converting faith included, but went beyond, belief in the rational and historic teaching of Christianity. For instance, Whitefield argued for a difference between a "bare historical faith" and a "lively faith" in the resurrection, saying that only those who had a lively faith would enter heaven.[108] In other words, a person could believe in the factuality of the miraculous event of Jesus' resurrection, but lively faith (to be discussed in the next paragraph) was more than factual agreement with events—even miraculous events (such as the resurrection) that attested to Jesus' divine nature. Elsewhere, Whitefield called for his hearers to distinguish between "true and divine faith" from that which is "historical."[109] In a straightforward comment on the difference between faith that is converting and historical faith, Whitefield wrote: "It is not sufficient to have an historical faith of CHRIST, without being born again from above."[110] The type of faith that brought about conversion, he argued, was a faith that, as Whitefield stated, "must therefore import something more."[111] Something more than historical faith was required in order to bring about conversion; Whitefield called this converting faith.

---

107. Whitefield, *The Works of the Reverend George Whitefield*, 6:56, 191, 347, 422.
108. Whitefield, *The Works of the Reverend George Whitefield*, 6:324.
109. Whitefield, *The Works of the Reverend George Whitefield*, 4:188.
110. Whitefield, *The Works of the Reverend George Whitefield*, 4:355.
111. Whitefield, *The Works of the Reverend George Whitefield*, 6:417.

Converting faith, for Whitefield, was a gift of God, worked in the heart to draw one to God.[112] The substance of this gift is trust in God that, by the merits of Christ, sins are forgiven. Whitefield's conception of convert-ing faith was not new; in fact, Whitefield articulated what had already been stated in the *Edwardian Homily* on salvation.[113] Whitefield wrote: "[True faith] is a sure trust and confidence in GOD, that by the merits of CHRIST, his sins are forgiven, and he reconciled to the favour of GOD."[114] Converting faith, for Whitefield, is a gift of God that goes beyond mere rational agreement with the historical beliefs of Christianity (such as the resurrection), in which trust and confidence are put (via the prevenient grace of God) in the work of Christ for the forgiveness of sins in order to be saved in an instant (synoptic statement 5: conversion arrives by faith in an instant).[115] Instantaneous conversion was not only preceded by preve-nient grace and faith; Whitefield taught that repentance preceded instan-taneous conversion.

3.1.3. Repentance (before conversion)

Repentance precedes instantaneous conversion in Whitefield's *ordo salutis*, but specifically he insisted on evangelical repentance in which a person had a genuine abhorrence of their own sin and resolved, through Christ's power, to change their actions.[116] Whitefield spoke of "repentance unto life" to describe the instrumental nature of repentance that brought eternal life via instantaneous conversion.[117] Whitefield's clearest articulation on

---

112. Whitefield, *The Works of the Reverend George Whitefield*, 4:16, 6:123. Schwenk argues that Whitefield believed that "God justifies in response to the believer's faith," but that "even the faith to believe is a gift of God." This statement melds with the understanding of preve-nient grace previously discussed in this section. Schwenk, *Catholic Spirit*, 33.

113. Church of England, *The Two Books of Homilies*, 34.

114. Whitefield, *The Works of the Reverend George Whitefield*, 4:241.

115. Whitefield implored his mother to convert to God by faith in a letter written on November 16, 1739: "Oh my honoured mother, my soul is in distress for you: Flee, flee I beseech you to JESUS CHRIST by faith. Lay hold on Him, and do not let Him go. GOD hath given you convictions. Arise, arise, and never rest till they end in a sound conversion." Whitefield, *The Works of the Reverend George Whitefield*, 1:122.

116. Whitefield understood repentance as a rudimentary concept. In his *Seventh Journal* Whitefield wrote: "Let a man go to the grammar school of faith and repentance, before he goes to the university of election and predestination." Whitefield, *Seventh Journal: From a Few Days after His Return to Georgia to His Arrival at Falmouth*, 66–67.

117. Whitefield, *The Works of the Reverend George Whitefield*, 1:283, 4:401, 6:158.

the topic of repentance, in the sermon *A Penitent Heart, the Best New Year's Gift*, dedicated nearly a quarter of the sermon to the topic "why repentance is necessary to salvation."[118] His pivotal point is that a person cannot love sin and love God at the same time; repentance is needed to orient oneself toward God in order to receive salvation.

Whitefield believed that a pre-converted person needed to repent,[119] but Whitefield distinguished between legal and saving repentance.[120] His clearest delineation between legal and saving repentance is found in the sermon *The True Way of Beholding the Lamb*. He preached:

> Through want of a due consideration of [sorrow for sin and the fear of hell], it is to be feared, many seeming converts have taken up with a few legal convictions, which never ended in savingly and truly beholding the LAMB of GOD. May none here present, by a half-way repentance, and hypocritical sorrow for sin, add to the unhappy number![121]

Whitefield agreed that sorrow for sin and fear of hell have a proper place in establishing the legal basis for repentance (that is, the rational recognition of the consequences of sin), but that evangelical repentance was needed in order to convert. Evangelical repentance, in Whitefield's theology, was not only the resolve to stop sinning but to do so through Christ's power. He wrote that repentance was "an abhorrence of all evil, and a forsaking of it,"[122] and "sorrow, hatred, and an entire forsaking of sin."[123] True evangelical repentance leads a person to, in Whitefield's words, "renounce, forsake, and abhor thy old sinful course of life, and serve GOD in holiness and righteousness all this remaining part of life."[124] Resolving to renounce sin and serve God was not complete evangelical repentance, Whitefield

---

118. Whitefield, *The Works of the Reverend George Whitefield*, 6:9-10.

119. Whitefield, *The Works of the Reverend George Whitefield*, 5:371.

120. While hyper-Calvinists used the distinction between legal and saving (or, "evangelical") repentance to distinguish repentance among the reprobate and the elect, Whitefield never made this distinction. Toon, *The Emergence of Hyper-Calvinism in English Nonconformity, 1689-1765*, 132–33.

121. Whitefield, *The Works of the Reverend George Whitefield*, 6:418; see also 5:381, 6:36, 192.

122. Whitefield, *The Works of the Reverend George Whitefield*, 6:5.

123. Whitefield, *The Works of the Reverend George Whitefield*, 6:5.

124. Whitefield, *The Works of the Reverend George Whitefield*, 6:7.

added: "Resolve, through grace, to do this, and your repentance is half done; but then take care that you do not ground your resolutions on your own strength, but in the strength of the LORD JESUS CHRIST."[125] Whitefield's understanding of evangelical repentance combined, first, the recognition and abhorrence of sin; second, the resolve to stop sinning and serve God; and, third, the recognition to do so through the strength that only Christ could give. This subsection has espoused from his operant corpus that Whitefield's *ordo salutis* begins with the prevenient grace of God that then enables the elect to respond via faith and repentance in order to experience instantaneous conversion.[126] Having established the theological actions that initialize instantaneous conversion, attention is now given to what occurs, theologically, in the moment of instantaneous conversion.

3.2. INSTANT OF INSTANTANEOUS CONVERSION: REGENERATION AND JUSTIFICATION

Faith and repentance preceded conversion in Whitefield's theology. In the moment of conversion two soteriological actions occurred in the life of the believer: regeneration (also called the new birth) and justification. This section will show that, for Whitefield, regeneration and the new birth are synonymous, while justification, though it happens in the same moment as regeneration, is quite different; during instantaneous conversion the new birth and regeneration bring about the inauguration of a new *nature* of the individual while justification alters the *standing* of the individual.

3.2.1. Regeneration and the New Birth (in the moment of instantaneous conversion)

Regeneration and the new birth represent the same idea in Whitefield's theology, which is the inauguration of a new nature given to a person in the moment of instantaneous conversion.[127] To understand this argument better, it will be shown via Whitefield's discussion of conversion that first,

---

125. Whitefield, *The Works of the Reverend George Whitefield*, 6:7.

126. For further examples of Whitefield's insistence that faith and repentance bring about eternal life found in salvation, see Whitefield, *The Works of the Reverend George Whitefield*, 1:23–24, 411, 5:15–16.

127. For more on Whitefield's view of the new birth in relation to conversion, see McGever, "The Vector of Salvation: The New Birth as (Only) the Beginning of Conversion for Wesley and Whitefield," 32–35, 37–41.

the new birth and regeneration are synonymous; second, the meaning and import of regeneration and the new birth as the inauguration of a new nature; and, third, regeneration and new birth arrive in the moment of instantaneous conversion.

Whitefield spoke synonymously of regeneration and the new birth; in his theology the terms are interchangeable. Whitefield often used the two terms to mean the same thing;[128] however, his clearest articulation of the synonymy of the terms is in his sermon *On Regeneration*. Whitefield originally titled this sermon *The Nature and Necessity of the New Birth in Christ Jesus in Order to Salvation*,[129] but later the sermon title was changed, for example, in Gillies collection, to *On Regeneration*.[130] The opening line of the sermon shows how Whitefield used the terms interchangeably: "The doctrine of our regeneration, or new birth in CHRIST JESUS, though one of the most fundamental doctrines of our holy religion ... is the very hinge on which the salvation of each of us turns."[131] Whitefield was not being innovative in his synonymous usage of the terms; he was being consistent with the articles of his church (Article XXVII, *Of Baptism*, also uses the terms interchangeably).[132]

Having established that Whitefield used the terms regeneration and new birth interchangeably, it is now possible to show that when Whitefield was talking about the new birth or regeneration, both of these terms meant the inauguration of a new nature in the life of the believer. Throughout Whitefield's preaching and writing, the new birth was understood in its most basic sense. The new birth was a metaphor for the delivery of a newborn baby, a mother birthing a child who was beginning its life (following Jesus' use of the concept in John 3).[133] This metaphor was then applied to

---

128. Whitefield, *A Further Account of God's Dealings with the Reverend Mr. George Whitefield*, 24; Whitefield, *Seventh Journal: From a Few Days after His Return to Georgia to His Arrival at Falmouth*, 25; Whitefield, *The Works of the Reverend George Whitefield*, 4:10, 6:197, 324.

129. George Whitefield, *Nature and Necessity of Our New Birth in Christ Jesus, in Order to Salvation* (Gloucester: Harris, 1737).

130. Whitefield, *The Works of the Reverend George Whitefield*, 6:257–72. Whitefield referred to the sermon by both names in Whitefield, *A Further Account of God's Dealings with the Reverend Mr. George Whitefield*, 19.

131. Whitefield, *The Works of the Reverend George Whitefield*, 6:257.

132. Church of England, *Book of Common Prayer, 1662 Edition*, 623.

133. Whitefield's sermon on regeneration and the new birth opens with a reference to

the new spiritual life in Christ a person received when he or she converted and became a true Christian.[134] Whitefield at times spoke of the new birth in terms such as the "new creation," "new man," "new heart," "new mind," and "new nature," all of which meant to communicate the totality of the new nature given through regeneration.[135] Whitefield taught that the new nature changes people's souls so that souls are "though still the same as to essence, yet are so purged, purified and cleansed from their natural dross, filth and leprosy, by the blessed influences of the Holy Spirit, that they may be properly said to be made anew."[136] The new birth, thus in Whitefield's theology, is a change that happens during instantaneous conversion in the inner person in which the soul is purified and a new nature is given by the Holy Spirit.[137]

The new birth was a key term within Whitefield's soteriological vocabulary and had a significant role in his theology of conversion.[138] Soon after his engagement with Charles Wesley and the Holy Club, Whitefield understood the importance of the new birth.[139] He wrote immediately to his family upon learning about the new birth as Scougal taught it: "I wrote letters to my relations, telling them there was such a thing as the new birth."[140] Later,

---

Jesus' conversation with Nicodemus; see Whitefield, *The Works of the Reverend George Whitefield*, 6:257.

134. Whitefield, *The Works of the Reverend George Whitefield*, 2:305.

135. Whitefield, *The Works of the Reverend George Whitefield*, 5:258, 260, 262, 267.

136. Whitefield, *The Works of the Reverend George Whitefield*, 6:260.

137. Whitefield described the "unregenerate unconverted sinner" in his early sermon, *The Necessity and Benefits of Religious Society*. In other words, to be unregenerate was to be unconverted. Whitefield, *The Works of the Reverend George Whitefield*, 5:118.

138. Lambert comments: "Although Whitefield did not invent the concept of the new birth, he constructed his own meaning of the conversion process. Proclaiming that salvation transcended traditional church boundaries, the revivalist delivered his message to a mass audience." Lambert, "The Great Awakening as Artifact," 226. Hindmarsh declared the new birth as Whitefield's "great theme." See Hindmarsh, *The Evangelical Conversion Narrative*, 104. Perhaps most significantly, in his funeral sermon for Whitefield, John Wesley declared the new birth and justification by faith the "fundamental doctrines which [Whitefield] everywhere insisted on." See Wesley, *Sermons*, 2:343. Kidd observed: "Preaching the new birth would become the center of Whitefield's gospel ministry and the defining cause of his life." Kidd, *George Whitefield*, 9.

139. Not only did his new understanding of the new birth inaugurate Whitefield's evangelical understanding of salvation, his view of the new birth did not change throughout his career. Smith wrote: "Neither Wesley nor the increasingly Calvinist Whitefield ever altered his basic stance on the primacy of the experience of the new birth." Timothy Lawrence Smith, *Whitefield & Wesley on the New Birth* (Grand Rapids: Asbury Press, 1986), 7.

140. Whitefield, *A Short Account*, 15.

in Whitefield's sermon, *All Men's Place*, Whitefield recalled: "Whenever I go to Oxford, I cannot help running to that place where Jesus Christ first revealed himself to me, and gave me the new birth."[141] Right from the outset of his ministry, the new birth was a major feature of his preaching and often a reason why he was banned from pulpits and the target of endless controversies with ministers.[142] Whenever Whitefield had the opportunity, he would preach on the new birth; this message was what he called the "one thing needful" (as described in a letter from October 2, 1738): "But what shall I write to you about? Why, of our common salvation, of that one thing needful, of that new birth in CHRIST JESUS, that ineffable change which must pass upon our hearts, before we can see GOD, and of which you have heard me discourse so often. Let this, this, my dear friends, be the end of all your actions."[143] The new birth was the focus of Whitefield's preaching and ministry. The new birth was the "one thing" that Whitefield expressed relentlessly anytime the opportunity arose.

The last aspect of Whitefield's theology of regeneration and new birth has already been established in the previous discussion on the instantaneous nature of regeneration in baptism.[144] Whitefield taught that regeneration and the new birth arrive in the moment of instantaneous conversion.[145] The moment of instantaneous conversion included not only regeneration (and the new birth); it also included the appropriation of justification in the life of the believer.

3.2.2. Justification (in the moment of instantaneous conversion)

Whitefield believed that justification (as the forensic declaration of forgiveness of sins as well as the imputation of the righteousness of Christ) was appropriated to the convert in the instant of instantaneous conversion and

---

141. Whitefield, *Eighteen Sermons*, 360.

142. In his *Further Account*, Whitefield recalled: "Two clergymen sent for me, and told me they would not let me preach in their pulpits any more, unless I renounced that part of my sermon on regeneration, wherein I wished, 'that my brethren would entertain their auditories oftener with discourses upon the new birth.' This I had no freedom to do, and so they continued my opposers." Whitefield, *A Further Account of God's Dealings with the Reverend Mr. George Whitefield*, 24.

143. Whitefield, *The Works of the Reverend George Whitefield*, 3:428–29.

144. See chapter five, section one.

145. See Whitefield, *Seventh Journal: From a Few Days after His Return to Georgia to His Arrival at Falmouth*, 25; Whitefield, *The Works of the Reverend George Whitefield*, 5:458.

justification did not occur again. When people converted they were fully justified, and the effects of justification continued. Whitefield often used the phrase "justification by faith" to denote the relationship and timing in which faith brought about justification in the moment of instantaneous conversion. Each of these claims will be articulated below.

Whitefield taught that justification was both the forensic declaration of the forgiveness of sins, as well as the imputation of the righteousness of Christ. Whitefield preached that justification "is a law-term, and alludes to a judge acquitting an accused criminal of the thing laid to his charge."[146] When one was justified, Whitefield taught, it was as though "you never had offended [God] at all."[147] With the removal of the offense of sin via God's acquittal, Whitefield taught that the sinner was declared legally justified. Justification, in Whitefield's theology, however, went further than the legal acquittal of sins; he defined justification as being "looked upon as righteous in GOD's sight."[148] Similarly, Whitefield stated: "GOD now sees no sin in them; the whole covenant of works is fulfilled in them; they are actually justified, acquitted, and looked upon as righteous in the sight of GOD."[149] Whitefield believed that to be justified was not only to be acquitted of sin but to be counted as righteous, so that the whole covenant of works had been fulfilled in the person who was justified by God. The application of the merits of Christ to the believer is what Whitefield described as the imputation of Christ's righteousness.[150] Whitefield boldly offered these benefits in the closing words of his sermon *The Righteousness of Christ*: "I now offer this righteousness, this free, this imputed, this everlasting righteousness to all poor sinners that will accept of it."[151] This sermon gives evidence not only to the meaning of Whitefield's view of justification, but also to its instantaneous nature, which he offered as something that could be received as long as his hearers would accept it.

---

146. Whitefield, *The Works of the Reverend George Whitefield*, 6:216. See also Schwenk, *Catholic Spirit*, 32.

147. Whitefield, *The Works of the Reverend George Whitefield*, 6:216.

148. Whitefield, *The Works of the Reverend George Whitefield*, 5:360.

149. Whitefield, *The Works of the Reverend George Whitefield*, 6:190.

150. Whitefield, *The Works of the Reverend George Whitefield*, 5:215–27, 6:223.

151. Whitefield, *The Works of the Reverend George Whitefield*, 5:249.

Whitefield taught that justification happened in the instant of instantaneous conversion, not at any point later. Justification was a one-time occurrence when one was acquitted and the merit of Christ was credited to the believer. Whitefield argued in the sermon, *The Good Shepherd*: "Some talk of being justified at the day of judgment, that is nonsense; if we are not justified here, we shall not be justified there."[152] Justification was not something to be hoped for in the future; Whitefield taught that justification was realized in the moment of faith via justification by faith. Whitefield used the phrase "justification by faith" dozens of times in his writing.[153] Whitefield held a defensive posture against those who denied justification by faith alone. He also frequently attempted to redeem what true faith meant for those who had a minimal and marginal faith but rested idly in their justification. Effectively, Whitefield was in a mediating position between the two extremes: those who denied justification by faith alone and those who approved of justification by faith alone and yet were idle in their faith, resulting in antinomianism.[154] In his sermon, *Dying Saint's Triumph*, Whitefield declared: "I do not know any one single thing more variously expressed in the scriptures than believing; why? because it is the marrow of the gospel. Without faith we cannot be justified."[155] Thus, Whitefield believed that faith was the catalyst which brought about justification.[156]

---

152. Whitefield, *Eighteen Sermons*, 447.

153. For example, in Whitefield's sermon, *What Think Ye of Christ*, he states: "This doctrine of our free justification by faith in CHRIST JESUS, however censured and evil spoken of by our present Masters of Israel, was highly esteemed by our wise fore-fathers: for in the subsequent words of the aforementioned article, it is called a most wholesome doctrine, and very full of comfort: and so it is to all that are weary and heavy laden, and are truly willing to find rest in JESUS CHRIST." See also Whitefield, *The Works of the Reverend George Whitefield*, 1:171, 4:15, 27, 81, 86, 115, 116, 118, 119, 151, 152, 153, 155, 156, 159, 168, 194, 5:221, 363, 6:59, 378, 419, 420. There are also at least a dozen instances of the phrase "justification by faith" in Whitefield's journals. It is quite peculiar that the phrase "justification by faith" does not show up once in the letters of Whitefield as published by Gillies.

154. A passage which summarizes Whitefield's definition of justification, the role of belief, and of faith, is found in the sermon *Abraham's Offering Up His Son Isaac*: "Thus it was that Abraham was justified before he did any good work: he was enabled to believe on the LORD CHRIST; it was accounted to him for righteousness; that is, CHRIST's righteousness was made over to him, and so accounted his. This, this is gospel; this is the only way of finding acceptance with GOD: good works have nothing to do with our justification in his fight. We are justified by faith alone." Whitefield, *The Works of the Reverend George Whitefield*, 5:49–50.

155. Whitefield, *Eighteen Sermons*, 91.

156. For more instances of faith being the catalyst of justification, see Whitefield, *The Works of the Reverend George Whitefield*, 6:56; Whitefield, *Eighteen Sermons*, 91; George

While regeneration and the new birth were synonyms for Whitefield, justification was not a synonym for the new birth or regeneration. As shown above, justification did happen in the moment of instantaneous conversion, just as regeneration did.[157] Yet, justification, for Whitefield, should be thought of in relation to sin and merit, regarding righteousness, while regeneration and the new birth should be thought of as the inauguration of a new nature. Justification and regeneration/new birth happened in the same moment in Whitefield's understanding, yet they described two different effects which were brought about in the moment of instantaneous conversion.

3.3. CONTINUING FROM CONVERSION: SANCTIFICATION (ONGOING FAITH AND REPENTANCE) AND GLORIFICATION

Conversion, in Whitefield's teaching, did not end in the moment of instantaneous conversion. Consistent with Whitefield's concept of conversion as a sustained orientation in which a convert turns, and keeps turning, toward the righteousness of Christ, conversion does not end with the new birth and the appropriation of justification. Instead, Whitefield taught that genuine conversion is a theological experience which continued. Whitefield articulated rich theological connections between conversion and the *ordo salutis* for the stages preceding conversion (prevenient grace, faith, and repentance) and in the instant of conversion (regeneration and justification). Whitefield, however, did not attend frequently to the theological loci that typically come after justification and regeneration, such as sanctification and glorification, in the midst of his direct discussions of conversion. Instead, in his direct discussions of that which comes after conversion, Whitefield focused on the motifs of continued evidence of conversion (chapter four, section four) and assurance (as examined in the previous section).

While Whitefield did not attend frequently to direct articulations of the *ordo salutis*, three observations can be made on this topic from related discussions. First, justification did not reoccur after the experience of

---

Whitefield, *An Exhortation to Come and See Jesus* (London: C. Whitefield, 1739), 10.

157. Justification spoken of here is applied or appropriated justification in the life of an individual. Whitefield taught that justification was accomplished upon Christ's resurrection. See Whitefield, *The Works of the Reverend George Whitefield*, 4:478, 6:128, 319.

instantaneous conversion. Justification, Whitefield taught, came merito-riously by the death of Christ, instrumentally by faith, and declaratively by good works (synoptic statement 7: conversion is marked by ongoing good works).[158] While good works continued for those who were genuinely justified by Christ, the evidence of good works merely pointed back to the once-for-all merit of Christ that was appropriated by faith in instantaneous conversion. Second, when Whitefield spoke about faith and repentance, he always meant that these activities would continue after instantaneous con-version. They were not merely instruments of instantaneous conversion; they were also the means of sanctification.[159] Third, Whitefield did men-tion the larger sequence of justification, sanctification, and glorification, but not in the direct context of his teaching on conversion.[160]

While Whitefield did not discuss directly an *ordo salutis* in relation to conversion (thus, making it an attendant theme, and not a primary motif), his operant discussions of the soteriological terminology related to con-version presents material which yields the following insights. Prevenient grace, faith, and repentance precede conversion (in a way which initial-izes instantaneous conversion). Faith that was converting was not mere intellectual agreement with historic Christianity. Converting faith, for Whitefield, was trust and confidence in the work of Christ for the forgive-ness of sins. Repentance that was converting was the renouncement of sin and commitment to serve God through the strength that only Christ could give. When a person responded in faith and repentance (by the prevenient grace of God), they, then, experienced instantaneous conversion. In the moment of instantaneous conversion, the person was regenerated (also called the new birth) and justified. Regeneration was the instantaneous inauguration of a new nature to become a new creation in which a person had a new heart and mind. Justification was the forensic declaration of forgiveness in which one was also imputed the righteous merits of Christ. Whitefield was clear that after instantaneous conversion a genuine convert would continue in their Christian growth (sanctification) in the journey toward glorification (as a reflection of the *telos* of conversion).

---

158. Whitefield, *The Works of the Reverend George Whitefield*, 5:366.
159. Whitefield, *The Works of the Reverend George Whitefield*, 1:22, 6:166.
160. Whitefield, *The Works of the Reverend George Whitefield*, 1:129, 6:196.

4. CONCLUSION

This chapter considered three attendant themes in Whitefield's theology of conversion. Beginning with the topic of baptismal regeneration, it was seen that Whitefield needed to attend to this topic since his church deemed all those who had been baptized as (already) regenerated. Whitefield justified his claim that baptized people needed to be born again through instantaneous conversion (the instantaneousness of which he supported through his exegesis of his church's baptismal rites). Thus, Whitefield taught that baptism was not necessarily the moment of one's conversion (synoptic statement 8). Whitefield's ample discussion of assurance of salvation was shown in the second section to conclude that Whitefield taught that assurance was the trust and knowledge that one's faith was genuine and salvific. This assurance was also called, by Whitefield, the witness of the Spirit, since assurance was given supernaturally (and not by human effort). Supernatural assurance was necessary since he taught that assurance was available even when one was cognizant of his or her ongoing battle with sinful choices. While assurance was available to all genuine converts, Whitefield recognized through his pastoral experience that assurance was not required for a person to be considered a genuine convert (synoptic statement 9). The second section showed Whitefield's affirmation of the doctrine of election as the source for assurance of salvation since election rested salvation not on human merit, but on God's appropriation of the merits of Christ to the elect. Whitefield held firmly to election as the basis for assurance (and not good works) while also insisting that genuine converts gave continued evidence of conversion through their good works (chapter four, section four). The second section concluded by arguing that Whitefield's hypothetical universal election was a source for the teleological aspect of conversion since it removed any lingering doubt that might remain for converts who were struggling in their sanctification. The discussion of regeneration in the first section and the prominence of Whitefield's adherence to the doctrine of election in the second section demanded an analysis of the soteriological terminology Whitefield used in his *ordo salutis*. The account of Whitefield's *ordo salutis* as it relates to conversion showed that, prior to conversion, a person needed faith and repentance (through the prevenient grace of God) as a catalyst for conversion. Converting faith was trust and confidence in the work of Christ for

the forgiveness of sins, while converting repentance was the renouncement of sin with a commitment to serve God through God's strength. In the
moment of instantaneous conversion, a person was justified (the forensic
declaration of forgiveness in which one was also imputed the righteousness
of Christ) and regenerated (given a new nature to become a new creation
in heart and mind). Sanctification and glorification followed instantaneous
conversion in Whitefield's theology, as indicative of the teleological aspect
of conversion. Having now given an account (in chapters two through
five) of the primary motifs and attendant themes of conversion for both
Wesley and Whitefield, we move now to a synthetic analysis of their theologies of conversion.

6

—

JOHN WESLEY AND GEORGE WHITEFIELD'S THEOLOGIES OF CONVERSION COMPARED

Despite a handful of well-known areas of disagreement, Wesley and Whitefield's operant teaching on conversion display overwhelming agreement in terms of a conversion theology which can be described as inaugurated teleology. The full meaning of conversion as inaugurated teleology emerged through the preceding analysis and is established fully in the nine synoptic statements.

The first section of this chapter will examine the continuity and discontinuity among the four primary conversion motifs identified in the operant theologies of Wesley and Whitefield as they relate to conversion. It will be shown that they were essentially univocal regarding the basic definition of conversion, the consistent precursors to conversion, the nature of instantaneous conversion, and the dynamics of ongoing conversion. Section two will examine continuity and discontinuity in relation to the three attendant conversion themes identified in the operant theologies of Wesley and Whitefield as they relate to conversion. This section will show that both Whitefield and Wesley approached the relationship between conversion and baptism, as well as conversion and assurance of salvation, in the same way. The comparison of Wesley's *via salutis* and Whitefield's *ordo salutis* will conclude that their views on the hidden decrees of God diverge but in relation to questions of the inauguration and *telos* of conversion there is a deep unity. Section three will summarize the espoused conversion theologies of Wesley and Whitefield by articulating overtly and together the nine synoptic statements of conversion which emerge from the previous

chapters. This section will give also a summative articulation of inaugurated teleology emerging from these statements.[1]

1. PRIMARY CONVERSION MOTIFS:
WESLEY AND WHITEFIELD

This section examines the continuity and discontinuity among the four primary conversion motifs identified in the operant theologies of Wesley and
Whitefield as they relate to conversion. By the end of this section, it will
be shown that Wesley and Whitefield were essentially univocal regarding
the basic definition of conversion, the consistent precursors to conversion
(conviction, convincing, and awakening), the nature of instantaneous conversion, and the dynamics of ongoing conversion.

1.1. CONVERSION AS AN EXPERIENCE FROM AND TO

Wesley and Whitefield shared the same basic definition of conversion:
conversion is an experience turning *from* and *to* something or someone.
Conversion is understood by Wesley and Whitefield as a turning *from* and
to because they considered this as the basic etymology of the word "conversion." In Wesley's 1753 dictionary, the etymological definition comes to the
fore. He wrote: "Conversion: 'a thorough change of heart and life from sin
to holiness; a turning.' "[2] Although Whitefield never produced a dictionary,
he too used the basic understanding of conversion as a turning *from* and *to*.[3]

At the most basic level, Wesley and Whitefield agreed on the general
usage of the word and concept of conversion. It is possible thus to state
that the most fundamental aspect of their agreement on the topic can be
summarized through one of the synoptic statements of their espoused conversion theologies: conversion is a turning *from* self and *to* Christ (labeled
as synoptic statement 3).[4] However, with the foundational agreement

---

1. This chapter will rely heavily on the research and conclusions identified in previous
chapters. The support for the various arguments and conclusions will not be retraced except
when a detailed comparison is required.

2. Wesley, *The Complete English Dictionary Explaining Most of Those Hard Words, Which
Are Found in the Best English Writers*. No pages are listed, only the alphabetical list of words.

3. See chapter four, section one.

4. The ordering of the numbering of the synoptic statements of conversion (1–9) has been
chosen for two reasons. First, the numbering of statements 4–9 has been given according
to their emergence in the exegesis of preceding chapters (chapters two to five). The reason

anchored in the general definition of conversion, this study has identified different emphases among Wesley and Whitefield on exactly what one converts *from* and *to*. Wesley's emphasis in the "from and to" motif was most often *from* heathenism and *to* Christ, while Whitefield's emphasis was regarding a conversion *from* the sinful nature and *to* the righteousness of Christ. This difference in emphasis leads to two observations.

First, Whitefield rarely spoke of heathens (or conversion from heathenism), while Wesley spoke of heathens (and conversion from heathenism) often. When Wesley spoke of heathens, he typically meant either people from a far-off land or people whose religious beliefs were different from Wesley's beliefs.[5] Wesley's use of "heathen language" began prior to his singular and ill-fated Georgian excursion and continued after his return from Georgia. Whitefield, however, spent much time in America and near those who could have been labeled as heathens in the "far-off land" sense, but did not speak of conversion *from* heathenism often.[6] It can be surmised that Whitefield's infrequent use of "heathen language" in the conversion motif is due to his sensitivities drawn from extensive travel in foreign lands, while Wesley's personal experience was far less settled and perhaps more idealized or theorized than Whitefield's. More pertinently, Wesley's imagination for the "conversion of the heathens" was more of a dream than a reality, and his language seemed to idealize the foreign mission scenario.

The second observation is that Whitefield's emphasis was a conversion *from* the sinful nature and *to* the righteousness of Christ.[7] This emphasis points to Whitefield's Calvinistic focus on the depraved and incapacitated human nature to convert oneself without divine grace. Wesley was not Pelagian and agreed with Whitefield about the depraved sinful nature, but it is not surprising that Whitefield highlighted, as a point of emphasis often found among Calvinists, the sinful nature as the state *from* which

---

statement 3 is given first in the above paragraph is because it provides the overarching logic upon which the other statements find their place; it has not been labeled as the first statement in order to prioritize the theological logic, which brings us to the second point. Second, the numbering aligns with the best way to present the statements in their entirety, as a narrative list according to their theological logic (for example, God's grace precedes [1] the experience [2] of conversion [3]). See section three in this chapter for this list and further discussion.

5. See chapter two, section 1.2.1.

6. See chapter four, section 1.1.

7. See chapter four, section 1.1.

one converts.[8] Wesley and Whitefield, therefore, agreed on the foundational meaning of conversion while maintaining their own distinct emphases. However, conversion was not merely a dusty theological term to be
mechanically defined but something, in Wesley and Whitefield's understanding, meant to be experienced.

Conversion, for both Wesley and Whitefield, must be understood as an
experience. Despite being pejoratively labeled as enthusiasts, Wesley and
Whitefield insisted that conversion was a genuine experience of God's *felt*
work in the life of those who converted.[9] Wesley and Whitefield embraced
the term enthusiasm as they understood it from Scripture.[10] Experiencing
God's work occurred not only from the beginning of the moment of instantaneous conversion (and ongoing after that moment), but also preceding
conversion. Thus, Wesley and Whitefield both understood conversion to
operate in the domain of experience. It will be shown in the discussions of
instantaneous conversion and the *via/ordo salutis* below that Wesley and
Whitefield believed that conversion is inaugurated by faith and repentance,
and that genuine conversion continues and is ongoing—all of which cor-
responds with the concept of salvation, or more precisely, the experience
of salvation. Salvation is not experienced, in Wesley and Whitefield's articulation, until faith and repentance commence in one's life. It is from this
correlative sense (the correlation between God's work of salvation and the
experience of conversion) that one might venture to form a further synoptic statement of the espoused theologies of conversion for Wesley and
Whitefield: conversion is the experiential correlate of salvation (labeled
as synoptic statement 2).

In order to experience instantaneous conversion via faith and repentance, Wesley and Whitefield both believed that God's grace had to go before,
or "prevent" in the older sense of the word, to enable the spiritually dead

---

8. Reist's analysis of the theology of Wesley and Whitefield concluded that both men
understood humanity as being totally depraved because of Adam and denied "any natural,
innate will power in man which enabled him to turn to God." Irwin W. Reist, "John Wesley
and George Whitefield: A Study in the Integrity of Two Theologians of Grace," *Evangelical
Quarterly* 47 (1975): 33.

9. For an analysis of the role of experience in conversion, see chapter two, section 1.1.
for Wesley and chapter four, section 1.2. for Whitefield.

10. Maddock wrote: "Like Wesley, Whitefield was convinced that genuine conversion
must to [sic] be 'felt' and 'experienced' in the life of those who claimed to have been born
again." Maddock, *Men of One Book*, 145.

sinner to be able to be receptive to the work of the Holy Spirit calling a person to convert. Wesley and Whitefield's belief in the work of God's grace to enable the spiritually dead sinner to "turn" is why it is possible to isolate the synoptic statement: conversion is initiated and sustained by the grace of God (labeled as synoptic statement 1).[11]

1.2. PRECEDING CONVERSION: CONVINCED, CONVICTED, AWAKENED

Wesley and Whitefield both believed that conversion was always preceded by God's work to convince, convict, and awaken individuals to their need of redemption.[12] Wesley and Whitefield agreed that the convincing, convicting, and awakening work included four conditions. First, convincing, convicting, and awakening were *experienced* for the human; they were not merely the objective work of God. These experiences were subjective, meaning that they were felt, noticeable, and identifiable. Second, these experiences did not always *end* in conversion. In other words, an individual may become convinced, convicted, and awakened and still not become converted. These components precede conversion but do not necessarily lead to conversion. Third, each of these experiences was linked to the conviction of sin. While one may become convinced of the truthfulness of Christianity, this collection of pre-conversion experiences always described engagement with the topic of sin, not merely objective information, but the *experience of sinfulness*. Fourth, Wesley and Whitefield consistently spoke of these activities as experiences one felt *before* conversion. Wesley and Whitefield taught that these experiences continued after conversion, but it is extremely rare to identify an instance where Wesley and Whitefield described conversion without the pre-converting work of convincing, convicting, and awakening. Collectively, Wesley and Whitefield's common ground related to being convinced, convicted, and awakened is that conversion is foreshadowed by a deep sense of sinfulness, which has already been articulated as an espoused synoptic statement of Wesley and Whitefield's theologies of conversion (labeled as synoptic statement 4).

---

11. See chapter two, section 2.1. for Wesley and chapter four, section 1.1. for Whitefield. Also see chapter three, section 3.1. for Wesley and chapter five, section 3.1.1. for Whitefield.

12. See chapter two, section two for Wesley and chapter four, section two for Whitefield.

In the midst of Wesley and Whitefield's overarching agreement on the experiences of convincing, convicting, and awakening as a deep sense of sinfulness which proceeded conversion, each man had his own nuances related to these terms. Wesley, unlike Whitefield, spoke of being convinced and convicted synonymously while emphasizing the experience to be a work of grace that, at times, produced visible manifestations such as crying and tears.[13] Whitefield understood conviction as an experience that pushed beyond simple rational agreement with the historic tenets of Christianity and convincing as an experience which emphasizes the gulf between human and Christ's righteousness.[14] The term "awakening" was used similarly for Wesley and Whitefield in contexts in which there was a notable gap of time between the initial onset of the sense of sinfulness and the experience of conversion. Whitefield's extensive evangelistic travel, often with prolonged gaps before his return trips, created ample anecdotal usage of the term awakening,[15] while Wesley's usage could take the form of a more prescriptive description that explained awakening as a preparative step before returning to deliver the gospel.[16]

Wesley and Whitefield's unanimity (with the nuances above as given) regarding the pre-converting experience of convincing, convicting, and awakening can be attributed to their shared foundation in the Holy Living tradition which stressed preparatory actions leading up to conversion.[17] While both Wesley and Whitefield moved on from the extreme asceticism of their early lives learned from the writings of Law, à Kempis, Castaniza, and others, Wesley and Whitefield did not throw the preparative baby out with the salvific bathwater. In other words, both Wesley and Whitefield no longer believed in a breakthrough converting moment which was based on preparationism. Rather than conversion being *based on* preparatory works (per the preparationism of the Holy Living tradition), conversion was *preceded by* foreshadowing experiences which came before conversion (such as

---

13. See chapter two, section 2.1.

14. See chapter four, sections 2.1–2.

15. See chapter four, section 2.3.

16. See chapter two, section 2.2.

17. See chapter two, section three for Wesley and chapter four, section 3.3.3.–6. for Whitefield's engagement with the Holy Living tradition (which included Law, à Kempis, Castaniza, and others) as well as Scougal.

being convicted, convinced, and awakened). One indicator of Wesley and Whitefield's homage to their formative Holy Living tradition roots while advancing their updated evangelical theologies is observed upon Wesley and Whitefield's issuing of edited versions of Law's *Serious Call* to remove theology which they understood as works-based righteousness in which conversion could be merited.[18]

Wesley and Whitefield believed that conversion was preceded not necessarily by the rigorous strain of preparationism (per the Holy Living tradition), but, instead, always by a deep sense of sinfulness (labeled as synoptic statement 4). They believed that the inauguration of conversion was foreshadowed by God's gracious work to give a deep sense of sinfulness prior to conversion that then initiated the convert into the purpose and aim of conversion, which is Christlikeness ending in perfection (the *telos* of conversion, as will be discussed in section 1.4. and section 2.3. later in this chapter). Having compared Wesley and Whitefield's understandings of the preparatory experience leading to instantaneous conversion, attention is now turned to comparing how they understood the moment of instantaneous conversion.

1.3. INSTANTANEOUS CONVERSION

Instantaneous conversion was the cornerstone doctrine of Wesley and Whitefield's theologies of conversion. They understood instantaneous conversion as the moment realized by faith when justification was applied and the new birth occurred in the convert.[19] Without instantaneous conversion, the primary and attendant themes in this study would essentially be moot. Without a definitive moment of transformation there was nothing to turn *from* and *to* which resulted in regeneration and justification; there was no need for anything to precede conversion such as convincing, convicting, and awakening; and there was little that needed to be re-examined in regard to infant baptism in the Anglican context (just to name a few key theological areas of consequence dependent upon instantaneous conversion). As such, Wesley and Whitefield agreed upon the need for

---

18. See chapter four, section 3.3.2. for more on Wesley and Whitefield's editorial editions of Law's work.

19. See section 3.2. in this chapter.

instantaneous conversion (as well as ongoing conversion, which will be examined in the next section).

The simple fact that both of these men experienced instantaneous conversions themselves is critical to the espousal of Wesley and Whitefield's theologies of instantaneous conversion.[20] Both men reflected theologically on the experience of instantaneous conversion before their personal conversion experiences, but it should be noted that both of their broader theologies which helped them understand their own conversions changed shortly after their conversion experiences. In other words, both Wesley and Whitefield understood instantaneous conversion differently after their own personal conversion experiences; their experiences became theological data. Before their conversions both Wesley and Whitefield were seeking ascetic Christian perfection in order to be assured that they were justified. Prior to their conversions, both Wesley and Whitefield understood instantaneous conversion as the full assurance of being justified, with assurance being rooted in good works found through the extreme use of the means of grace. Essentially they understood sanctification to precede justification. Shortly after their conversions, both Wesley and Whitefield reframed their understandings of instantaneous conversion as an experience which did not depend upon assurance and did not require the extreme use of the means of grace in order to be found. They both came to understand instantaneous conversion as being available via justification through faith alone. Instantaneous conversion via justification through faith alone found an easy and comfortable home in Whitefield's growing Calvinistic theology. Instantaneous conversion via justification through faith alone took longer to settle in Wesley's Arminian theology. Wesley's challenge had nothing to do with the theological meaning of justification through faith alone; Wesley's challenge was to reconcile his personal experience with his theology of the assurance of salvation.

In their mature understandings, Wesley and Whitefield held two key beliefs in regard to instantaneous conversion. First, instantaneous conversion was the normative mode in which conversion occurred, which is

---

20. Maddock wrote: "[Wesley and Whitefield's] shared history also included dramatic conversion experiences that became paradigmatic for their own proclamation of the necessity of regeneration and of being justified by faith, not works." Maddock, *Men of One Book*, 1.

the reason we can articulate the espoused synoptic statement (labeled as synoptic statement 5): conversion arrives by faith in an instant.[21] But, this claim was held in tension with, second, that there were some exceptional cases in which a genuinely converted person could not pinpoint when they converted. Hence, we can offer another synoptic statement (6): conversion is instantaneous but is not always recognizable on behalf of the genuine convert.[22] Lacking a recollection of a specific moment of conversion did not negate the reality of instantaneous conversion. Whether instantaneous conversion was recognizable (which was normative in the mature theologies and ministries of Wesley and Whitefield) or unrecognizable (which was not normative), instantaneous conversion was the inauguration of conversion which brought with it the *telos* of conversion: Christ-likeness. Following the inauguration of conversion via instantaneous conversion, Wesley and Whitefield both insisted that genuine conversion continued toward this *telos*.

1.4. CONTINUED EVIDENCE OF CONVERSION

Wesley and Whitefield taught that the *telos* of conversion was the journey toward perfection which was evidenced progressively by good works. Instantaneous conversion inaugurated the *telos* of conversion (perfection), but this inauguration was not the end itself.[23] Continued evidence (of good works) was required by both Wesley and Whitefield in their teaching on conversion and was necessary for an individual to be a genuine convert; if an individual lacked the ongoing continuance of Christian growth, the genuineness of their present-tense and initial conversion may be doubted.[24] To build upon the directionality of conversion using the turning motif, if a pilgrim was on a pilgrimage toward a destination, but turned back

---

21. See chapter two, section 3.2. for Wesley and chapter four, sections 3.2.–3. for Whitefield.

22. See chapter two, section 3.3. for Wesley and chapter four, section 4.1. for Whitefield.

23. See chapter two, sections 3.2. and 4.1. for Wesley and chapter four, section four for Whitefield.

24. See chapter two, section 4.2. for Wesley and chapter four, section 4.3. for Whitefield. Schwenk wrote: "Both Whitefield and Wesley agreed that good works should follow conversion. Yet Whitefield saw them as 'privileges,' things a Christian did out of obedience and love for Christ. Wesley saw them more as spiritual gauges that believers could use to check the depth of their relationship with Christ." It is true that Whitefield and Wesley insisted upon good works and that Wesley understood good works as gauges of spiritual health, but Whitefield understood good works to be more than a "privilege," as Schwenk indicates;

around and started heading home, they would no longer technically be considered a pilgrim. Conversion, for Wesley and Whitefield, requires directionality, not unlike in physics where a *vector* requires a velocity and a *direction*. When the directionality of a vector is changed (even when the velocity is maintained), the vector ceases to be and a different vector has been initiated; so it is with conversion in their articulation. Good works orient the directionality of the *telos* of a Christian toward Christlikeness in a genuine convert; when good works no longer accompany the activity of the convert (even in the continued ongoing activity of the person), the status of their identification as a convert is in flux.[25]

Good works and continued evidence of conversion were indicative of the *telos* of conversion that Wesley and Whitefield taught but were not related to assurance of salvation. They both taught that assurance of salvation was to be sought, but that assurance was not required for one to be a true convert.[26] While assurance of salvation was optional, continued evidence of salvation, however, was not optional for a person to be a true convert. In other words, a person might doubt their subjective feelings and self-perception regarding conversion, but the objective nature of his or her actions left much less to doubt regarding conversion; the sources of data for the continued evidence mattered for Wesley and Whitefield.

The sources of continued evidence differed in emphasis between Wesley and Whitefield. Wesley's recognition of the continued work of conversion was outward and inward. Wesley looked to both good works (outward) and the inner witness of the Spirit (inward) as continued evidence of conversion.[27] While Whitefield maintained his belief in the inner work of the Spirit, his focus was on the marks of a sound conversion; these marks were indicated by the forsaking of sin through repentance, bringing forth

---

Whitefield understood good works as indicators of genuine conversion. See Schwenk, *Catholic Spirit*, 46.

25. Note that in this analogy of a vector, velocity is equated to Christian activity while directionality is compared to good works. A person, thus, could be very active in their "Christianity" via activities such as church attendance, Bible reading, community involvement, etc., while lacking good works. Wesley and Whitefield challenged and attacked "active" Christians who thought that they were secure in their salvation, but had not converted and, in turn, did not produce good works evident of genuine conversion.

26. For more on Wesley and Whitefield's view on assurance of salvation in relation to conversion, see section 2.2. in this chapter.

27. See chapter two, section 4.1.

fruit in godly living, and going beyond general civility toward actual godliness.[28] Whitefield put more stress on the continued, external, outward
evidence of conversion than Wesley; this is because Whitefield tended to
put less stress on identifying the exact moment of conversion than Wesley.[29]
Since Whitefield put less stress on identifying the precise moment of conversion than did Wesley, Whitefield put more stress on continued good
works to identify a genuine convert. In this regard, Whitefield's theology
of conversion was not antinomian.[30] Despite being accused of antinomianism often as a derivative of his Calvinistic theology, Whitefield was a
moderate Calvinist and not a hyper-Calvinist.[31] Whitefield advocated an
ongoing second conversion evidenced by good works which did not *merit*
but *marked* a genuine conversion as the fruit of his belief in the doctrine of
election.[32] But, what is certain for both Wesley and Whitefield is that they
agreed that conversion was marked by ongoing good works (a principle
which gives rise to synoptic statement 7).[33]

2. ATTENDANT CONVERSION THEMES:
WESLEY AND WHITEFIELD

Having examined continuity and discontinuity among the four primary
conversion motifs identified in Wesley and Whitefield's operant theologies of conversion, this section will examine continuity and discontinuity
among the three attendant conversion themes identified in their theology.
It will be shown that Whitefield and Wesley approached the relationship

---

28. See chapter four, section 4.3.

29. It should be stated again that both Wesley and Whitefield understood identifiable
instantaneous conversion as the overwhelming normative mode of conversion. In Wesley
and Whitefield's theology of conversion it was rare and exceptional for an individual to *not*
be able to pinpoint the moment of their conversion. See chapter four, section 4.1. and chapter
two, sections 3.2.–3.

30. Whitefield's requirement for continued evidence of conversion parallels Calvin's third
use of the law in which believers were instructed in living righteousness out of gratitude for
the grace they had received from God. Whitefield claimed that he had not read any of Calvin's
works, but Whitefield would have differed from Calvin on this topic. Whitefield went further
than Calvin and understood acts of righteousness not only as an act of gratitude but an act
(and confirmation) of the genuineness of conversion. Whitefield, *The Works of the Reverend
George Whitefield*, 1:205; Calvin, *Calvin*, 2.7.12 (1:360–61).

31. See chapter four, section 1.2.

32. See chapter four, section 4.4.

33. See chapter two, section four for Wesley and chapter four, section 4.3. for Whitefield.

between conversion and baptism, as well as conversion and assurance of salvation, in the same way.

The comparison of Wesley's *via salutis* and Whitefield's *ordo salutis* will conclude that while they disagree on the hidden decrees, their disagreement is a relative disagreement which does not affect the primary concerns which each of them have with regard to conversion theology (which is inaugurated teleology). There is disagreement over this area, but more profound and deep agreement over the vast majority of their conversion theologies. Emphasis is often placed on the differences that rest between Wesley and Whitefield;[34] however, both of them focus on conversion's orientation toward its ultimate end rather than the exact process of and divine decress behind its beginning. It is in the hidden decrees of the *arché* that the two are divided, but in relation to questions of *telos* there is a deep unity.

2.1. CONVERSION AND BAPTISM

Wesley and Whitefield told their audiences that they were not to depend on their baptism for their salvation; in order to be saved they needed to experience the new birth through conversion. For Wesley and Whitefield, the regenerative work of conversion demanded a re-visioning of the Anglican rite of baptism. Wesley and Whitefield had inherited and participated in a church which understood baptism as the point of inauguration for the Christian life. Upon their experiences of conversion, however, the topic of baptism required further analysis in their soteriology.

Wesley and Whitefield continued to officiate baptisms, both infant and adult, throughout their lives. Wesley and Whitefield's preaching for adult conversion located baptism to be the introduction of the individual to the church with the seeds of regeneration placed but not necessarily germinated in the act of baptism. Regeneration and justification took place upon the appropriation of faith in the life of the new convert. Wesley and Whitefield believed that regeneration was not necessarily synchronized with the *act* of baptism.

---

34. See the literature review in chapter one, section five for instances of scholars who highlight difference between Wesley and Whitefield (such as Coppedge, Maddock, and Schwenk).

Wesley took over forty-five years to articulate fully how his view of conversion influenced baptism. It was not until the 1784 *Sunday Service* when Wesley carefully adjusted the precise tense of the statements regarding regeneration in the baptismal service that Wesley's mature outworking of conversion melded with his practice and theology of baptism.[35] Effectively, for Wesley, regeneration was not tied chronologically to the moment of baptism. Instead, regeneration, and, thus, instantaneous conversion, was synchronized with the arrival of personal, genuine faith.[36]

Unlike Wesley, Whitefield did not attempt to change the baptismal service as a consequence of his view of conversion. Whitefield was not afforded the unique opportunity to change the baptismal service to fit the contours of his theology of conversion which Wesley seized via the re-appropriation of Methodism amidst the American Revolution. Instead, Whitefield's understanding of baptism must be induced indirectly from his sermons and letters.[37] One move that Whitefield made was to understand that the baptized individual was initially baptized in the *name* but not the *nature* of the Father, Son, and Holy Spirit. Baptism into the *nature* of the Father, Son, and Holy Spirit was what Whitefield considered the baptism of the Holy Spirit, a work subsequent to initial baptism.[38] Whitefield believed that faith brought about instantaneous conversion, which brought with it baptism into the nature of the Father, Son, and Holy Spirit.

Whitefield never delineated a thorough explanation for how his theology of conversion fully melded with the Anglican baptismal rites. Instead, he simply continued to use the baptismal rites, together with their espousal of regeneration terminology. Whitefield could have seized the baptismal language of the Westminster Confession of Faith, which states: "The efficacy of baptism is not tied to that moment of time wherein it is administered."[39] However, it does not appear that Whitefield ever engaged *directly* with the Westminster Confession of Faith, and even if he did, it is unlikely

---

35. See chapter three, section 1.4.

36. See chapter three, section 1.5.

37. See chapter five, section 1.1.

38. See chapter five, section 1.3.

39. Westminster Confession of Faith 28.5–6, found in Leith, *Creeds of the Churches*, 224–25. The suggestion that Whitefield could use the concept embedded in the Westminster Confession is built upon the suggestion Campbell gave to reconcile Wesley's view on baptism. See Campbell, "Conversion and Baptism in Wesleyan Spirituality," 167–69.

that Whitefield would have strayed from his priestly orders to baptize using the rites from the *Book of Common Prayer*; he was firmly committed to the baptismal teaching of his church.[40] The interpretive key to understanding how Whitefield could understand a subsequence regeneration via baptism in the nature of the Holy Spirit is to recognize a difference between baptismal regeneration and regeneration. Whitefield did not invent the bifurcation of regeneration conceptuality; he inherited it from his Anglican predecessors. For Whitefield, baptismal regeneration represented alignment with baptism as an ordinance of Christ as well as the imparting of preparatory grace.[41]

Nevertheless, with or without an adjusted baptismal service, Wesley and Whitefield agreed: one should not rest in one's baptism, and a further work was needed after one had sinned away the benefits of one's baptism. Instead, for them, baptism provides the seeds which germinate upon subsequent conversion. In other words, Wesley and Whitefield believed that baptism marked one's entrance to the church but was not chronologically tied to conversion (the idea which forms synoptic statement 8).[42]

2.2. CONVERSION AND ASSURANCE

Baptism was no longer (necessarily) the inauguration of the Christian life in Wesley and Whitefield's theologies. Instead, conversion through personal faith and repentance had become the point of inauguration of salvation in the life of the believer (as will be shown in the next section). It was, thus, natural for people to desire a reference point for their assurance of salvation. Baptism, with its certificate, date, and godparents (for those who were baptized as infants) no longer provided a shibboleth for the assurance of salvation. Wesley and Whitefield's understandings of assurance of salvation, therefore, are critical to understanding their views on conversion, especially because conversion was a *felt* experience; it was natural for a convert to want to *feel* assured of their salvation.[43] The challenge of discussing Wesley and Whitefield's theologies of conversion together is complicated

---

40. See chapter five, section 1.1.
41. See chapter five, section 1.3.
42. See chapter three, section 1.5. for Wesley and chapter five, section 1.4. for Whitefield.
43. See chapter five, section 2.1.

by the fact that Wesley's views on assurance changed significantly over his lifetime,[44] with one prominent Wesleyan scholar indicating that Wesley's view on assurance changed more than any other of Wesley's soteriological beliefs.[45] Whitefield's views on assurance remained much more static than those of Wesley.[46] Given Wesley's shifting views on assurance, the analysis of their theologies of assurance must proceed diachronically.[47]

Prior to their respective conversions, both Wesley and Whitefield's religious efforts could be described as desperate searches for their assurances of salvation. Wesley sought assurance first through assent to truth,[48] next via the witness of the Spirit,[49] and finally, in the era of Aldersgate, through the pursuit of removing fear and doubt.[50] Whitefield, too, sought assurance that he was saved initially through the extreme engagement with the means of grace, whereby his hopes for salvation were continually thwarted by his inability to maintain extreme piety and impeccability.[51]

Whitefield changed his view on assurance after his conversion; he no longer understood assurance of salvation to hinge upon the frequency and severity of his sin.[52] Whitefield taught that assurance was still a *felt* experience, but the feeling could be sustained through the valleys of personal sin.[53] In the early years following Whitefield's conversion, it is unclear why Whitefield could theologically justify his sense of assurance in the midst of his own personal battles with sin.[54] Two to three years after his conversion, however, Whitefield began to lean more and more upon Calvinistic theology. Whitefield's growing confidence in the doctrine of election became the surety of his sense of assurance despite his ongoing

---

44. For this development, see chapter three, sections 2.1.–4.

45. Collins wrote: "Wesley's teaching on assurance underwent more modifications and was sustained by more nuances than any other single element in his doctrine of salvation." Collins, *The Scripture Way of Salvation*, 136.

46. See chapter five, section two.

47. See chapter three, section two for Wesley and chapter five, section two for Whitefield's views on assurance.

48. See chapter three, section 2.1.

49. See chapter three, section 2.2.

50. See chapter three, section 2.3.

51. See chapter four, section 3.3.5.

52. See chapter five, section 2.2.

53. See chapter five, section 2.1.

54. See chapter five, section 2.2.

struggles with personal sin.[55] While Whitefield spoke of assurance of salvation being rooted in the doctrine of election, he also held that good works were required for a person to be considered a genuine Christian—this is a tension that Whitefield did not resolve.[56]

Wesley was confident that his sense of assurance was settled immediately after his heart was strangely warmed. But, as his journal shows, even the next morning after Aldersgate, Wesley had lost his sense of assurance because at that time Wesley based his assurance on whether or not he had fear and doubt in regard to his salvation and faith.[57] Wesley continued to wrestle with his views on assurance until 1747, nine years after Aldersgate, at which time Wesley concluded personally and in his public preaching that assurance of salvation was not required for one to be saved.[58]

Wesley and Whitefield shared two principle commonalities in their mature theologies of assurance. First, assurance of salvation, like conversion, is an experiential component of salvation.[59] Assurance, for them, is the subjective attestation to the objective salvation of God for an individual. While external works may play a part in assessing obedience, external works can be performed by a regenerate or unregenerate person. Thus, both Wesley and Whitefield put less emphasis on external works and more emphasis on the internal experience and feeling of assurance, which was the witness of the Spirit that one had truly become a child of God.[60] Second, and directly related to their theologies of conversion, the mature Wesley and Whitefield both taught that assurance of salvation was not required for an individual to be a genuine convert (labeled as synoptic statement 9).[61] Assurance was always to be sought since assurance provided peace for the believer, but some simply might not experience a sense of assurance. Both Wesley and Whitefield understood assurance of salvation initially to be a requirement for a true convert; however, eventually both

---

55. See chapter five, section 2.4.
56. See chapter four, section 4.4. and chapter five, sections 2.4.
57. See chapter three, section 2.3.
58. See chapter three, section 2.4.
59. See chapter three, section 2.3. for Wesley and chapter five, section 2.1. for Whitefield.
60. See chapter three, section 2.2. for Wesley and chapter five, section 2.1. for Whitefield.
61. See chapter three, section 2.4. for Wesley and chapter five, section 2.3. for Whitefield.

discarded this requirement.[62] Wesley and Whitefield's pastoral experiences brought the realization that not all people with genuine faith had a sense of assurance. Wesley's ongoing personal doubts and fears led him to discard the requirement of assurance in order to recognize an individual to be saved. Whitefield's growing commitment to election strengthened his view that assurance was not required to denote a genuine convert. The mature Wesley and Whitefield agreed, therefore, that assurance was to be sought in order to bring personal peace, but assurance was not required for a person to be considered a genuine convert to Christ.

2.3. CONVERSION AND THE VIA/ORDO SALUTIS

Wesley and Whitefield taught that conversion was essentially an experience, and being such, conversion had a particular relationship with the *ordo salutis*, or preferable in Wesley's understanding, the *via salutis*.[63] Wesley and Whitefield both taught that the emphasis in conversion was on what was felt and experienced in an individual.[64] Thus, Wesley and Whitefield's theologies of conversion dealt primarily with the experiential application of God's work. Conversion can be thought of as the experiential correlate to God's work of saving humans. Humans are the subject of conversion: humans convert. But it is also true that humans are the object of salvation: humans are converted through God's saving activity, God saves humans. Therefore, God saved, is saving, and will save humans. Even in speaking of humans as the subjects of conversion, one cannot forget God's saving activity through prevenient grace. Neither Wesley nor Whitefield were Pelagian. They both claimed that all people need God's grace to convert, and thus, conversion was always the subjective experiential *response* to God's work of salvation. To better understand the relationship between conversion and the *via/ordo salutis*, this section will compare the larger scope of theological inquiry which goes beyond the experiential aspect of conversion in Wesley and Whitefield's theologies.

Both men held to a soteriological three-fold sequence of justification, sanctification, and glorification, with justification occurring at

---

62. See chapter three, section 2.4. for Wesley and chapter five, section 2.3. for Whitefield.

63. For more on the relationship between the *via salutis* and *ordo salutis*, see chapter three, section three.

64. See chapter two, section 1.1. for Wesley and chapter four, section 1.2. for Whitefield.

instantaneous conversion, sanctification as a description of the ongoing work of conversion, and glorification as the glorified state that one enters in the eventual presence of the Lord.[65] One *ante* stage should also be added to help understand the place of conversion in the *via/ordo salutis*.[66] This stage is where Wesley and Whitefield diverged: the hidden decrees of God.[67]

Wesley and Whitefield had considerable differences related to their articulations of God's work in the hidden decrees.[68] Wesley included within the hidden decrees preventing grace, the foreknowledge of God, and predestination (conditional predestination based upon the foreknowledge of God).[69] Whitefield understood the hidden decrees to include sovereign grace, election, and predestination.[70] Wesley's use of preventing grace and Whitefield's use of sovereign grace essentially accomplished the same task:

---

65. See, for Whitefield, chapter five, section 3.3., and for Wesley, his *Sermons*, 2:417-21.

66. Perhaps the best explication of Wesley's *via salutis* is found in his sermon *On Predestination*. Wesley, *Sermons*, 2:417-21. Whitefield's general structure to his *ordo salutis* can be found in his letter to Rev. R. E. on November 28, 1739, as well as Whitefield's comments about Thomas Boston's *Four Fold State of Man* and John Edwards's *Veritas Redux*. See Whitefield, *The Works of the Reverend George Whitefield*, 1:128-29, 4:55. Boston's work focuses on the four states of human nature: (1) Initial innocence, (2) Entire depravity, (3) Grace through regeneration and union with God, and (4) Eternal state. John Edwards's work describes the decrees of: (1) Election/Reprobation, (2) Grace and Conversion, (3) Efficacy of Redemption, and (4) Perseverance in Grace. It is significant that in Edwards's strongly Calvinistic scheme, Edwards still emphasizes the role of human response for conversion. Edwards wrote: "Tho conversion be by grace alone, yet there is a persona and proper action belonging to those that are converted." Edwards continued: "For man being acted by God, doth really and properly act; it is he that believes and repents, and not God; and therefore believing and repenting are man's proper acts." John Edwards, *Veritas Redux* (London: Jonathan Robinson, John Lawrence, and John Wyat, 1707), 315-16, 344-45.

67. After the Free Grace controversy, Wesley and Whitefield appeared reticent to belabor the discussion of the decrees since it distracted from the missional work of evangelism and discipleship. In the sermon *The Holy Spirit Convincing the World of Sin, Righteousness, and Judgment*, Whitefield wrote: "Do not go and quarrel with God's decrees, and say, if I am a reprobate I shall be damned; if I am elected, I shall be saved; and therefore I will do nothing. What have you to do with God's decrees? Secret things belong to him; it is your business to 'give all diligence to make your calling and election sure.'" Whitefield, *The Works of the Reverend George Whitefield*, 6:140.

68. Whitefield, for example, avoided the direct discussion of the decrees in the introduction to his letter responding to Wesley's *Free Grace* sermon. Whitefield directed Wesley to Edwards's *Veritas Redux* instead. See Whitefield, *The Works of the Reverend George Whitefield*, 4:55.

69. Wesley, *Sermons*, 3:553; Wesley, *Doctrinal and Controversial Treatises II*, 13:555.

70. Whitefield, *The Works of the Reverend George Whitefield*, 4:58, 71.

attributing all grace and goodness to God alone.[71] On rare occasions, Wesley spoke of sovereign grace,[72] and Whitefield spoke of preventing grace.[73] Wesley and Whitefield articulated their views of divine grace differently. Wesley believed that predestination was based upon the divine foreknowledge of God,[74] and that the only proper understanding of election was conditional election based upon human response to divine grace.[75] Whitefield believed that predestination was based upon the grace of God exhibited in the unconditional election of God (apart from divine foreknowledge).[76]

Wesley and Whitefield had considerable agreement in their articulation of justification (less their differences on imputation)[77] and sanctification as it related to conversion, with the significant exception being the extreme edge of sanctification (Christian perfection in Wesley's theology and perseverance in Whitefield's theology). Their agreement in the area of justification began with the necessity of repentance and faith as a catalyst to the

---

71. Reist wrote: "The difference between Wesley and Whitefield is not about the source of salvation, which is grace, but in its mode of operation. For Wesley grace is operative positively on all men; for Whitefield it is applied redemptively only to the eternally elect in Christ." Reist, "John Wesley and George Whitefield: A Study in the Integrity of Two Theologians of Grace," 34.

72. Wesley, *Doctrinal and Controversial Treatises II*, 13:550.

73. Whitefield, *The Works of the Reverend George Whitefield*, 4:190, 452, 6:40.

74. Wesley, *Sermons*, 2:417.

75. Wesley, *Doctrinal and Controversial Treatises II*, 13:268.

76. Whitefield, *The Works of the Reverend George Whitefield*, 4:70.

77. One area of divergence among Wesley and Whitefield regarding justification is what they meant by imputation. Wesley and Whitefield believed that Jesus Christ's righteousness was imparted to the genuine believer. By impartation Whitefield meant that the believer was justified by the merits of Christ juridically for his or her sins past, present, and future. Wesley differed from Whitefield gently, and James Hervey forcibly, in regard to viewing justification as automatically applying Christ's righteousness to the future state of the convert. Theologically and scripturally Wesley saw no merit for extending imputed righteousness beyond the moment of justification at instantaneous conversion; Wesley was extremely concerned pastorally about the antinomian potential of the Reformed view of impartation. Wesley taught that beyond the juridical benefit of justification in conversion, justification enabled an inherent righteousness which gave the new believer the capacity, through God's grace, to overcome sin, with no merit coming back to the believer, but to Christ's enabling work. McGonigle wrote regarding Wesley: "Thus justification is sanctification begun, that is, the sinner is not merely accounted righteous, he is made righteous." Herbert Boyd McGonigle, *Sufficient Saving Grace: John Wesley's Evangelical Arminianism* (Carlisle: Paternoster, 2001), 227. For further analysis of Wesley and Whitefield on the topic of justification and imputed righteousness, see Maddock, *Men of One Book*, 205–11; Coppedge, *John Wesley in Theological Debate*, 157–74, especially 166–67; Schwenk, *Catholic Spirit*, 32–35; McGonigle, *Sufficient Saving Grace*, 217–40; Alan P. F. Sell, *The Great Debate: Calvinism, Arminianism, and Salvation* (Eugene, OR: Wipf & Stock, 1998), 64–66.

moment of instantaneous conversion.[78] As noted in the summary above, Wesley and Whitefield both discussed faith as an immediately preceding catalyst to instantaneous conversion. Wesley is clear, however, that faith is instantaneous in the moment of instantaneous conversion. Whitefield does not attend to this level of specificity so, while they are not in disagreement, Wesley is more specific (see chapter two, section 3.2). In the moment of instantaneous conversion they both believed that justification was appropriated to the believer and that regeneration (also called the new birth) occurred.[79]

Wesley and Whitefield aligned on the foundational aspects of sanctification, which included continued repentance, faith, and good works.[80] Where they disagreed on sanctification was on the topics of Christian perfection and perseverance.[81] Whitefield understood perseverance to be linked to election; as such, he rooted perseverance in the hidden decrees (which were already noted as an area of difference).[82] In Wesley's journal entry on August 32, 1743, written *after* the Free Grace controversy of 1739–1741, he clarified his remaining three points of dispute with Whitefield: unconditional election, irresistible grace, and final perseverance.[83] Irresistible grace logically depends upon the doctrine of election. However, it is important to note that the research for this study could only locate one instance of Whitefield discussing irresistible grace directly, and this instance was only a passing reference.[84] While adhering boldly to the doctrine of unconditional election, Whitefield did not appear comfortable to extrapolate the logical implications of election into the domain of human experience, hence the apparent lack of engagement with the concept of irresistible grace on Whitefield's behalf. Whitefield's emphasis on experience in

78. See chapter three, sections 3.1.–2. for Wesley and chapter five, sections 3.1.2.–3. for Whitefield.

79. See chapter three, section 3.2. for Wesley and chapter five, section 3.2. for Whitefield.

80. See chapter three, section 3.3. for Wesley and chapter five, section 3.3. for Whitefield.

81. Coppedge, *John Wesley in Theological Debate*, 160–68; Maddock, *Men of One Book*, 224–30; McGonigle, *Sufficient Saving Grace*, 153–77. The best recent discussion may be found in Joel Houston, "A Decade of Difference: Predestination and Early Methodist Identity in the 'Free Grace' Controversy, 1739–1749" (PhD diss., University of Manchester, 2017).

82. See Whitefield, *The Works of the Reverend George Whitefield*, 1:101, 129, 140, 156, 182, 204, 206, 212, 4:58.

83. Wesley, *Journals and Diaries*, 19:332.

84. See Whitefield, *The Works of the Reverend George Whitefield*, 1:182.

conversion and the necessity of genuine faith appears to have tempered the
logic of irresistible grace. Perseverance is also a logical implication of the
doctrine of unconditional election. Whitefield exhorted his people to not
speculate about their own election, but to, instead, continue in their ongoing conversion.[85] Thus, while the doctrine of perseverance could provide
comfort for Whitefield's devotees, perseverance is a decree and not a performance or experience. Perseverance can *operate* in the domain of human
experience, yet perseverance is *ordered* in the hidden decrees. Whitefield's
doctrine of perseverance is distanced from the experiential nature of his
concept of conversion.[86] Thus, on the topic of their theologies of conversion,
neither Christian perfection, nor perseverance, played a significant role
regarding conversion except that Wesley did believe that a person could
backslide to the point of apostasy and effectively un-convert due to having
"made shipwreck of faith" through unrepentant sin and disbelief in Christ.[87]

Wesley and Whitefield disagreed on the topic of Christian perfection.[88]
It may seem that this disagreement runs contrary to the argument of this
study (that profound agreement exists between them concerning the *telos*
of salvation). However, while their disagreement had been terse and livid
at times, an important kernel of agreement is at its core: the *telos* of conversion as the journey of Christian growth through ongoing sanctification.
Christian perfection is less connected to the hidden decrees, with the possible exception of the determination of the limits of theological anthropology.

Christian perfection, more so than perseverance, overlaps with the
domain of experience and deserves further attention as it relates to conversion. Any discussion of Wesley's doctrine of Christian perfection must

---

85. See chapter four, section 4.4. for more on this topic. Whitefield did claim to know of
one person who did not doubt their election and final perseverance: himself. Whitefield, *The
Works of the Reverend George Whitefield*, 1:76.

86. It should be noted that Wesley said "that all those eminently styled the elect will
infallibly persevere to the end." But, Wesley's view of election was based in foreknowledge
and not unconditional election. In Wesley's 1774 edition of his *Works* he deleted the phrase just
mentioned, likely to avoid confusion regarding unconditional election and foreknowledge
election. Wesley, *Journals and Diaries*, 19:333.

87. See Wesley's sermons *On Sin in Believers* and *A Call to Backsliders*. Wesley, *Sermons*,
1:332, 3:224.

88. Coppedge, *John Wesley in Theological Debate*, 160–68; Maddock, *Men of One Book*, 224–
30; McGonigle, *Sufficient Saving Grace*, 153–77. The best recent discussion may be found in
Houston, "A Decade of Difference: Predestination and Early Methodist Identity in the 'Free
Grace' Controversy, 1739–1749."

take into account that Wesley's views and articulation of Christian perfection changed over time.[89] Whitefield noted this change over time, as he observed in a letter to Wesley on September 11, 1747: "I rejoice to hear, that you and your brother are more moderate with respect to sinless perfection."[90] Wesley's mature view of conversion and Christian perfection share an important feature: they both occur instantaneously.[91] However, and of critical importance, the instantaneousness of both conversion and Christian perfection, for Wesley, are only the *beginning* and not the *end* of their aims. Further, Wesley (and Whitefield) understood conversion as instantaneous *and* ongoing.[92] While Whitefield shared Wesley's understanding of conversion as ongoing, Whitefield failed to understand Wesley's conception of Christian perfection as ongoing. Scholars have pointed out that Wesley and Whitefield's divergence on Christian perfection is partially rooted in Whitefield's misunderstanding of Wesley's view (and, perhaps, also rooted in Wesley's evolving articulation of Christian perfection).[93]

Whitefield perceived the doctrine of Christian perfection as a threat in two ways. First, Christian perfection seemed practically impossible since perfection belongs only to God.[94] Second, Christian perfection confused the imputed righteousness of Christ with attempts at human works-based righteousness.[95] Wesley countered both of Whitefield's arguments by clarifying that, in the first case, Christian perfection is not defined as the *full* attainment of the perfection of God's perfection;[96] in the second

---

89. For a discussion of the transitions in Wesley's emphases concerning Christian perfection, see Wesley, *A Plain Account of Christian Perfection*, 21–26.

90. Whitefield, *The Works of the Reverend George Whitefield*, 2:126–27.

91. See Wesley, *A Plain Account of Christian Perfection*, 27.

92. See chapter two, sections 3.–4. for Wesley and chapter four, sections 3.–4. for Whitefield.

93. For example, see Maddock, *Men of One Book*, 225–30.

94. Whitefield, *The Works of the Reverend George Whitefield*, 6:413.

95. Whitefield, *The Works of the Reverend George Whitefield*, 3:337, 6:413.

96. Wesley's mature and clearest articulation of what he meant by perfection is summarized well by Maddox and Chicote: "Christian perfection does not bestow omniscience or infallibility ... [Wesley] dismissed any suggestion that the perfect have no need of the merits of Christ. And it is why he emphasized that Christian perfection was an essentially dynamic reality—ever open to richer development in grace and always capable of being lost if it is not nurtured." This summary sets apart the type of perfection that Wesley meant by Christian perfection from the perfection of God, which is omniscient, infallible, and in no need of merit or richer development in grace. Wesley, *A Plain Account of Christian Perfection*, 26–27.

case, Wesley disagreed on the nature of imputed righteousness.[97] The broad contours of the theologies of conversion for Wesley and Whitefield are best espoused through the concept of inaugurated teleology. While they did disagree on perfection, their disagreement was not complete. In fact, they agreed on the *telos* of conversion, but not the timing of when the *telos* was humanly possible (for Wesley perfection was possible before death, for Whitefield only after death). They also misunderstood each other.

Their misunderstanding of each other on the topic of perfection is unfortunate, especially in relation to their views on conversion. Whitefield would have found more common ground if he understood Wesley's doctrine of Christian perfection as being more synonymous with Whitefield's view of ongoing conversion. Whitefield was not opposed to articulating perfection in terms of ongoing Christian growth. For instance, Whitefield recorded in his journal on November 10, 1739: "Oh that they may not only receive the Word with joy for a season, but bring forth fruit unto perfection."[98] Similarly, in the sermon, *Thankfulness for Mercies Received, a Necessary Duty*, Whitefield wrote: "But few are arrived to such a degree of charity or love, as to rejoice with those that do rejoice, and to be as thankful for others mercies, as their own. This part of christian perfection, though begun on earth, will be consummated only in heaven."[99] Whitefield also spoke of the "highest pitch of perfection" to describe the aims of Christian growth.[100] While Whitefield used "perfection" terminology in a way consistent with ongoing conversion, Whitefield was clear that he rejected Wesley's view of Christian perfection. Wesley's view of Christian perfection was, in Whitefield's words, "unattainable," "absurdity," "that pernicious weed," "a monsterous doctrine," and "apt to lead men into spiritual pride," while attributing the doctrine to Satan![101] Wesley and Whitefield never reconciled their differences on the topic of Christian perfection, but it may be suggested that the concept of the instantaneousness and the continued

97. See footnote 78 earlier in this chapter.

98. Whitefield, *Fifth Journal: From His Embarking after the Embargo, to His Arrival at Savannah in Georgia*, 32.

99. Whitefield, *The Works of the Reverend George Whitefield*, 5:95.

100. Whitefield, *The Works of the Reverend George Whitefield*, 6:333, 413.

101. Whitefield, *The Works of the Reverend George Whitefield*, 1:209, 222, 361, 3:337, 4:151; George Whitefield, "Newly Discovered Letters of George Whitefield, 1745-1746," ed. John W. Christie, *Journal of the Presbyterian Historical Society* 32, no. 3 (September 1954): 162.

nature of conversion could have provided the structure for Whitefield to understand Wesley's doctrine of Christian perfection as having an instantaneous beginning which then continued. While Whitefield disagreed with Wesley on the extent of Christian perfection that could be attained before glorification, both agreed on the aim, or *telos*, of Christian perfection, which was conformity to the image of God.[102] Thus, while Wesley and Whitefield disagreed on the articulation of Christian perfection, both men were committed to a vision of conversion in which a *telos* was embedded whose end can be described as Christian perfection.

Inaugurated teleology is an accurate term to describe Wesley and Whitefield's theologies of conversion because of the overwhelming homogeny they articulated regarding justification, sanctification, and glorification (with the exceptions of imputation and Wesley's doctrine of Christian perfection, though an explanation has been given how they may have agreed more than they realized on Christian perfection). Wesley and Whitefield diverged in their doctrines of the hidden decrees, but their emphases on the experiential nature of conversion made the topic of conversion functionally independent of their divergent understandings of the hidden decrees. The *via salutis* of Wesley and *ordo salutis* of Whitefield synthesize with the overarching claim of this study: the espousal of their theologies of conversion can be articulated as inaugurated teleology. Synthesis is possible because inauguration is a punctiliar human experience that comes chronologically after the hidden decrees. In other words, Wesley and Whitefield agree on what happens in the moment of instantaneous conversion, which can be described as the inauguration of conversion. Similarly, they agree on the requirement for ongoing good works and Christian growth as an expression of the *telos* of conversion (though they differ on the humanly possible extent of this *telos* before glorification). Thus, the analysis of their respective orders of salvation synthesize with the articulation of conversion as inaugurated teleology while respecting the differences they held.

Below is a summary of Wesley's *via salutis* and Whitefield's *ordo salutis* (with areas of agreement in *italics*):

---

102. See chapter two, sections 3.2. and 5. for Wesley and chapter four, section 3.3.5. for Whitefield.

Wesley's Via Salutis	Whitefield's Ordo Salutis

1. Hidden decrees
    Preventing grace
    Foreknowledge of God
    Predestination (based on fore-
    knowledge)
	1. Hidden decrees
	    Sovereign grace
	    Election
	    Predestination (based on
	    election)

2. *Justification*
Leading to justification:
    Repentance
 	
    Moment of instantaneous
    conversion
    Faith
    Justification
    Regeneration / New Birth
	2. *Justification*
	Leading to justification:
	    Repentance
	    Faith[103]
	    Moment of instantaneous
	    conversion
	
	    Justification
	    Regeneration / New Birth

3. Sanctification
    Continued repentance
    Continued faith
    Continued good works
    Possibility of Christian perfection
	3. Sanctification
	    Continued repentance
	    Continued faith
	    Continued good works
	    Perseverance

4. *Glorification*	4. *Glorification*

3. SUMMARY OF THE ESPOUSED CONVERSION THEOLOGIES OF WESLEY AND WHITEFIELD

This account has sought to show that Wesley and Whitefield had largescale agreement in their theological understanding of conversion as inaugurated teleology. The description of conversion as inaugurated teleology emerged in chapters two to five as these offered a careful exegesis of Wesley and Whitefield's operant material on conversion, which was organized into primary motifs and attendant themes in order to espouse theologies of conversion for Wesley and Whitefield. Emerging from the exegesis of their operant theologies, nine synoptic statements have been espoused to give further clarification and specificity to the nature of conversion as a theological trope. The current chapter has brought the individual material of

---

103. Wesley and Whitefield both discussed faith as an immediately preceding catalyst to instantaneous conversion. Wesley is clear, however, that faith is instantaneous in the moment of instantaneous conversion. Whitefield does not attend to this level of specificity, so while they are not in disagreement, Wesley is more specific (see chapter two, section 3.2.).

Wesley and Whitefield into conversation and compared them within the broad parameters of their theological agreement for areas of similarity and departure. This chapter has given a particular account of dissimilarities that exist within their broad agreement in their operant theologies of conversion related to Wesley's Arminianism and Whitefield's Calvinism. However, these differences between the two revivalists are not ones which affect directly their theologies of conversion, and it is possible therefore to offer a summary of the theological category of conversion with which they both work. These nine articulated theological statements can be thought of as the unpacking of a theological account of conversion best understood in broadest terms in terms as inaugurated teleology of the Christian life. Where differences exist between them, it is within these broader contours of a theological account of conversion.

1. Conversion is initiated and sustained by the grace of God.

2. Conversion is the experiential correlate of salvation.

3. Conversion is a turning *from* self and *to* Christ.

4. Conversion is foreshadowed by a deep sense of sinfulness.

5. Conversion arrives by faith in an instant.

6. Conversion is instantaneous but is not always recognizable on behalf of the true convert.

7. Conversion is marked by ongoing good works.

8. Baptism marks one's entrance to the church but is not chronologically tied to conversion.

9. Assurance of salvation is available but not required for a genuine convert.

These nine synoptic statements of the theology of conversion obviously align with the overarching theme of inauguration in conversion, as one might expect given the emphasis on the instantaneous nature of conversion. The inauguration of conversion is initiated through grace (statement 1) in the midst of an experience which is the onset of the experience of salvation (statement 2). This inauguration happens in the moment and instant when one turns to Christ (statement 3) in a movement from self which was preceded by a deep sense of sinfulness (statement 4). The actual moment of inauguration, or moment of instantaneous conversion, arrives by faith and happens in an instant (statement 5), though, in some cases, the convert may not recognize this precise moment (statement 6). Thus, the first six statements unpack and articulate the claim that a theological account of conversion for Wesley and Whitefield must attend to the inauguration and beginning of conversion. The final three statements, while not primarily oriented toward the inaugural moment of conversion, relate in an accompanying way to the inauguration of conversion. Good works attest to the genuineness of the inauguration of conversion (statement 7) but take time to emerge. However, the necessity of good works points back to the reality of an inaugural moment of conversion because something has changed the behavior of the person which has brought with it good works. The inauguration of conversion locates baptism as the mark of one's entrance to the church, but the act of baptism does not necessarily chronologically demarcate the moment of conversion (statement 8); it is the moment of conversion which is key to salvation. Last, since assurance of salvation is not required to be a genuine convert (statement 9), the importance of an inaugural moment is heightened all the more: if a person traverses back and forth from having assurance of salvation to lacking assurance of salvation (or never having assurance at all), then the non-requirement of assurance of salvation makes the inaugural moment of conversion pivotal for one's experience of conversion. The theological accounts of conversion in Wesley and Whitefield (while acknowledging certain differences), therefore, show reference to the inaugural nature of conversion. Yet, the inauguration of conversion is only the beginning and not the end of conversion. It is inaugural: that is, it inaugurates something else. A theological account of conversion for Wesley and Whitefield is incomplete if it only attends to its inaugural aspect. Therefore, what does conversion inaugurate?

While the account of these nine synoptic statements may look as though they are focused on an instantaneous moment of conversion, nevertheless, a key issue to recognize with both Wesley and Whitefield's theologies of conversion is that for them, the instantaneous moment of conversion is not understood apart from the life of faith, and its direction is, therefore, an inauguration which is only meaningful in relation to its teleology (that to which the inauguration points). Conversion does not replace teleology: it *initiates* it. So, while conversion is initiated (inaugurated), it is sustained by the grace of God to its teleological end (statement 1). While conversion happens in a moment, it is an experiential correlative of salvation which is ongoing (statement 2). While conversion involves an initial turning from self to Christ, this turn is something which goes on (that is, turning to God over and over) throughout the life of the believer (statement 3). While conversion has a momentary aspect, it is, nevertheless, foreshadowed by a proceeding moment which orientates it toward its own end (statement 4). While conversion arrives by faith in a moment, the life of faith continues and is ongoing (statement 5). A convert must not fixate upon an inaugural moment, or his or her baptism, but, instead, commit to the directionality of their life toward God (statements 6 and 8) indicated by ongoing good works (statement 7). While assurance of salvation may be held in a particular moment, if assurance is lost, the *telos* of conversion is not impinged by the lack of assurance (statement 9). What conversion does is to orientate a believer toward a life of faith unpacked throughout one's existence. Therefore, for all that these nine motifs seem to point toward a momentary instantaneous account of conversion, there is, nevertheless, a correlative in each of them which pulls out the teleological aspect in relation to the life of faith as has been seen in the foregoing.

Each one of these tropes, for all of the focus on the instantaneous moment, should always be understood even internal to itself in terms of its teleology. It is strictly within these broad parameters that Wesley and Whitefield's demarcations over the decrees should be seen and the relative importance of them can be identified. For all that their differences are significant, they do not actually affect directly their theologies of conversion because the way that conversion operates as a theological trope for them is always orientated toward the moment of conversion and (as teleology) the end, not the hidden decrees of God.[104] It is possible to see a broader parameter with which Wesley and Whitefield work in regards to a theological account of conversion best articulated as inaugurated teleology.

---

104. To attend to the decrees is to focus on theology proper (a different locus), not conversion which relates more to the locus of salvation.

4. CONCLUSION

This chapter has shown that there is overwhelming continuity within the operant material of Wesley and Whitefield's teaching on conversion which can be described in the term inaugurated teleology. Any disagreement takes place *within* this conceptuality. The first section showed that they were univocal on the overarching nature of conversion as an experience, preceded by a deep sense of sinfulness, in which one turns *from* self and *to* Christ through an instantaneous conversion which is followed by continued evidence of conversion. The second section demonstrated the continuity, though through different emphases and approaches, between Wesley and Whitefield on the topics of baptism and assurance. The comparison of Wesley's *via salutis* and Whitefield's *ordo salutis* revealed the most significant differences between their theologies in relation to conversion (due to Wesley's Arminianism and Whitefield's Calvinism, as well as Wesley's unique and evolving articulation of Christian perfection). These differences, however, exist within, rather in contrast to, Wesley and Whitefield's conception of conversion as a human experience of salvation known in an instant as it is ordered to its end.[105] The third section summarized the nine synoptic statements and concluded with an analysis showing how the nine synoptic statements relate not only to the inaugural moment of instantaneous conversion, but, also, always to the *telos* of conversion. This analysis sustains the primary claim of this study, which is, that Wesley and Whitefield's theological articulation of conversion is best described as inaugurated teleology.

---

105. Wesley and Whitefield did disagree on the timing of Christian perfection, which for Wesley (via his own unique definition) was possible before glorification, but otherwise, for Wesley and Whitefield, was a realization of the teleological aspect of conversion after death.

7

—

CONVERSION AS INAUGURATED TELEOLOGY FOR WESLEY AND WHITEFIELD

Wesley and Whitefield understood conversion as inaugurated teleology. This challenges modern evangelical understandings of conversion which focus on the inauguration (beginning) of conversion at the expense (or exclusion) of the teleological aspect found in Wesley and Whitefield's theology of conversion.

The exegesis of Wesley and Whitefield's operant material on conversion espoused nine synoptic statements of their theologies of conversion. Each of these nine statements relate not only to an instantaneous (inaugural) moment of conversion but also continually, to the *telos* of conversion.

1. Conversion is initiated and sustained by the grace of God.

2. Conversion is the experiential correlate to salvation.

3. Conversion is a turning *from* self and *to* Christ.

4. Conversion is foreshadowed by a deep sense of sinfulness.

5. Conversion arrives by faith in an instant.

6. Conversion is instantaneous but is not always recognizable on behalf of the convert.

7. Conversion is marked by ongoing good works.

8. Baptism marks one's entrance to the church but is not chronologically tied to conversion.

9. Assurance of salvation is available but not required in order
to be a genuine convert.

While Wesley and Whitefield disagreed on certain topics (particularly the hidden decrees of God and the timing of full sanctification), they
expressed conversion theologically as the inauguration (through instantaneous conversion) and *telos* of salvation (evidenced by the life of faith).
Wesley and Whitefield had overarching agreement on the theological
understanding of conversion as inaugurated teleology, but on topics related
to the hidden decrees they were divided (on the topics of election, foreknowledge, predestination, irresistible grace, and perseverance). In relation to questions of the *telos* of conversion, however, there is a deep unity.
Their unity in the *telos* of conversion exists with an exception regarding the
timing of Christian perfection. Wesley, in his unique understanding of the
concept, believed perfection was possible before glorification. Whitefield
believed that Christian perfection was possible only upon glorification.
However, these differences exist within, rather than in contrast to, Wesley
and Whitefield's conception of conversion as inaugurated teleology.

1. CONVERSION IN MODERN EVANGELICALISM

The unearthing of Wesley and Whitefield's theologies of conversion as
a datum point for early evangelical conversion motivates a brief reappraisal of the modern conception of conversion among evangelicals.[1] In
brief, Wesley and Whitefield and modern evangelicals would generally
align theologically on the inauguration of conversion while modern evangelicals have largely discarded the *telos* in conversion articulated by Wesley
and Whitefield.[2]

---

1. A fuller treatment assessing conversion among early and modern evangelicals is beyond
the scope of this book and this chapter. I hope, however, to do exactly this in the future.

2. A major challenge for this assessment is to determine which modern statements by
evangelicals qualify as representative of modern evangelicalism. The question of defining
early evangelicalism was introduced in chapter one of this book and aligned with Bebbington's
analysis regarding early evangelicalism. The question of how to define modern evangelicalism
is fluid, complex, and passionate. For the sake of this brief chapter, I will address concep-
tions of conversion which fall in the shadow cast by the ethos of Billy Graham upon modern
North American evangelicalism. This group is largely comprised of non-mainline churches
in America as well as prominent evangelical ministries such as Campus Crusade for Christ.

An influential example of the modern evangelical understanding of conversion is found in Campus Crusade for Christ's *The Four Spiritual Laws*.[3] In 1957, Bob Ringer, a salesman and member of Hollywood Presbyterian Church, spoke at Campus Crusade for Christ's conference about "presentation fatigue," and urged their staff to stick to one pitch, one version of the gospel.[4] Two years later, this "pitch" was condensed to *The Four Spiritual Laws*. The core of the pamphlet invites the participant to say, "I open the door of my life and receive [Jesus] as my Savior and Lord. Thank you for forgiving my sins and giving me eternal life."[5] The pamphlet then gives "suggestions for Christian growth" as well as encourages the reader to "make plans to attend [church] regularly."[6] The booklet has been translated into more than 200 languages, and more than 2.5 billion copies have been distributed worldwide.[7] Despite its success, Bill Bright, the founder of Campus Crusade for Christ (now Cru), "admitted that his pamphlet was a drastic oversimplification of the Christian faith."[8] He believed this was particularly true with those who had no exposure to Christianity, while those with a broader background in Christianity would have more of a foundation for its message.

Scot McKnight argues that "salvation" has become the entirety of the gospel for modern evangelicals and can be summarized through "four simple (and thin) points: God loves you, you are messed up, Jesus died for you, accept him and (no matter what you do) you can go to heaven."[9]

The limited size of this chapter is a significant impingement upon the conclusions but it is undertaken nonetheless.

3. Campus Crusade for Christ, *Have You Heard of the Four Spiritual Laws?* (Campus Crusade for Christ, 1965). In 2011, Campus Crusade for Christ renamed their organization Cru. Campbell's analysis of the gospel and conversion in evangelical communities highlights the role of Campus Crusade for Christ. Ted A. Campbell, *The Gospel in Christian Traditions* (Oxford: Oxford University Press, 2009), 75-99, esp. 77, 94-95.

4. John G. Turner, *Bill Bright & Campus Crusade for Christ: The Renewal of Evangelicalism in Postwar America* (Chapel Hill: University of North Carolina Press, 2008), 99.

5. Bill Bright, *Have You Heard of the Four Spiritual Laws?* (Bright Media and Campus Crusade for Christ, 2007), 10.

6. Bright, *Have You Heard of the Four Spiritual Laws?*, 14-15.

7. "About | Cru," *cru.org*, accessed February 19, 2019, www.cru.org/us/en/about.html.

8. David Harrington Watt, *A Transforming Faith: Explorations of Twentieth-Century American Evangelicalism* (New Brunswick, NJ: Rutgers University Press, 1991), 30.

9. Scot McKnight, *The King Jesus Gospel: The Original Good News Revisited* (Grand Rapids: Zondervan, 2011), 73.

McKnight's summary mirrors the message of *The Four Spiritual Laws* and is, in my opinion, an accurate snapshot of the modern North American evangelical conception of conversion.

The Four Spiritual Laws encodes a theology of conversion that isolates conversion from Christian growth, or in other words, sanctification.[10] The modern bifurcation of conversion from sanctification is widespread and can be seen in robust modern evangelical theological works such as the chapter entitled "Conversion and Sanctification" by Miyon Chung. Chung writes: "In conversion, the sinner is turned and surrendered to God for a radically different way of life. Through sanctification, the Christian learns that living by faith means embarking on a pilgrimage of growing trust in God's power of grace amidst ever encroaching legalism and apostasy."[11] Richard Lovelace named the modern evangelical bifurcation of conversion from sanctification the "sanctification gap."[12] This gap within modern evangelical conversion theology creates what is sometimes called "easy-believe-ism," in which the "sinner's prayer" functions as a ticket to heaven to stow away until death with no further action required.[13]

Modern evangelicals sometimes show the sanctification gap in their separation of conversion from discipleship. Richard Peace, a self-identified evangelical missiologist, makes this distinction while defining conversion for modern evangelicals as merely "a tentative step toward Jesus," while calling discipleship "actively and consciously following the way of Jesus."[14] Peace's research on conversion in a five-year study of a recent well-known

---

10. Conversion has been isolated from Christian growth by many evangelists, theologians, and organizations prior to modern evangelicalism. The limited point being made in this chapter, however, is that modern North American evangelicalism also does this.

11. Miyon Chung, "Conversion and Sanctification," in *The Cambridge Companion to Evangelical Theology*, ed. Timothy Larsen and Daniel J. Treier (Cambridge: Cambridge University Press, 2007), 121.

12. Richard F. Lovelace, *Dynamics of Spiritual Life* (Downers Grove, IL: InterVarsity Press, 1979), 232–34.

13. Billings's recent work resources modern evangelical bifurcation of justification and sanctification through Calvin's concept of union with Christ in which "substantial participation" replaces mere "imitation." J. Todd Billings, *Calvin, Participation, and the Gift: The Activity of Believers in Union with Christ* (Oxford: Oxford University Press, 2008), 61.

14. Richard V. Peace, "Conflicting Understandings of Christian Conversion: A Missiological Challenge," *International Bulletin of Missionary Research* 28, no. 1 (2004): 9. As shown in this book, and will be evaluated below, Wesley and Whitefield's view of conversion massively transcends a mere "tentative step toward Jesus."

evangelical crusade in America reveals that roughly 10% of conversions resulted in long-term changes in behavior. In other words, many converts made in modern evangelicalism did not become disciples.[15]

Gordon T. Smith has produced the most robust systematic theological studies on conversion to date.[16] In his chapter in the *Oxford Handbook of Evangelical Theology*, he describes the standard modern evangelical conception of conversion as a punctiliar experience often marked by the "sinner's prayer" with a focus so that one could "go to heaven after death."[17] Smith adds that this view of conversion is spoken of in "escapist terms, as a means by which one gets on the life raft before the ship goes down."[18] Smith calls for evangelicals to move "toward a thorough reenvisioning of the nature of conversion and redemption."[19]

2. WESLEY AND WHITEFIELD'S THEOLOGIES OF CONVERSION COMPARED TO MODERN EVANGELICALISM

This reenvisioning can be accomplished by reassessing the modern evangelical view of conversion with the nine synoptic statements of conversion of Wesley and Whitefield:

Conversion is initiated and sustained by the grace of God (statement 1). Modern evangelicals would agree that conversion is initiated by the grace of God, but some might hesitate to say that conversion is sustained by the grace of God. Sanctification and discipleship are often seen among modern evangelicals as the responsibility of the Christian rather than an act of God's ongoing grace toward the Christian.

Conversion is the experiential correlate to salvation (statement 2). Salvation often collapses into a past-tense experiential verb (for example, "I was

---

15. Peace, "Conflicting Understandings," 8.

16. Gordon T. Smith, *Beginning Well: Christian Conversion & Authentic Transformation* (Downers Grove, IL: InterVarsity Press, 2001); Gordon T. Smith, *Transforming Conversion: Rethinking the Language and Contours of Christian Initiation* (Grand Rapids: Baker Academic, 2010).

17. Gordon T. Smith, "Conversion and Redemption," in *Oxford Handbook of Evangelical Theology*, ed. Gerald R. McDermott (Oxford: Oxford University Press, 2010), 210. Note that Smith's chapter is on "conversion and redemption" *and not* "conversion and sanctification." Smith frames his understanding of evangelical conversion differently than Chung given above.

18. Smith, "Conversion and Redemption," 219.

19. Smith, "Conversion and Redemption," 210.

saved") for modern evangelicals at the expense of the present and future
tense of "I am saved" and "I am being saved." The lack of an ongoing and
future salvation restricts modern evangelicals from understanding conversion in its ongoing and teleiotic sense.

Conversion is a turning from self and to Christ (statement 3). Modern evangelicals align with early evangelicals: conversion is a "turn" from self and
to Christ. What is lost among modern evangelicals is the ongoing sustain-
ment, directionality, and orientation of the turn of conversion, not unlike
a person on a pilgrimage—to abandon the destination is to no longer be a
pilgrim. This is why, for example, Whitefield spoke of himself needing to
be converted "more and more every day and hour!"[20]

Conversion is foreshadowed by a deep sense of sinfulness (statement 4). Not
only do modern evangelicals collapse the *ongoing* sense of conversion
which Wesley and Whitefield articulated, modern evangelicals truncate the
expectation of a sense of sinfulness that *precedes* conversion. For example,
when *The Four Spiritual Laws* are used as an evangelistic tract, virtually no
time is allowed for a foreshadowing "deep sense of sinfulness." Certainly
the Holy Spirit is able to instantaneously give a deep sense of sinfulness
and could prepare a person before encountering *The Four Spiritual Laws*.
Modern evangelicalism, however, tends to emphasize emotional and cir-
cumstantial appeal in a way that departs from Wesley and Whitefield's
emphasis on the foreshadowing of sinfulness upon the potential convert.

Conversion arrives by faith in an instant (statement 5). Early and modern
evangelicals likewise hold to the essential requirement of faith in instantaneous conversion. What is sometimes lacking in modern evangelicals is
an insistence for genuine converts to maintain a life of faith. Modern evangelicals, again, think of conversion as a past tense occurrence which was
sparked by faith. Further, some modern evangelicals like Richard Peace
highlight studies which claim that no more than 30 percent of conversions are instantaneous; he concludes, "For most people, conversion is a
process, not an event."[21] Wesley and Whitefield's theology undergirding
conversion, in which conversion is brought about instantaneously through

---

20. Whitefield, *The Works of the Reverend George Whitefield*, 2:463. See chapter four, section 4.2.

21. Peace, "Conflicting Understandings," 9.

instantaneous justification, contradicts claims that evangelical conversion is a "process."

Conversion is instantaneous but is not always recognizable on behalf of the convert (statement 6). For modern evangelicals who perceive conversion as a process, Wesley and Whitefield would have denied that conversion was a process and, instead, explained that conversion was simply not always recognizable to the convert. They did agree that there were rare instances (though, certainly not 70 percent as Peace explains above) when the "perception" of conversion did not feel or appear instantaneous.

Conversion is marked by ongoing good works (statement 7). The "sanctification gap" of modern evangelicals creates a divide between conversion and good works in which good works are a second agenda disassociated with conversion. For Wesley and Whitefield, good works are a function of instantaneous conversion and an indicator that conversion was genuine. For modern evangelicals, good works become something to begin rather than something that has already begun by God's grace in the convert.

Baptism marks one's entrance to the church but is not chronologically tied to conversion (statement 8). Modern evangelicals who are credo-baptistic can lack a crucial connection and entrance to the church which baptism provides. For modern evangelicals, a conversion experience can operate entirely independent from the church due to a view of baptism in which baptism is virtually meaningless. For whatever tensions Wesley and Whitefield left in their views of baptism and conversion, they would have cringed at the modern practice of the "sinner's prayers" which has no connection to church and sacrament. Modern evangelicals who are paedo-baptistic vary how they understand the connection between baptism and conversion.

Assurance of salvation is available but not required in order to be a genuine convert (statement 9). Wesley and Whitefield recognized that assurance of salvation was not an essential experience of genuine converts. Modern evangelicals stress that assurance is certain for those who had a prior experience such as a "sinner's prayer." For example, *The Four Spiritual Laws* teach that "we do not depend on feelings or emotions" because they can contradict the "trustworthiness of fact and the promises of His Word."[22]

---

22. Bright, *Have You Heard of the Four Spiritual Laws?*, 12.

The Four Spiritual Laws cite 1 John 5:13: "that you may **know** that you have eternal life."[23] In other words, a tool distributed by modern evangelicals to 2.5 billion people around the world requires converts to discard their experience and to believe "as fact" that they are assured of their salvation.

———

This closing chapter does not provide the space to reappraise thoroughly the theology of conversion for evangelicals. Indeed, *The Four Spiritual Laws*, while massively influential and, in my opinion, indicative of the prevailing currents of modern evangelical conversion theology, are only a sliver of the modern evangelical landscape (which also happens to currently be a combustive label in of itself). I hope that the detailed primary source research and analysis of the conversion theologies of Wesley and Whitefield given in this study will prompt further discussion not only of what early evangelicals meant by conversion, but also that modern evangelicals might reencounter the work of God, perhaps even a revival similar to what Wesley and Whitefield saw unfold in front of their eyes. Lord willing, there will be theologians, pastors, and evangelists who will echo the booming voice of George Whitefield across the fields: "But that there is really such a thing, and that each of us must be spiritually born again, I shall endeavour to shew."[24]

23. Bright, *Have You Heard of the Four Spiritual Laws?*, 11. Bold in the original.
24. Whitefield, *The Works of the Reverend George Whitefield*, 6:261.

BIBLIOGRAPHY

—

"About | Cru." *cru.org*. Accessed February 19, 2019. www.cru.org/us/en/about.html.

Abraham, William J. "The Epistemology of Conversion." In *Conversion in the Wesleyan Tradition*, edited by Kenneth J. Collins and John H. Tyson. Nashville: Abingdon Press, 2001.

Anonymous. *Country Parson's Advice to His Parishioners.* London: Benjamin Tooke, 1680.

Armstrong, Michael. "Ordinary Theologians as Signal Processors of the Spirit." In *Exploring Ordinary Theology: Everyday Christian Believing and the Church*, edited by Leslie J. Francis and Jeff Astley. London: Routledge, 2016.

Astley, Jeff. *Ordinary Theology: Looking, Listening, and Learning in Theology.* London: Ashgate, 2002.

Baker, Frank. "John Wesley's Introduction to William Law." *Wesley Historical Society* 36, no. 3 (1969): 78–82.

———. "John Wesley's Introduction to William Law: A Reconsideration." *Wesley Historical Society* 37, no. 6 (1970): 173–77.

Barton, J. Hamby. "The Two Versions of the First Edition of John Wesley's 'The Sunday Service of the Methodists in North America.' " *Methodist History* 23, no. 3 (April 1985): 153–62.

Bebbington, David W. *Evangelicalism in Modern Britain: A History from the 1730s to the 1980s.* London: Routledge, 2004.

———. "Evangelicalism in Modern Britain and America: A Comparison." In *Amazing Grace: Evangelicalism in Australia, Britain, Canada, and the United States*, edited by Mark A. Noll and George A. Rawlyk. Grand Rapids: Baker, 1993.

———. "The Evangelical Quadrilateral: A Response." *Fides et Historia* 47, no. 1 (Winter 2015): 87–96.

Beebe, Keith Edward. "The McCulloch Manuscripts of the Cambuslang Revival, 1742: A Critical Edition." PhD diss., Kings College, University of Aberdeen, 2003.

Bhatti, Deborah, Catherine Duce, James Sweeney, and Clare Watkins. *Talking about God in Practice: Theological Action Research and Practical Theology.* London: Hymns Ancient and Modern, 2010.

Billings, J. Todd. *Calvin, Participation, and the Gift: The Activity of Believers in Union with Christ.* Oxford: Oxford University Press, 2008.

Borgen, Ole E. *John Wesley on the Sacraments: A Definitive Study of John Wesley's Theology of Worship.* Grand Rapids: Francis Asbury Press, 1985.

Boultbee, Thomas Pownall. *A Commentary on the Thirty-Nine Articles: Forming an Introduction to the Theology of the Church of England.* London: Longmans, 1877.

Brauer, Jerald C. "Conversion: From Puritanism to Revivalism." *The Journal of Religion* 58, no. 3 (1978): 227–43.

Bright, Bill. *Have You Heard of the Four Spiritual Laws?* Bright Media and Campus Crusade for Christ, 2007.

Calvin, John. *Calvin: Institutes of the Christian Religion.* Translated by Ford Lewis Battles. Louisville, KY: Westminster John Knox Press, 2001.

———. *Institutes of the Christian Religion: 1541 French Edition.* Translated by Elsie Anne McKee. Grand Rapids: Eerdmans, 2009.

Campbell, Ted A. "Conversion and Baptism in Wesleyan Spirituality." In *Conversion in the Wesleyan Tradition,* edited by Kenneth J. Collins and John H. Tyson. Nashville: Abingdon Press, 2001.

———. *The Gospel in Christian Traditions.* Oxford: Oxford University Press, 2009.

———. *John Wesley and Christian Antiquity: Religious Vision and Cultural Change.* Nashville: Kingswood Books, 1991.

———. *Wesleyan Beliefs: Formal and Popular Expressions of the Core Beliefs of Wesleyan Communities.* Nashville: Kingswood Books, 2010.

Campus Crusade for Christ. *Have You Heard of the Four Spiritual Laws?* Campus Crusade for Christ, 1965.

Castaniza, John. *Spiritual Combat: Or, the Christian Pilgrim in His Spiritual Conflict and Conquest.* 2nd ed. London: Sam Keble, 1710.

Chamberlain, Jeffrey S. "Moralism, Justification, and the Controversy over Methodism." *Journal of Ecclesiastical History* 44, no. 6 (1993): 10–25.

Chapman, Mark. *Anglican Theology*. London: T&T Clark, 2012.

Cherry, Conrad. *The Theology of Jonathan Edwards: A Reappraisal*. Garden City, NY: Doubleday, 1990.

Chung, Miyon. "Conversion and Sanctification." In *The Cambridge Companion to Evangelical Theology*, edited by Timothy Larsen and Daniel J. Treier. Cambridge: Cambridge University Press, 2007.

Church of England. *Book of Common Prayer, 1662 Edition*. Cambridge: Cambridge University Press, 2005.

———. *The Two Books of Homilies*. Oxford: Oxford University Press, 1859.

Collins, Kenneth J. "A Hermeneutical Model for the Wesleyan Ordo Salutis." *Wesleyan Theological Journal* 19, no. 2 (Fall 1984): 23–37.

———. "Other Thoughts on Aldersgate: Has the Conversionist Paradigm Collapsed?" *Methodist History* 30, no. 1 (October 1, 1991): 652–78.

———. "A Reply to Randy Maddox." *Methodist History* 31, no. 1 (October 1992): 51–54.

———. *The Scripture Way of Salvation: The Heart of John Wesley's Theology*. Nashville: Abingdon Press, 1997.

———. *The Theology of John Wesley: Holy Love and the Shape of Grace*. Nashville: Abingdon Press, 2007.

Conn, Walter E., ed. *Conversion: Perspectives on Personal and Social Transformation*. New York: Alba House, 1978.

Cooke, Mary. "Mr Wesley Letterbook: Cooke and Clarke Family Documents and Images at Bridwell Library." Accessed December 22, 2016. digitalcollections.smu.edu/cdm/ref/collection/cooke/id/446.

Coppedge, Allan. *John Wesley in Theological Debate*. Wilmore, KY: Wesley Heritage Press, 1987.

Cornwall, Robert. "The Rite of Configuration in Anglican Thought during the Eighteenth Century." *Church History* 68, no. 2 (June 1999): 359–72.

Crisp, Oliver D. *Deviant Calvinism: Broadening Reformed Theology*. Minneapolis: Fortress Press, 2014.

Crisp, Oliver D., and Kyle Strobel. *Jonathan Edwards: An Introduction to His Thought*. Grand Rapids: Eerdmans, 2018.

Dallimore, Arnold. *George Whitefield: The Life and Times of the Great Evangelist of the Eighteenth-Century Revival.* Vol. 1. London: Banner of Truth Trust, 1970.

———. *George Whitefield: The Life and Times of the Great Evangelist of the Eighteenth-Century Revival.* Vol. 2. Edinburgh: Banner of Truth Trust, 1980.

Davies, Rupert E. "Introduction." In *The Methodist Societies: History, Nature, and Design.* The Bicentennial Edition of the Works of John Wesley, vol. 9. Nashville: Abingdon Press, 1989.

Dochuk, Darren. "Revisiting Bebbington's Classic Rendering of Modern Evangelicalism at Points of New Departure." *Fides et Historia* 47, no. 1 (Winter 2015): 63–72.

Downey, James. *The Eighteenth Century Pulpit. A Study of the Sermons of Butler, Berkeley, Secker, Sterne, Whitefield and Wesley.* Oxford: Clarendon Press, 1969.

Edwards, John. *Veritas Redux.* London: Jonathan Robinson, John Lawrence, and John Wyat, 1707.

Elliot, Robert. "A Summary of Gospel Doctrine Taught by Mr. Whitefield." In *Select Sermons of George Whitefield*, edited by J. C. Ryle. Carlisle, PA: The Banner of Truth Trust, 1953.

English, John C. "The Sacrament of Baptism according to the Sunday Service of 1784." *Methodist History* 5, no. 2 (1967): 10–15.

Fisher, John Douglas Close. *Christian Initiation: Confirmation Then and Now.* Chicago: Hillenbrand Books, 2005.

Francke, August Hermann. *Nicodemus: Or, a Treatise Against the Fear of Man.* London: Joseph Downing, 1706.

Gatiss, Lee. "The Anglican Doctrine of Baptism." *Foundations: An International Journal of Evangelical Theology* 63 (Autumn 2012): 65–89.

Gillies, John. *Memoirs of the Life of the Reverend George Whitefield.* London: Charles Dilly, 1772.

Gillies, John, and Aaron C. Seymore. *Memoirs of the Life of the Reverend George Whitefield, A.M.* Philadelphia: Simon Probasco, 1820.

Goode, William. *The Doctrine of the Church of England as to the Effects of Baptism in the Case of Infants.* London: J. Hatchard and Son, 1850.

Hambrick-Stowe, Charles E. *The Practice of Piety: Puritan Devotional*

Disciplines in Seventeenth-Century New England. Chapel Hill, NC: University of North Carolina Press, 1982.

Hand, Bill. "The Return of George Whitefield." *New Bern Sun Journal*, April 28, 2013. www.newbernsj.com/20130428/bill-hand-the-return-of-george-whitefield/304289940.

Haykin, Michael A. G. *The Revived Puritan: The Spirituality of George Whitefield*. Dundas, Ontario: Joshua Press, 2000.

Haykin, Michael A. G., and Kenneth J. Stewart, eds. *The Emergence of Evangelicalism: Exploring Historical Continuities*. Nottingham: Apollos, 2008.

Heitzenrater, Richard P. "Great Expectations: Aldersgate and the Evidences of Genuine Christianity." In *Aldersgate Reconsidered*, edited by Randy L. Maddox, 49–91. Nashville: Kingswood Books, 1990.

———. "John Wesley and the Oxford Methodists." PhD diss., Duke University, 1972.

Henry, Matthew. *Matthew Henry's Commentary on the Whole Bible: Complete and Unabridged in One Volume*. Peabody, MA: Hendrickson, 1994.

Henry, Stuart C. *George Whitefield: Wayfaring Witness*. New York: Abingdon Press, 1957.

Hindmarsh, D. Bruce. *The Evangelical Conversion Narrative: Spiritual Autobiography in Early Modern England*. Oxford: Oxford University Press, 2005.

———. *The Spirit of Early Evangelicalism: True Religion in a Modern World*. Oxford: Oxford University Press, 2018.

Hohenstein, Charles R. "The Revisions of the Rites of Baptism in the Methodist Episcopal Church, 1784–1939." PhD diss., University of Notre Dame, 1990.

Hooker, Richard. *The Works of Mr. Richard Hooker in Eight Books of Ecclesiastical Polity*. London: Thomas Newcomb, 1666.

Houston, Joel. "A Decade of Difference: Predestination and Early Methodist Identity in the 'Free Grace' Controversy, 1739–1749." PhD diss., University of Manchester, 2017.

Hunter, Fredrick. "John Wesley's Introduction to William Law (Response)." *Wesley Historical Society* 37, no. 5 (1970): 143–50.

Johnson, Maxwell E. *The Rites of Christian Initiation: Their Evolution and Interpretation*. Collegeville, MN: Liturgical Press, 2007.

Jones, David Ceri. *The Fire Divine: An Introduction to the Evangelical Revival*. Nottingham: InterVarsity Press, 2015.

———. "George Whitefield and the Revival of Calvinism in Eighteenth-Century Britain." *International Congregational Journal* 14, no. 1 (Summer 2015): 97–115.

Jones, David Ceri, Eryn Mant White, and Boyd Stanley Schlenther. *The Elect Methodists: Calvinistic Methodism in England and Wales, 1735–1811*. Cardiff: University of Wales Press, 2012.

Kidd, Thomas S. "The Bebbington Quadrilateral and the Work of the Holy Spirit." *Fides et Historia* 47, no. 1 (Winter 2015): 54–57.

———. *George Whitefield: America's Spiritual Founding Father*. New Haven, CT: Yale University Press, 2014.

———. *The Great Awakening*. New Haven, CT: Yale University Press, 2007.

Lambert, Frank. "The Great Awakening as Artifact: George Whitefield and the Construction of Intercolonial Revival, 1739–1745." *Church History* 60, no. 2 (June 1991): 223–46.

———. *Pedlar in Divinity: George Whitefield and the Transatlantic Revivals, 1737–1770*. Princeton, NJ: Princeton University Press, 1994.

———. "Whitefield and the Enlightenment." In *George Whitefield: Life, Context, and Legacy*, edited by David Ceri Jones and Geordan Hammond. Oxford: Oxford University Press, 2016.

Lavington, George. *The Enthusiasm of Methodists and Papists Compar'd*. London: Knapton, 1749.

Law, William. *A Practical Treatise Upon Christian Perfection*. London: William and John Innys, 1726.

———. *A Serious Call to a Devout and Holy Life*. London: William Innys, 1729.

———. *A Serious Call to a Holy Life [Abridgement by John Wesley]*. Edited by John Wesley. Newcastle upon Tyne: John Gooding, 1744.

Leith, John H. *Creeds of the Churches: A Reader in Christian Doctrine, from the Bible to the Present*. Atlanta: John Knox Press, 1982.

Loane, Edward. "Wesley, Whitefield, and the Church of England." In *Wesley and Whitefield? Wesley versus Whitefield?*, edited by Ian J. Maddock. Eugene, OR: Pickwick Publications, 2018.

Lovelace, Richard F. *Dynamics of Spiritual Life.* Downers Grove, IL: InterVarsity Press, 1979.

Lucas, Richard. *Religious Perfection, or, a Third Part of the Enquiry after Happiness.* London: S. Smith and B. Walford, 1704.

Maddock, Ian J. *Men of One Book: A Comparison of Two Methodist Preachers, John Wesley and George Whitefield.* Eugene, OR: Pickwick Publications, 2011.

Maddox, Randy L. *Aldersgate Reconsidered.* Nashville: Kingswood Books, 1990.

———. "Continuing the Conversation." *Methodist History* 30, no. 4 (July 1992): 235–41.

———. "John Wesley—Practical Theologian?" *Wesleyan Theological Journal* 23 (1988): 122–47.

———. "The Recovery of Theology as a Practical Discipline: A Contemporary Agenda." *Theological Studies* 51 (1990): 650–72.

———. *Responsible Grace: John Wesley's Practical Theology.* Nashville: Kingswood Books, 1994.

———. "An Untapped Inheritance: American Methodism and Wesley's Practical Theology." In *Doctrines and Disciplines: Methodist Theology and Practice,* edited by Dennis Campbell, 19–52, 292–309. Nashville: Abingdon Press, 1999.

Malony, H. Newton, and Samuel Southard, eds. *Handbook of Religious Conversion.* Birmingham, AL: Religious Education Press, 1992.

Mather, Increase. *Ichabod or, A Discourse, Shewing What Cause There Is to Fear That the Glory of the Lord Is Departing from New-England.* Boston, 1702.

McDermott, Gerald R. "A Possibility of Reconciliation: Jonathan Edwards and the Salvation of Non-Christians." In *Edwards in Our Time: Jonathan Edwards and the Shaping of American Religion,* edited by Sang Hyun Lee and Allen C. Guelzo. Grand Rapids: Eerdmans, 1999.

McGever, Sean. "The Vector of Salvation: The New Birth as (Only) the Beginning of Conversion for Wesley and Whitefield." In *Wesley and Whitefield? Wesley versus Whitefield?,* edited by Ian J. Maddock. Eugene, OR: Pickwick Publications, 2018.

McGonigle, Herbert Boyd. *Sufficient Saving Grace: John Wesley's Evangelical*

Arminianism. Carlisle: Paternoster, 2001.

McKnight, Scot. *The King Jesus Gospel: The Original Good News Revisited.* Grand Rapids: Zondervan, 2011.

McKnight, Tim. *No Better Gospel: George Whitefield's Theology and Methodology of Evangelism.* Timmonsville, SC: Seed Publishing Group, 2017.

Noll, Mark A. *The Rise of Evangelicalism: The Age of Edwards, Whitefield, and the Wesleys.* Downers Grove, IL: InterVarsity Press, 2003.

Oden, Thomas C. *Doctrinal Standards in the Wesleyan Tradition.* Nashville: Abingdon Press, 2008.

Old, Hughes Oliphant. *The Reading and Preaching of the Scriptures in the Worship of the Christian Church: Moderatism, Pietism, and Awakening.* Vol. 5. Grand Rapids: Eerdmans, 2004.

Olson, Mark K. "Exegeting Aldersgate: John Wesley's Interpretation of 24 May 1738." PhD diss., University of Manchester, 2016.

———. "Whitefield's Early Theological Formation." In *George Whitefield: Life, Context, and Legacy,* edited by David Ceri Jones and Geordan Hammond. Oxford: Oxford University Press, 2016.

Olson, Roger E., and Christian T. Collins Winn. *Reclaiming Pietism: Retrieving an Evangelical Tradition.* Grand Rapids: Eerdmans, 2015.

Outler, Albert C. *John Wesley.* Oxford: Oxford University Press, 1964.

Packer, J. I. "The Spirit with the Word: The Reformational Revivalism of George Whitefield." In *Honouring the People of God: The Collected Shorter Writings of J. I. Packer,* vol. 4. Carlisle: Paternoster, 1999.

Peace, Richard V. "Conflicting Understandings of Christian Conversion: A Missiological Challenge." *International Bulletin of Missionary Research* 28, no. 1 (2004): 8–14.

Perkins, William. *A Golden Chain, or The Description of Theology.* Edited by Greg Fox. Cambridge: Puritan Reprints, 2010.

Pew Research Center. "The Size and Distribution of the World's Christian Population (2010)." Accessed February 20, 2017. www.pewforum.org/2011/12/19/global-christianity-exec/.

Rack, Henry D. *Reasonable Enthusiast.* 3rd ed. Peterborough, UK: Epworth Press, 2014.

Reist, Irwin W. "John Wesley and George Whitefield: A Study in the Integrity of Two Theologians of Grace." *Evangelical Quarterly* 47

(1975): 26–40.

Rightmire, R. David. "Holiness and Wesley's 'Way of Salvation.' " *Word and Deed* 13, no. 1 (November 2010): 39–53.

Rivers, Isabel. "Scougal's *The Life of God in the Soul of Man.*" In *Philosophy and Religion in Enlightenment Britain*, edited by Ruth Savage, 29–55. Oxford: Oxford University Press, 2012.

Runyon, Theodore. "The Importance of Experience for Faith." In *Aldersgate Reconsidered*, edited by Randy L. Maddox. Nashville: Kingswood Books, 1990.

———. *The New Creation: John Wesley's Theology Today*. Nashville: Abingdon Press, 1998.

Ryle, J. C. *The Upper Room*. Edinburgh: Banner of Truth Trust, 1990.

Schwenk, James L. *Catholic Spirit: Wesley, Whitefield, and the Quest for Evangelical Unity in Eighteenth-Century British Methodism*. Lanham, MD: Scarecrow Press; Center for the Study of World Christian Revitalization Movements, 2008.

Scougal, Henry. *The Life of God in the Soul of Man with Nine Other Discourses on Important Subjects*. London: J. Downing and G. Strahan, 1726.

Scupoli, Lorenzo. *The Spiritual Combat*. Translated by James William Lester and Robert Paul Mohan. London: Catholic Way Publishing, 2013.

Sell, Alan P. F. *The Great Debate: Calvinism, Arminianism, and Salvation*. Eugene, OR: Wipf and Stock Publishers, 1998.

Shantz, Douglas H. *A Companion to German Pietism, 1660–1800*. Leiden: Brill, 2015.

Sherriff, Collin Bedford. "The Theology of George Whitefield (1714–1770)." PhD diss., University of Edinburgh, 1950.

Smith, Gordon T. *Beginning Well: Christian Conversion & Authentic Transformation*. Downers Grove, IL: InterVarsity Press, 2001.

———. "Conversion and Redemption." In *Oxford Handbook of Evangelical Theology*, edited by Gerald R. McDermott. Oxford: Oxford University Press, 2010.

———. *Transforming Conversion: Rethinking the Language and Contours of Christian Initiation*. Grand Rapids: Baker Academic, 2010.

Smith, John E., Harry S. Stout, and Kenneth P. Minkena, eds. *A Jonathan*

Edwards Reader. New Haven, CT: Yale University Press, 2003.

Smith, Josiah. *The Character, Preaching, &c, of the Reverend Mr. George Whitefield, Impartially Represented and Supported, in a Sermon*. Boston: G. Rogers, 1740.

Smith, Timothy Lawrence. *Whitefield & Wesley on the New Birth*. Grand Rapids: Asbury Press, 1986.

Stout, Harry S. *The Divine Dramatist: George Whitefield and the Rise of Modern Evangelicalism*. Grand Rapids: Eerdmans, 1991.

Strobel, Kyle. "By Word and Spirit: Jonathan Edwards on Redemption, Justification, and Regeneration." In *Jonathan Edwards and Justification*, edited by Josh Moody. Wheaton, IL: Crossway, 2012.

Thomas, Page A. "The Wesley Center Online: John Wesley: Spiritual Advisor To Young Women As He Speaks Through His Letters." Accessed December 22, 2016. wesley.nnu.edu/?id=4723.

Thomas, W. H. Griffith. *The Principles of Theology: An Introduction to the Thirty-Nine Articles*. Eugene, OR: Wipf & Stock, 2005.

Thorsen, Donald A. "Experimental Method in the Practical Theology of John Wesley." *Wesleyan Theological Journal* 24 (1989): 117–41.

Toon, Peter. *The Emergence of Hyper-Calvinism in English Nonconformity, 1689–1765*. Eugene, OR: Wipf & Stock, 2011.

Turner, John G. *Bill Bright & Campus Crusade for Christ: The Renewal of Evangelicalism in Postwar America*. Chapel Hill: University of North Carolina Press, 2008.

Tyerman, Luke. *The Life of the Rev. George Whitefield*. 2 vols. London: Hodder and Stoughton, 1876.

Tyson, John H. "John Wesley's Conversion at Aldersgate." In *Conversion in the Wesleyan Tradition*, edited by Kenneth J. Collins and John H. Tyson. Nashville: Abingdon Press, 2001.

Wallace, Dewey D. *Shapers of English Calvinism, 1660–1714: Variety, Persistence, and Transformation*. New York: Oxford University Press, 2011.

Ward, Pete. "Seeing and Believing." In *The End of Theology: Shaping Theology for the Sake of Mission*, edited by Jason S. Sexton and Paul Weston, 145–70. Minneapolis: Fortress Press, 2016.

Ward, W. Reginald. *Early Evangelicalism: A Global Intellectual History, 1670–1789*. Cambridge: Cambridge University Press, 2006.

Watt, David Harrington. *A Transforming Faith: Explorations of Twentieth-Century American Evangelicalism*. New Brunswick, NJ: Rutgers University Press, 1991.

Wesley, John. *The Appeals to Men of Reason and Religion and Certain Related Open Letters*. Edited by Gerald Cragg. The Bicentennial Edition of the Works of John Wesley, vol. 11. Nashville: Abingdon Press, 1989.

———. *A Collection of Hymns for the Use of the People Called Methodists*. Edited by Franz Hildenbrandt and Oliver A. Beckerlegge. The Bicentennial Edition of the Works of John Wesley, vol. 7. Nashville: Abingdon Press, 1983.

———. *The Complete English Dictionary Explaining Most of Those Hard Words, Which Are Found in the Best English Writers*. London: W. Strahan, 1753.

———. *Doctrinal and Controversial Treatises I*. Edited by Randy L. Maddox. The Bicentennial Edition of the Works of John Wesley, vol. 12. Nashville: Abingdon Press, 2012.

———. *Doctrinal and Controversial Treatises II*. Edited by Paul Wesley Chilcote and Kenneth J. Collins. The Bicentennial Edition of the Works of John Wesley, vol. 13. Nashville: Abingdon Press, 2013.

———. *Explanatory Notes Upon the New Testament*. New York: J. Soule and T. Mason, 1818.

———. *Explanatory Notes upon the Old Testament*. Salem, OH: Schmul Publishers, 1975.

———. *Journals and Diaries*. Edited by W. Reginald Ward and Richard P. Heitzenrater. The Bicentennial Edition of the Works of John Wesley, vols. 18–24. Nashville: Abingdon Press, 1988.

———. *Letters*. Edited by Frank Baker and Ted A. Campbell. The Bicentennial Edition of the Works of John Wesley, vols. 25–27. Nashville: Abingdon Press, 1980.

———. *The Letters of John Wesley*. Edited by John Telford. London: The Epworth Press, 1931.

———. *The Methodist Societies: History, Nature, and Design*. Edited by Rupert E. Davies. The Bicentennial Edition of the Works of John Wesley, vol. 9. Nashville: Abingdon Press, 1989.

———. *The Methodist Societies: The Minutes of Conference*. Edited by Henry D. Rack. The Bicentennial Edition of the Works of John Wesley, vol. 10. Nashville: Abingdon Press, 2011.

———. *A Plain Account of Christian Perfection.* Edited by Randy L. Maddox and Paul Wesley Chilcote. Kansas City, MO: Beacon Hill Press, 2015.

———. *Sermons.* Edited by Albert C. Outler. The Bicentennial Edition of the Works of John Wesley, vols. 1–4. Nashville: Abingdon Press, 1984.

———, ed. *Thoughts Upon Infant-Baptism (Extracted from a Late Writer).* Bristol: Felix Farley, 1751.

———. *The Works of John Wesley.* Edited by Thomas Jackson. 3rd ed. 14 vols. London: Methodist Reading Room, 1872.

Wesley, Samuel. *The Pious Communicant Rightly Prepar'd.* London: Charles Harper, 1700.

Whitefield, George. *A Brief and General Account of the First Part of the Life of the Reverend Mr. George Whitefield, From His Birth, to His Entering into Holy Orders.* Boston: Kneeland & Green; Edwards & Eliot, 1740.

———. *Eighteen Sermons Preached by the Late Rev. George Whitefield.* Edited by Joseph Gurney. London: Joseph Gurney, 1771.

———. *An Exhortation to Come and See Jesus.* London: C. Whitefield, 1739.

———. *Fifth Journal: From His Embarking after the Embargo, to His Arrival at Savannah in Georgia.* London: James Hutton, 1740.

———. *First Journal: A Voyage from London to Savannah in Georgia.* London: James Hutton, 1738.

———. *Fourth Journal: During the Time He Was Detained in England by the Embargo.* London: James Hutton, 1739.

———. *A Further Account of God's Dealings with the Reverend Mr. George Whitefield.* London: W. Strahan, 1747.

———. *Nature and Necessity of Our New Birth in Christ Jesus, in Order to Salvation.* Gloucester: Harris, 1737.

———. "Newly Discovered Letters of George Whitefield, 1745–1746." Edited by John W. Christie. *Journal of the Presbyterian Historical Society* 32, no. 3 (September 1954): 159–86.

———. *Seventh Journal: From a Few Days after His Return to Georgia to His Arrival at Falmouth.* London: W. Strahan, 1741.

———. *A Short Account of God's Dealings with the Reverend Mr. George Whitefield.* London: James Hutton, 1740.

———. *Sixth Journal: After His Arriving at Georgia, to a Few Days after His Second Return Hither from Philadelphia*. London: James Hutton, 1741.

———. *Third Journal: His Arrival at London to His Departure from Thence on His Way to Georgia*. London: James Hutton, 1739.

———. *The Two First Parts of His Life, with His Journals, Revised, Corrected, and Abridged, by George Whitefield*. London: W. Strahan, 1756.

———. *The Works of the Reverend George Whitefield*. Edited by John Gillies. 6 vols. London: Printed for Edward and Charles Dilly, 1771.

Yates, Arthur S. *The Doctrine of Assurance: With Special Reference to John Wesley*. Reprint edition. Eugene, OR: Wipf & Stock, 2015.

SUBJECT INDEX

—

A

à Kempis, Thomas, 129, 195
activism, 3
Aldersgate, 14, 21–24, 29, 31–40, 77,
    79–80, 82, 87, 148, 204–5
Andrews, Lancelot, 151
Anglican Church, 129, 151, 203
  and baptism, 148–51, 156, 196, 201–2
  sacramental theology of, 66
  and "sinning away," 62
  view on regeneration, 151–53, 203
  and Wesley, 63
  and Whitefield, 148–51
antinomianism, 53, 134, 143–45, 185,
    200
apostasy, 210, 222
Arminianism, 8, 172, 197, 215, 218
asceticism, 127–29, 195, 197
assurance, 2, 10–11, 52, 61, 77–84, 94,
    125, 147, 161–73, 186–88, 197–99,
    203–6, 215–17, 220, 225
  and continued sin, 165–67
  as divine, 164, 169
  and election, 169–73
  experiential nature of, 162–65, 169,
    203–4
  felt, 17, 105, 165
  full, 43, 78, 81, 83–84, 130, 165, 168, 171,
    197
  and good works, 80
  and the gospel of new birth, 162
  and the Spirit, 162
  supernatural, 164–66

  and true conversion, 77, 83, 163,
    167–69, 205–6
  and trust, 162
  Wesley's views on, 204
  Whitefield's definition of, 161–62
awakening, 28–29, 105, 110–13

B

backsliding, 84, 91–94, 210
baptism, 2, 10, 33, 35, 61–77, 94, 148–61,
    188, 190, 201–3, 215–17, 219, 225
  Anglican view of, 148–51, 156, 196,
    201–2
  benefits of, 33, 74, 156–57, 160
  and Christian life, 201
  and entrance to church, 74–76, 161,
    203
  inward verses outward, 157
  in name verses nature, 11, 153, 156–61,
    202
  and preparatory grace, 153
  renunciation of, 157
  and repentance, 64
  Roman Catholic view of, 153
  and salvation, 201
  "sinning away" the benefits of, 10, 33,
    37, 39, 62–63, 75, 134, 203
  Wesley's theology of, 202
  Wesley's view of, 61
  Zwinglian view of, 153
baptismal regeneration, 61, 114, 148–61,
    173, 188, 203
  and spiritual regeneration,
    distinction between, 152

SCRIPTURE INDEX

—

Old Testament

New Testament